Insured to Death

How Health Insurance Screws Over
Americans - And How We Take It Back

Neal K. Shah

Foreword by David Casarett, M.D.

MERIDIAN POLICY PRESS

Copyright © 2025 by Neal K. Shah

All rights reserved. No part of this book may be used or reproduced without written permission from the publisher except in the case of brief quotations embodied in critical articles or reviews.

Published by Meridian Policy Press

ISBN: 979-8-9990224-0-0 (hardcover)
ISBN: 979-8-9990224-1-7 (paperback)
ISBN: 979-8-9990224-2-4 (e-book)

All names and identifying characteristics have been changed to protect the privacy of the individuals involved. In some cases, composite characters have been created by combining details from multiple real-life individuals to illustrate systemic issues more effectively. While the events and experiences described are based on thorough research, journalistic reporting, and verified case studies, certain identifying details have been altered for confidentiality. Any resemblance to specific persons, living or deceased, is purely coincidental unless explicitly stated.

The software tools and resources mentioned in this book are provided for informational purposes only. Their inclusion is solely intended to highlight potentially helpful options for readers navigating insurance challenges.

While every effort has been made to ensure the accuracy of the information contained in this book, the publisher and author assume no responsibility for errors or omissions, or for outcomes arising from the application of this information. This book is not intended to substitute for legal, financial, or medical advice.

To view references and supporting documentation related to the content of this book, please visit www.insuredtodeath.org.

> *"Each time someone stands up for an ideal, or acts to improve the lot of others, or strikes out against injustice, he sends forth a tiny ripple of hope."*
>
> \- Robert F. Kennedy

To the millions of Americans denied essential care every year.

To every parent who has held a sick child while fighting faceless bureaucrats on the phone. To every patient who has rationed medication because an algorithm deemed their prescription "unnecessary." To every family driven to bankruptcy not by illness, but by a system that profits from denial.

To those who have died waiting for approval that never came.

To the healthcare workers who entered medicine to heal, only to spend their days battling insurance companies instead of diseases.

You are not alone.

This fight is yours. This voice is yours. These tools are yours.

The system is broken, but we are not powerless. Together, we will reclaim what is rightfully ours - one successful appeal, one overturned denial, one victory at a time.

Your health is not their profit margin.

Table of Contents

Acknowledgements	vii
Foreword by David Casarett, M.D.	xi
Before You Dive In	xvii
Introduction A Shot Heard Across the System	1
PART I: The Patient Trap	**27**
1 The Denial Industry	28
2 Profits Over Patients	47
3 The Great American Health Scam	65
PART II: The Human Cost	**90**
4 Voices from the Battlefield	91
5 Doctor in Handcuffs	109
6 Inside the Industry	123
PART III: Fighting Back	**141**
7 Your Healthcare Rights Playbook	142
8 The Tech Revolution	165
9 The Power of the People	182
10 The Three-Layer Solution	201
Conclusion Taking Back Control	220
A Note from the Author	225
About the Author	227

Acknowledgements

"Truth and love will overcome lies and hatred."
— *Václav Havel*

I begin with gratitude to God, whose quiet grace transformed personal pain into public mission, and whose divine presence calls us to serve those who suffer. In alleviating the pain of others, we discover our own highest purpose. This book emerges from a sacred conviction: that healing the sick and caring for the vulnerable is not just good policy, but a moral imperative that transcends all boundaries of faith, politics, and circumstance.

Every insight in these pages was forged from real human experience, from the countless families we've served who opened their hearts and shared their struggles, to the healthcare warriors on the front lines who refuse to accept a broken status quo. This book is both an exposé of a broken system and a blueprint for the healthcare revolution that's already beginning. I write to create hope for a transformed future and to inspire each reader to discover their own role in reshaping healthcare for the better.

My deepest gratitude begins at home. To my father, whose brilliant mind shaped my own from our earliest conversations. He challenged me to think deeper, question assumptions, and never accept easy answers. The analytical skills that allowed me to dissect the complexities of our healthcare system, the confidence to take on powerful interests, and the ability to synthesize complex ideas into actionable solutions - all of these trace back to the foundation he built through countless hours of teaching and inspired conversation. To my mother, who instilled in me the values of kindness, compassion, and unwavering moral courage. She saw in me, from childhood, a calling to serve others and reinforced that prophecy through her own example of selfless dedication. The empathy that allows me to truly hear the pain in families' voices flows from the wellspring of love and wisdom she poured into my heart. To my sister, who taught me that healthcare reform begins with questioning everything we've been told about what makes us sick and what makes us well, showing me that real change requires reclaiming our right to define health on our own terms. To my wife, whose own battle with our healthcare system revealed its cruelest contradictions and whose courage in overcoming them showed me what real strength looks like. And to my daughter, whose very existence fills me with the optimism and determination needed to fight for the world she deserves.

This mission could never have succeeded without extraordinary partners. Gavry Eshet, my longtime collaborator and technological visionary, has brought practical idealism to every innovation we've created together, proving that technology can indeed change the world for the better. Maggie Xu's multidisciplinary brilliance shines throughout this work, from meticulous research and tireless drafting to the creative vision that shaped how these ideas came to life on the page. Frances Chiu's editorial expertise transformed our passion into prose worthy of the families whose stories we tell.

The teams at CareYaya and Counterforce Health represent the beating heart of this movement. I've learned that when your mission is true, remarkable people emerge to help you achieve it. To Nirvana Tari, Roxy Garrity, Dezarae Stone, Riyaa Jadhav, and the many others who work tirelessly on the front lines of America's care crisis: you are the embodiment of change in action. Dr. David Casarett leads an extraordinary coalition of advisors and supporters who have been instrumental in shaping our mission and accelerating our impact across the country.

To the visionary organizations that believed in our work from the early days - the American Heart Association, Johns Hopkins University, University of Pennsylvania, the National Institutes of Health, AgeTech Collaborative from AARP, and many others. Your support reminds us that even within our flawed system, countless people are working every day to transform it. You prove that hope and progress are not naive ideals but achievable realities.

Most inspiring of all are the tens of thousands of college students who power CareYaya's mission, caring for older adults living with dementia and serious illness across America. You represent the future of healthcare - a generation that understands care as a calling. Your daily acts of compassion remind us why this fight matters.

To the millions of healthcare professionals, from physicians and nurses to home health aides and hospital staff, your dedication deserves celebration, not the corporate interference that has sadly corrupted your noble work. And to our colleagues within the insurance industry: I know many of you entered healthcare to help people. The system's fundamental brokenness extends far beyond any individual's actions. As we expose these failures together, I hope we can create opportunities for all of us to align our careers with our values.

This book is ultimately for the patients and families who have suffered - emotionally, financially, and physically - under a system that was supposed to protect you. Your stories fuel our determination. We will not forget your struggles, and we will not rest until we create the healthcare system you deserve. The transformation begins now, with each of us, in service to all of us.

Neal K. Shah

INSURED TO DEATH

Foreword

BY DAVID CASARETT, M.D.

When my mother was dying of multiple myeloma, fights with insurance companies were the bane of her existence and my father's. But as with most things in their lives, they loved a challenge. The bigger, the better. So, they attacked those insurance denial letters with the same rigor and organization and determination that they brought to bear in fighting her disease. My mom was less like a patient and more like a coach marshaling her team. I swear it was almost like a sport to them. Albeit a sport with consequences that are deadly if you lose. So a high stakes game for sure.

They took on a series of insurance companies, and for the most part, surprisingly, they won. Their track record in appealing insurance company denials was maybe not 100%, but far closer to perfect than most of us ever are going to get.

Why? Why did they do so well? Well, the easiest answer, and the most straightforward, is that they tried. Where other people would've given up and simply written a check that would nudge them that much closer to bankruptcy, my parents fought. It didn't matter whether the amount was big or small, or even whether they could afford the cost. It was the principle of the thing for them. And so, if my mom was getting a treatment that was known to be effective and an insurance company refused to pay for it, that insurance company could expect to receive a letter. So just making an effort to fight is an essential first step.

But that's not enough. The other superpower that my parents had, aside from their teamwork, was the fact that both were retired researchers. Between the two of them, they had what was probably more than 100 years of experience

conducting lab research, which was funded by numerous grants from prestigious funders like the National Institutes of Health and the National Science Foundation. They harnessed all of that experience in academia, plus their ability to dive into the weeds of what is often highly technical science, to fight back against insurance companies that were refusing to pay for my mom's care.

In the same way that they used that scientific knowledge and expertise to figure out what treatment options were best, they used those same skills to force insurance companies to pay for those treatments. That was all well and good for them, because organizing those fights was well within their expertise. And, to be frank, they were retired. So they had the time and energy and resources to take that fight to the insurance company. But the rest of us, and by that I mean the vast majority, have neither their skills nor their time and energy. So, while my parents took that fight to the insurance companies and won, most of the rest of us, when faced with a denial letter, will simply throw up her hands, write a check, and try to get back to our lives.

As Shah writes in this excellent book, that's exactly what insurance companies rely on us to do. Their entire model is based on creating obstacles that, well, not insurmountable, are high enough, and for boating enough, that most people, when face with the denial letter, we'll give up. But that has to change. The power differential is so enormous between insurance companies that have all the time in the world, and seemingly endless resources and strategies to create obstacles that your average patient is going to lose. The differential so great, in fact that most of the time it doesn't make sense for the average patient to get in the game.

But that is changing. Patient organizations, online information, and new tools are making it significantly easier for patients to stand up to insurance companies. In particular, AI tools have the potential to level the playing field by giving patients more information at their fingertips. The fight with insurance companies is still a fight, and it's one that insurance companies will continue to win more often than not. But we are making progress.

David Casarett, M.D.
Section Chief of Palliative Care
Professor of Medicine
Duke University

Disclaimer:

All names and identifying characteristics have been changed to protect the privacy of the individuals involved. In some cases, composite characters have been created by combining details from multiple real-life individuals to illustrate systemic issues more effectively. While the events and experiences described are based on thorough research, journalistic reporting, and verified case studies, certain identifying details have been altered for confidentiality. Any resemblance to specific persons, living or deceased, is purely coincidental unless explicitly stated.

The software tools and resources mentioned in this book are provided for informational purposes only. Their inclusion is solely intended to highlight potentially helpful options for readers navigating insurance challenges.

While every effort has been made to ensure the accuracy of the information contained in this book, the publisher and author assume no responsibility for errors or omissions, or for outcomes arising from the application of this information. This book is not intended to substitute for legal, financial, or medical advice.

To view references and supporting documentation related to the content of this book, please visit www.insuredtodeath.org.

Before You Dive In

Thanks for picking up this book!

Health insurance is broken, but there's a growing community of patients, caregivers, and advocates pushing for something better. If you'd like to be part of that conversation, I'd love to hear from you!

Please visit insuredtodeath.org to stay in the loop and drop your email so we can send a complimentary companion guide with templates, checklists, and tips as a small thank you.

If this book ends up helping you, it means a lot when readers share their thoughts on Amazon, Goodreads, or even Reddit. It helps more people discover the book and allows us to build something that lasts beyond the final page. Let's get started.

Neal

Scan QR code for relevant links

Introduction

A SHOT HEARD ACROSS THE SYSTEM

"The only thing necessary for the triumph of evil is for good men to do nothing."

— *Edmund Burke*

On a cold December morning in 2024, a single act of violence laid bare the deep wounds in America's healthcare system. UnitedHealthcare CEO Brian Thompson had just left his Midtown hotel for an investor conference where he would tout another record-breaking quarter. He never made it. Three gunshots rang out, killing him on the spot.

Here was one of America's most powerful healthcare executives lying on the sidewalk, with each spent cartridge telling a story. The words "delay," "deny," and "depose" exposed the dark workings of an industry that pushed far too many Americans to the brink of bankruptcy, if not death.

While police launched a manhunt for the shooter, Americans processed what had happened. Stories of delays and denials they had encountered suddenly surged all over social media and comment sections of newspapers. For a divided country still reeling over the recent national election, Americans seemed almost united in their anger, regardless of their political ideology.

After a five-day search, police would arrest a young man at a Pennsylvania

McDonald's. Luigi Mangione did not fit the stereotype of a violent extremist at all. If anything, he appeared to be the exact opposite as a 26-year-old Ivy League graduate and app developer from a very affluent family. Yet, like many other Americans, he suffered not only chronic pain but frustration with the healthcare system.

~~~

None of this was particularly surprising to me as the husband of a young woman who had suffered from cancer and as the founder of CareYaya, a healthcare technology company connecting families with affordable care provided by pre-health college students. Over the years, I've heard countless stories of Americans battling a labyrinthine system supposedly designed to help them as they struggled with their illnesses. I've witnessed firsthand how insurance denials pushed families to the breaking point financially and emotionally. Even though Mangione's violent actions can never be justified, they nonetheless led the way for a much-needed conversation on our unpredictable health insurance industry where treatments are anything but guaranteed in spite of high premiums.

I understand this reality all too intimately. Ten years ago, I was living what many would consider the American dream as a successful hedge fund manager in Manhattan focused on maximizing returns and scaling investment strategies.

Then came the phone call that would shatter my world. My wife Katie, just 34 years old, had been diagnosed with aggressive triple-negative breast cancer. All too quickly, we veered from planning our future to fighting for her survival. Despite having what we thought was premium insurance coverage through my job, we soon discovered the brutal reality of American healthcare from the other side.

First came the fight over her MRI scan deemed "not medically necessary" despite her oncologist's insistence. Then came the denial of coverage for a clinical trial drug that offered her best chance of survival. The genetic testing that could determine her optimal treatment plan? "Experimental," according to our insurer. Each denial required hours of appeals, medical records submissions, and tearful calls with indifferent customer service representatives who continually referenced "policy guidelines" while my wife grew weaker.

I still remember sitting on our bathroom floor at 2 a.m., holding Katie as she vomited from chemotherapy, while simultaneously being put on hold by our insurance company about a denied anti-nausea medication.

Through the exceptional medical care that we received, a good portion of which was personally funded, Katie survived. But our experience permanently colored my perspective: I knew I had a mission to fulfill for the many who shared my struggles. So, I left the hedge fund world and founded CareYaya, a tech-enabled platform that connects families with compassionate college students to provide affordable, companionship-level care. What started as a simple idea has grown into a national movement of over 40,000 student caregivers helping thousands of families across the country. Along the way, we've earned the support of leading organizations like the American Heart Association, Johns Hopkins University, the University of Pennsylvania, the National Institute on Aging, and the AgeTech Collaborative from AARP.

What began as a solution to help families find affordable care opened my eyes to a stream of American healthcare failures. I soon realized I was not alone as I heard story after story from families on our platform about the struggle to find care and, arguably just as frustrating, the endless battles with insurance denials that left them exhausted and financially drained.

That's why we launched Counterforce Health, a new CareYaya venture offering a suite of AI-driven tools to help patients and families fight back against wrongful insurance denials. Our caregiving platform grew into a broader mission: empowering people to navigate, challenge, and ultimately overcome the systemic barriers of our broken healthcare system.

WHAT YOU'LL DISCOVER IN THIS BOOK

This book is divided into three parts that will arm you with the knowledge and tools to fight back against a broken system while working toward meaningful reform.

In Part I, "The Patient Trap," you'll discover exactly how the denial industry operates. **Chapter 1** exposes the deliberate complexity of denial letters, the common reasons insurers use to reject claims, and the automated systems that deny care in seconds without human review. **Chapter 2** follows the money, revealing how insurance executives earn millions by limiting your care while Wall Street rewards companies that deny claims. **Chapter 3** traces how we built the only healthcare system in the developed world that routinely bankrupts families for getting sick.

Part II, "The Human Cost," puts faces to these failures. **Chapter 4** shares stories from real families: cancer patients denied life-saving treatments, parents crowdfunding their children's care, and middle-class families destroyed by medical bills despite having "good insurance." **Chapter 5** takes you inside the examining room to hear from physicians who've become prisoners of prior authorization requirements and productivity quotas that prioritize billing over healing. **Chapter 6** offers unprecedented insights from insurance industry insiders—the claims adjusters, medical directors, and customer service representatives who implement the denial machinery but often struggle with the moral injury it causes.

Part III, "Fighting Back," provides your action plan. **Chapter 7** is your comprehensive playbook for challenging denials, with step-by-step instructions for appeals, templates for effective letters, and strategies that win. **Chapter 8** reveals the technological tools that are leveling the playing field, from price transparency platforms that expose hidden costs to AI systems that help you craft winning appeals. **Chapter 9** shows how individual resistance becomes collective power through social media campaigns, community organizing, and legislative advocacy that forces change. **Chapter 10** presents a practical three-layer solution that could transform American healthcare while preserving what actually works in our current system.

By the end of this book, you'll understand not just why the system fails but how to navigate it successfully while joining the movement to transform it. You'll have specific tools to challenge denials, reduce costs, and access quality care. Most importantly, you'll discover that you're not alone in this fight, and that together, we have the power to take back control of American healthcare.

THE LUIGI MANGIONE CASE: PROFILE OF A BREAKING POINT

But back to Mangione.

The story of this intelligent and athletic man, pieced together from court records and investigative reporting, reads like a case study in American healthcare vexation. In his early twenties, he suffered a debilitating back injury that led to spinal surgery. According to family members, he became increasingly withdrawn over the following years, frustrated by his health insurance coverage and the broader medical system that seemed more focused on procedure codes and profits than addressing his persistent pain.

In November 2024, Mangione went "underground," losing touch with friends and family while also nursing a growing resentment toward the health insurance industry. A month later, when police arrested Mangione, they found more than just the murder weapon. In his backpack was a manifesto railing against killer health insurance companies and referencing filmmaker Michael Moore's critiques of the industry. While acknowledging he wasn't the "most qualified person" to make the case against for-profit healthcare, Mangione credited Moore's film *Sicko* as evidence of "the corruption and greed" in the current system. This manifesto helps explain why Mangione targeted the UnitedHealthcare CEO despite having a different provider. Thompson epitomized a system "that profits from denying care." In other words, Mangione viewed his act of violence as a political statement against an insurance system that had failed numerous patients.

Nonetheless, as shocking as Mangione's actions were, millions of Americans recognized the sentiment behind them. Even today, he continues to invoke sympathy as donations pour in for his legal funding.

~~~

I think about Hannah, one of the many family caregivers CareYaya has supported in Georgia, whose husband needed specialized physical therapy after a stroke. Their insurer denied the treatment despite their neurologist's recommendation, dismissing it as "experimental" despite extensive research supporting its efficacy. After three months of appeals that went nowhere, they paid $22,000 out of pocket while Hannah juggled caregiving duties with her job. The treatment worked as her husband regained significant mobility, but their retirement savings were decimated. "Sometimes I think about driving to the insurance company's headquarters and just screaming in their lobby until someone listens," Hannah told me during her CareYaya onboarding call.

Hannah's words sent a chill through me. They echoed my own darkest thoughts during Katie's treatment. I understood the primal frustration of watching someone you love suffer while faceless bureaucrats determine their fate based on profit calculations. Hannah would never commit violence. Neither would the vast majority of Americans frustrated by insurance denials. But her fantasy of making someone, anyone, in the system truly understand her family's suffering resonates with countless others who've found themselves shouting into the void.

A NATION DIVIDED

The media coverage following Thompson's murder revealed a nation wrestling with complicated emotions. Politicians, reporters, and other commentators uniformly condemned the violence, yet many contextualized it within widespread frustrations over the American healthcare system. Major news organizations like *Reuters* observed how Mangione's act resonated with segments of the public fed up with soaring medical costs and insurance claim denials.

What truly shocked establishment figures was the public response. A NORC survey found that while about 8 in 10 Americans placed significant responsibility on Mangione himself, a striking 70% also believed insurance companies' coverage denials and profit-driven practices bore at least moderate responsibility for Thompson's death. This nuanced reaction, condemning the act while understanding the underlying grievances, revealed much about America's relationship with its healthcare system.

Even more revealing was the generational divide. Young adults under 30 were far less inclined to find fault with Mangione as only about 40% said he deserved "a great deal" of blame, compared to 80% of seniors. These younger Americans were also more likely to distribute blame more evenly between the killer and an insurance industry they perceived as putting profits over people.

Social media told an even more disturbing story. Despite the quick removal of content explicitly celebrating violence, mainstream platforms couldn't contain the flood of personal insurance horror stories shared with hashtags like #DeniedToDeath and #InsuranceNightmare.

Television and print outlets struggled with how to frame the story. Some focused on Mangione's personal journey: a brilliant student from a privileged background who unraveled due to chronic pain. Others zeroed in on UnitedHealthcare's business practices, with headlines pointing out controversies such as algorithm-driven claim denials and hefty insurer profits while patients struggled to afford care. A *Vanity Fair* piece reported that "Luigi Mangione isn't solely responsible" for the CEO's death based on a non-partisan survey where participants also responded that insurance companies "bear a moderate amount of responsibility."

Comparisons with other countries' health systems provided a particularly stark perspective. In no other wealthy nation would an insurance executive be targeted because in those countries, insurers do not wield as much power in approving or denying essential treatment. This comparative angle has further fueled U.S. media debates on whether the outrage behind the crime, while misdirected into violence, stemmed from legitimate grievances unique to the American system.

HEALTHCARE PROFESSIONALS CAUGHT IN THE MIDDLE

The reaction from medical professionals revealed another layer of complexity. Healthcare leaders denounced the violence and expressed their condolences to Thompson's family, yet in quieter tones, many frontline healthcare workers acknowledged the underlying frustrations highlighted by Mangione's actions. On private physician forums and in staff lounges, conversations turned to the daily barriers insurance companies erect between doctors and patients.

During Katie's cancer treatment, I witnessed this firsthand. Her oncologist would spend her lunch breaks on the phone appealing denials for her patients. One afternoon, after a particularly frustrating call about Katie's case, she confessed to me: "Your wife's treatment plan was denied by a general practitioner who hasn't practiced medicine in eight years and now works full-time for the insurance company. He overruled my recommendation in less than two minutes without even reviewing her full file."

The defeated look in her eyes, a brilliant physician rendered powerless by an insurance algorithm, is something I'll never forget.

~~~

This experience is common. Nearly one in four physicians report that prior authorization delays or denials have led to serious adverse outcomes for their patients. This statistic, from an AMA survey, was frequently cited by doctors commenting on the case; it underscored how insurance hurdles can literally put lives at risk.

Insurers and industry representatives reacted defensively. UnitedHealth Group and other insurance companies emphasized that Mangione had no direct claim dispute with UnitedHealthcare, portraying him as a disturbed individual driven by personal demons. In public statements, insurance executives expressed fear that they could become targets, noting an uptick in threats against health insurance personnel after the shooting.

Some industry lobbying groups warned that demonizing insurers in public discourse could incite further violence, urging a focus on facts not rage. At the same time, some insurance executives acknowledged public dissatisfaction. In a guest essay in the *New York Times*, the CEO of UnitedHealth Group, Andrew Witty, wrote, "... we need to improve how we explain what insurance covers and how decisions are made. Behind each decision lies a comprehensive and continually updated body of clinical evidence focused on achieving the best health outcomes and ensuring patient safety."

This defensive posture, insisting denials are only for inappropriate services, was met with skepticism by providers who had fought insurers on necessary care. Privately, industry insiders indicated companies were in damage control, worried that Mangione had unexpectedly made them villains in the public eye.

The policy community, lawmakers, regulators, think tanks, also responded along predictable lines. Progressive politicians seized the moment to renew calls for health insurance reform. Several senators and representatives pointed to the case as proof that the for-profit insurance model is broken. Senator Chris Murphy stated that while he will never condone violence, policymakers need to listen to the visceral anger Americans feel toward insurance denials.

On the other side of the aisle, conservative lawmakers emphasized law and order. Some framed Mangione as a terrorist and cautioned against using his crime to justify expanding government healthcare programs. Still, a few acknowledged the rage and frustration fueled by rising premiums and opaque billing fuel resentment. Even those who opposed big government solutions admitted the industry should police itself better to avoid a public backlash.

THE DISAPPEARING ACT YOU PAY PREMIUMS FOR

WHEN DENIALS TURN DEADLY

As the initial shock faded, commentators began to connect the dots between the shooting and systemic failures in the U.S. healthcare and insurance system. One glaring issue was the practice of coverage denials for medically recommended treatment. Thompson's death shone a harsh light on how insurers routinely decide what to approve or deny, decisions that can mean life-or-death to patients.

For example, 17% of insured working-age adults reported having had an insurance claim denied for care their doctor deemed necessary. Many Americans began sharing their own stories of denials: a cancer patient whose MRI scan was initially refused as "not medically necessary," a diabetic person denied a newer insulin because of cost, a family billed thousands after an insurer declined coverage for a specialist surgery.

The MRI scan denial story hit particularly close to home. When Katie's oncologist ordered her first follow-up scan after treatment, our insurer denied it as "premature" despite her high risk of recurrence. I spent two weeks fighting the denial while my wife lay awake at night wondering if her cancer was silently returning. The insurer eventually approved the scan only after I threatened legal action and media exposure, but those two weeks of unnecessary anxiety remain one of the cruelest experiences of our journey. No algorithm can calculate the psychological torture of waiting for a scan that could determine your survival.

The Mangione case also exposed the practice of prior authorization, the insurer requirement that doctors obtain approval before prescribing certain treatments or medications. Originally intended as a cost-control measure, prior authorization has expanded into a major obstacle to timely care.

~~~

James, whose mother receives home care through CareYaya, told me how prior authorization nearly cost his mother her life. "Mom needed a specialized heart medication, but the insurance company denied it three times. They wanted her to try two other medications first, both of which her cardiologist already knew wouldn't work with her other conditions. By the time we finally got approval, she'd been hospitalized twice. Each hospitalization cost the insurance company far more than the medication would have."

I sat with James in his mother's living room as he told me this story, watching his hands tremble with suppressed rage. His mother, a retired schoolteacher, dozed in her recliner, still recovering from her most recent hospitalization.

"Know what the insurance company told me when I pointed out how much money they wasted by denying the medication?" he asked me. "They said it wasn't relevant because hospitalizations and prescriptions come from different budget categories. The left hand doesn't care what the right hand is doing, as long as they both maximize profit."

Drawing on my former career, I explained to James that he'd identified one of the system's most perverse incentives. Insurance companies operate in silos; the department denying medications rarely coordinates with the department paying hospital claims. Each is incentivized to minimize its own costs, even if the total cost to the system (and human suffering) increases. It's a fundamental design flaw that prioritizes departmental metrics over patient outcomes.

Another systemic failure highlighted by the Mangione case was the lack of transparency and accountability in insurance decisions. When state insurance commissioners and federal regulators are pressed on questions like: How often do insurers deny claims? Do they track patient outcomes after denials? The uncomfortable answer in many cases was that no one knows precisely. In California, for instance, health plans are not required by the state to report on a regular basis how often they deny treatment, which means there's limited oversight on patterns.

This opacity allows potentially harmful practices to continue unchecked. The lack of a robust, transparent system to address grievances may have intensified Mangione's exasperation. Had there been easier ways for patients to get unjust denials reviewed by an independent party, or for insurers to communicate their rationale and work with patients more proactively, extreme distrust of the industry might not have taken root. In short, the event revealed the alienation and powerlessness felt by many people when dealing with large insurance corporations.

A PATTERN OF SUFFERING

Across the country, insurance denials or bureaucratic hurdles have led to devastating consequences, including deaths.

One harrowing example is the case of Nataline Sarkisyan, a 17-year-old California girl whose story became national news in 2007. Nataline needed a liver transplant after complications from leukemia, but her insurer, Cigna, initially denied coverage for the transplant, deeming it experimental. Only after massive public outcry and protests with nurses and classmates picketing the insurer did Cigna reverse its decision. Tragically, the reversal came too late as

Nataline died only hours after the company belatedly approved the procedure.

Her death sent shockwaves through the healthcare system and became a rallying cry in health reform debates. The Sarkisyan family's grief was compounded by rage at a system that, in their view, sentenced their daughter to death. The case highlighted how an insurance denial for a recommended treatment can have fatal consequences.

More recently, consider the story of Kathleen Valentini, a 47-year-old wife and mother in New York. When her doctors feared her hip pain could be cancer and ordered an MRI, the imaging request required a third-party utilization review (a form of outsourced prior authorization). The company handling the review denied the MRI for weeks, requesting more documentation and second-guessing the need. During the wait, Kathleen's condition worsened; by the time she finally got approval, the MRI revealed an aggressive cancer that had spread. She underwent amputation, which doctors believed could have been avoided had there been no delays due to prior authorization, but ultimately passed from cancer. After her death, Kathleen's husband sued the review company, arguing their refusal to promptly authorize care essentially killed her.

Another case is that of Ryan Matlock, a young man in California struggling with opioid addiction. Determined to get clean, Ryan sought inpatient rehabilitation for fentanyl addiction. His doctors recommended an extended stay at a residential treatment facility specialized for his condition. However, his insurance plan, administered by Optum (a UnitedHealth Group subsidiary), denied the extended inpatient coverage, asserting that he no longer met the criteria since he was medically stable after a short detox stay.

In reality, while his acute withdrawal symptoms had subsided, he was far from cured of addiction, still requiring weeks of therapy and support. Forced to leave treatment early for financial reasons, Ryan relapsed. Heartbreakingly, within days of being discharged due to the insurance refusal, he died of a fentanyl overdose.

His case revealed with startling clarity the deadly gap between what medical professionals know a patient needs and what insurers are willing to cover. "Leaving could kill them," one expert said about patients in Ryan's situation, and in his case, it tragically did.

There are countless other less-publicized cases: a New Hampshire man who committed suicide when he couldn't afford his heart medication after an insurance denial; a Texas mother whose cancer became terminal as she waded through appeals to get an experimental therapy covered; a Florida family whose child died of a chronic illness complication after home nursing hours were cut by Medicaid managed care.

DON'T WORRY, WE'LL GET YOUR LIFE-SAVING MEDICATION APPROVED... IF YOU LIVE LONG ENOUGH TO COMPLETE THE PAPERWORK!

In many of these cases, the common thread is bureaucratic barriers to care or cost considerations overriding medical necessity. Each incident may differ in specifics, but collectively, they paint a picture of a health insurance landscape that sometimes yields tragic outcomes.

The comparisons to similar cases nationwide bolster the argument that Mangione's rage, while misdirected into violence, was rooted in very real, very pervasive failures of the status quo.

LONG-TERM IMPACT ON HEALTHCARE POLICY DISCUSSIONS

If the assassination of Brian Thompson sent immediate shockwaves through the healthcare industry, its ripples in policy discussions and reform debates will most likely be felt for years to come. Already, we can discern a change in tone where insurance policies and procedures are concerned. Although issues like coverage denials and insurer overreach had long been discussed in technocratic terms, they suddenly gained moral and emotional gravity in the halls of Congress and state legislatures. As American magazine *Jacobin* wrote, "the assassination of UnitedHealthcare CEO Brian Thompson in Manhattan last week has drawn more media scrutiny of America's healthcare system than we saw in the entire 2024 presidential election."

One tangible impact was a flurry of legislative proposals and inquiries. In late December 2024, within weeks of the incident, a bloc of lawmakers wrote to regulators demanding a thorough review of UnitedHealth Group's practices—everything from how it handles claims, to its use of algorithms in care decisions, to its growing acquisitions of medical providers.

Citing UnitedHealth's enormous market share, the lawmakers argued that such concentration can undermine competition and hurt patients, prior to floating the once-unthinkable idea of breaking up the company. While trust-busting an insurer is a long shot, the fact it was even suggested shows how the policy window opened.

I was struck by their new boldness. Until the Thompson shooting, most lawmakers would nod sympathetically but cite "political realities" that prevented meaningful action. Now, the same politicians were suddenly calling for structural reform. It was both encouraging and frustrating, but why did it take violence to spark the urgency these issues have always deserved?

~~~

Crucially, the case also reinvigorated calls for broader healthcare reform, including proposals that had stalled in recent years. Advocates of a single-payer system (Medicare for All) and public-option plans seized on the public outrage. They argued that a system removing for-profit insurers from the equation would prevent the kind of denial-driven despair that seemingly motivated Mangione. Senator Bernie Sanders referenced the case in advocating for Medicare for All, stating that "the current system is broken, it is dysfunctional, it is cruel, and it is wildly inefficient—far too expensive." He emphasized that real reform will require "a political revolution" to confront the power of insurance and pharmaceutical companies. Indeed, commentators observed that Thompson's murder generated more media scrutiny of the U.S. health system than the entire 2024 presidential election did.

Conservative reformers, while condemning the violence, also capitalized on the moment to advance their own vision for healthcare transformation. Republican leaders and conservative think tanks renewed calls for consumer-directed healthcare. Central to their response was an aggressive push to expand Health Savings Accounts (HSAs), which they claim lower healthcare spending by giving individuals more control over their dollars and incentivizing smarter choices. The Heritage Foundation and other groups proposed doubling HSA contribution limits and allowing their use for insurance premiums and direct care services. Reflecting these priorities, House Republicans' 2025 budget bill would raise annual HSA caps by roughly $4,300 for individuals and $8,550 for families, while decoupling them from high-deductible plans so that more Americans could contribute pre-tax funds for expenses like telehealth, direct primary care, or even health sharing ministries. GOP lawmakers also revived the Health Care PRICE Transparency Act, which would require hospitals and insurers to post real-time, payer-specific prices for shoppable services, enabling consumers, not prior authorization clerks, to influence costs at the point of purchase. Market-oriented policy groups like the Niskanen Center proposed layering universal catastrophic coverage on top of expanded HSAs, seeking to provide a safety net without crowding out consumer choice. While opinions diverged on the role of government, the incident exposed rare bipartisan agreement on one point: the system is deeply broken. Even conservative Reddit users voiced that "the healt[h]care system is beyond f---ed," sharing stories of denials and delays alongside their liberal counterparts.

This heightened awareness created political space to discuss reforms that had been on the back burner. By early 2025, there were renewed pushes for legislation to rein in prior authorization requirements (e.g., the "Safe Step Act" in Congress, that aims to limit step-therapy and ease overrides for insurers' denial decisions). Calls for transparency also grew louder. Some lawmakers now want insurers to publicly report their denial rates and clinical justifications, a measure directly responsive to the opacity highlighted by the case.

However, there are also signs of political gridlock and entrenched opposition. Insurance industry allies caution against "over-regulation" in reaction to a singular event, framing Mangione as an outlier. They argue that the focus should be on mental health and security, not overhauling insurance.

These voices have slowed the momentum of sweeping reforms. For instance, while prior-authorization reform bills gained co-sponsors, they faced pushback from committees influenced by insurance lobbyists. Similarly, proposals for a public insurance option at the state level (like in Connecticut and Colorado) saw invigorated public support after the shooting, but they, too, encountered familiar roadblocks. The conversation has changed, but converting that into policy change remains an ongoing battle.

The Mangione case has carved a place in the cultural and political narrative that will likely influence elections and policy making. Healthcare has long been a top voter issue, but typically the focus is on premiums and coverage. Now, the issue of "abusive insurance practices" has been thrust into that arena, and candidates may need to take a stance on it.

It's not hard to imagine campaign ads referencing the case, or candidates declaring "No one should have to do what Luigi did to be heard. We need change through legislation, not violence." In that sense, the case's legacy might be a sustained and sharpened dialogue on making the healthcare system more humane.

THE FINANCIAL PRECIPICE

The United States healthcare system not only poses risks to health but also to financial stability. Studies over the past decade have consistently found that medical bills are a leading cause of personal bankruptcy in the U.S. In one study, researchers estimated that as many as 66.5% of personal bankruptcies are tied to medical issues like high bills or lost income due to illness. This translates to roughly 550,000 families filing for bankruptcy each year because of medical costs.

To put that in perspective, that's like the entire population of a city the size of Atlanta financially collapsing annually under the weight of medical debt. It's a uniquely American problem; in most other wealthy countries, virtually no one goes bankrupt over healthcare. Here, however, the phenomenon is so common that "medical bankruptcy" is part of our vocabulary, and insurance claim denials contribute significantly to it.

A Kaiser Family Foundation (KFF) analysis found that about 40% of insured adults who faced problems paying medical bills usually experienced a claim denial. In many cases, these denials were for services the patients believed were covered, like an insurer deeming a procedure "not medically necessary" despite a doctor's recommendation, or not covering an out-of-network emergency bill.

Statistics on medical debt illustrate how precarious the situation is. As of 2022, around 100 million people in America (roughly 41% of adults) carry some amount of medical debt, from a lingering $200 lab bill to tens of thousands for surgery.

Once in debt, many face aggressive debt collection or must choose between paying medical bills and basic needs. Medical debt has become so widespread that platforms like GoFundMe have essentially turned into a shadow healthcare safety net. It's a grim reflection of our system that millions of Americans must ask strangers online for money to afford treatments, medications, or surgeries.

When those measures fail, bankruptcy becomes the last resort. Behind bankruptcy statistics are human stories: families selling belongings, parents skipping their own meals to pay for a child's therapy, individuals moving back in with relatives because medical debt cost them their home. Each insurance denial that leads to a major unexpected expense can trigger a cascade of financial trauma.

What's more, even the fear of financial ruin can affect health decisions. Surveys indicate that large numbers of Americans delay or skip medical care due to cost concerns. In 2022, about 38% of adults reported delaying or avoiding medical care because of cost. The fear of incurring large bills can turn small health issues into bigger, costlier ones. It's a vicious cycle: fear of denials and bills leads to worse health, which then leads to higher bills.

PROJECTED HEALTHCARE EXPENSES

The cost of healthcare in the United States keeps climbing, and all signs suggest it will continue to do so over the next decade. This escalation has wide-ranging implications: higher premiums, higher taxes for government programs, and likely more aggressive cost-control measures by insurers, which could translate to more denials if nothing else changes. It's a cycle that worries economists and strikes fear into patients and providers alike.

Let's talk numbers first. Healthcare spending in the U.S. is already the highest in the world in absolute terms and as a share of our economy. In 2023, national health expenditures were around $4.9 trillion (about 17.6% of GDP). Projections from the Centers for Medicare & Medicaid Services Office of the Actuary indicate that annual health spending is expected to grow by 5.6% per year over the next decade, outpacing the average GDP growth of 4.3%. As a result, health spending is projected to account for 19.7% of GDP by 2032.

Some analyses which factor in the aging Baby Boomer population paint an even more dramatic picture: one study suggested that by 2030, health spending could consume 32% of GDP if unchecked. While that figure might be an upper-bound scenario, it underscores the trajectory; healthcare is eating up a larger and larger share of our national resources.

What drives these cost increases? Several factors: an aging population (older people need more medical care), advances in medical technology and specialty drugs (which often come with high price tags), chronic disease prevalence (e.g., diabetes, heart disease remain widespread and expensive to manage), and general price inflation in the healthcare sector (hospital prices, drug prices, etc.). There's also the administrative overhead and profit margins of our complex system adding to costs.

For insured Americans, these rising costs are most obvious in rising insurance premiums and cost-sharing. The average employer-sponsored family premium in 2023 was about $24,000 a year, and early reports for 2024 show it creeping towards $25,000. Employers typically pay most of that, but workers' share (which was around $6,500 on average for a family plan in 2023) has been going up too, along with deductibles.

If trends persist, we might see family premiums well over $30,000 by decade's end. That's the equivalent to buying a new car every year just for health insurance. For those in the individual market or small group plans, premium hikes and high deductibles continue to be a challenge, sometimes pricing people out of coverage.

~~~

Mrs. Smith, a 78-year-old widow, came to us after her Medicare Advantage (MA) plan hiked her out-of-pocket costs for the third straight year. "When I first signed up five years ago, my maximum out-of-pocket was $3,400," she told me. "Now it's $7,550. My Social Security hasn't doubled, so where am I supposed to find that extra money if I get sick?"

Now, if healthcare costs double or triple over the next decade (as some projections suggest in total spending), insurance companies will undoubtedly implement measures to control their payouts. Historically, insurers have three main levers: increase premiums, shift more cost to patients (through higher deductibles/copays), or tighten utilization management (more prior auth, narrower networks, stricter denials for what they consider low-value care). We're likely to see more of all three if nothing systemic changes. That means the issues of coverage denials and delays could intensify—more stories of people being told "no" because the insurer is trying to keep costs down.

Moreover, as costs escalate, there's the possibility that employers and individuals will gravitate towards cheaper plans, which often entails plans with skimpier coverage, narrower networks, and higher cost-sharing. These plans keep premiums somewhat in check but at the expense of generous coverage. People might opt for them thinking they'll save money, only to be hit with more denials (because the plan might not cover, say, an out-of-network specialist or a brand-name drug) and more out-of-pocket when they do need care.

On the public side, government healthcare programs (Medicare, Medicaid) will also face cost pressures. Medicare is a huge spender, and as Baby Boomers age, its rolls will swell. If costs rise dramatically, the government might implement cost-control in Medicare that mirrors private insurance tactics (indeed, MA plans run by private insurers already use lots of prior authorization). Or there could be cuts to provider payments, which might indirectly affect patients if doctors refuse Medicare or if services become financially unviable.

One cannot talk about future costs without mentioning drug prices. The next decade promises incredible new therapies—gene therapies, personalized medicine, novel biologics—which can save lives but are often accompanied by six- or even seven-figure price tags. For instance, there's a newly approved gene therapy for a rare disease with a one-time cost of $2.1 million. Imagine many such treatments coming to market.

Insurers will have to decide: cover them and absorb the cost (raising premiums for everyone) or deny/limit them citing cost-effectiveness or experimental status. We may see more high-profile battles between patients wanting cutting-edge treatments and insurers reluctant to pay.

All these projections and possibilities underscore that without significant reform, rising healthcare costs could make the current problems of insurance denials and medical debt even worse. On the other hand, the unsustainability of cost growth might force changes. It could push policymakers to consider larger interventions (like price controls on drugs, a public option to compete with private insurers, more antitrust enforcement to reduce hospital or insurer monopolies).

Some analysts suggest that if we don't curb costs, we'll eventually hit a breaking point where the system simply cannot function. Too many people will be priced out, or we'll sacrifice other societal needs because health care consumes too much of the budget. In summary, the next decade is poised to test our system. If healthcare costs escalate as projected, Americans could face higher premiums and out-of-pocket costs, and insurers might respond with stricter cost controls (potentially more denials).

POLITICAL GRIDLOCK AND CORPORATE LOBBYING: THE BARRIERS TO CHANGE

When examining why meaningful health insurance reform has been so difficult, one must confront the twin elephants in the room: political gridlock and the power of corporate lobbying. These forces have long maintained the status quo, and they continue to shape what changes are (or aren't) possible in the aftermath of events like the Mangione case.

First, political gridlock: The U.S. political system is highly polarized, with healthcare reform often falling victim to partisan stalemates. Major changes typically require alignment of the Presidency and Congress, and even then, razor-thin margins can doom proposals. This was seen with the Affordable Care

Act's (ACA) passage and the later failed repeal attempt.

On issues of insurance regulation, such as tighter rules on denials or establishing a public option, there's a deep ideological divide. Democrats tend to push for more government oversight or involvement to protect consumers, while Republicans push back, warning against government overreach and defending free-market approaches. This has led to considerable paralysis on bold reforms.

This political divide has been strategically exploited by health insurance companies for over a century. Since the early 1900s, when progressive reformers first proposed state-based compulsory health insurance, insurers have actively opposed public health insurance measures that threatened their business. Their political influence has evolved from early lobbying efforts to a sophisticated operation involving campaign donations, direct lobbying, and public messaging campaigns.

For instance, even though surprise billing was something hated by voters from both parties, years of haggling and lobbying fights were spent in passing legislation—and that was for a relatively narrow issue. For broader issues like creating a public insurance plan or allowing Medicare to cover everyone (Medicare for All), the gridlock is even more pronounced. Politically powerful stakeholders can find allies on both sides of the aisle to halt proposals that threaten their interests.

This is where corporate lobbying comes in. The health insurance industry, along with pharmaceutical companies and hospital systems, form one of the most potent lobbying forces in Washington and state capitals. Healthcare is consistently the top sector for federal lobbying spending, shelling out over $600 million in 2019 alone.

The scale of this influence is staggering. Campaign contributions from the insurance industry have grown exponentially over decades, from about $14.4 million in the 1990 election cycle to a record $128 million in the 2020 cycle. The industry has historically favored Republicans with its donations, giving them approximately 55-60% of contributions in most election cycles since 1992, though insurers strategically adjust their giving based on which party controls Congress and key committees.

These dollars fund armies of lobbyists who work to influence legislation and regulation in ways favorable to industry players. America's Health Insurance Plans (AHIP), the main insurance industry trade group, spent over $13 million on lobbying in 2022. This is just the tip of the iceberg. In 2024 alone, AHIP spent $11.77 million on lobbying, while major insurers added much more: UnitedHealth Group spent $10.76 million in 2023, Cigna spent $8.25 million in

2024, and the Blue Cross Blue Shield system collectively spent a massive $27.1 million in 2024. That's just one organization. Individual insurance companies also spend millions, and that's not counting campaign contributions and PR campaigns. The effect is that many promising reforms get watered down or never see the light of day.

A concrete example: Medicare for All or single-payer proposals have massive lobbying opposition. It's not just insurers who fight it. Pharma, device makers, and even some provider groups fear it could reduce payments or profits. In 2019, when Medicare for All was a hot topic, the industry coordinated through the Partnership for America's Health Care Future (a coalition of insurers, hospitals, and pharma) to run ads and lobby lawmakers to oppose it. This coalition was explicitly formed in 2018 to combat Medicare for All and public option proposals, mirroring tactics from earlier battles. When President Bill Clinton proposed health reform in the 1990s, the Health Insurance Association of America (AHIP's predecessor) spent $14-15 million on the infamous "Harry and Louise" advertising campaign that helped sink Clinton's plan. That same year, under intense political pressure and industry influence, several high-profile presidential candidates, including Pete Buttigieg and Kamala Harris, initially voiced support for Medicare for All but later reversed or softened their positions. Buttigieg pivoted to advocating for a "Medicare for All Who Want It" public option, while Harris introduced a compromise plan that preserved a role for private insurance, a notable shift from her earlier full-throated support for single-payer.

Similarly, even incremental reforms like a "public option" health plan or expanding Medicare eligibility to younger people have been stymied by industry pressure. Insurers worry these would undermine their market share, so they invest heavily in convincing lawmakers (and the public via ads) that such moves are dangerous or unworkable.

Conservative proposals for consumer-directed healthcare and HSA expansion face their own forms of opposition, though often from different quarters than those fighting Medicare for All. Critics argue that HSA expansions benefit people with higher incomes, with 77 percent of the total deductible value of HSA contributions going to households with incomes over $100,000. Progressive groups like the Center on Budget and Policy Priorities actively lobby against HSA expansions, arguing they could crowd out policies that help people with low and moderate incomes afford health coverage and medical needs. Interestingly, the insurance industry itself, through America's Health Insurance Plans (AHIP), has shown mixed enthusiasm for consumer-directed reforms. This lukewarm support from the industry's own lobby reflects insurers' concern that truly empowered consumers with transparent pricing might actually reduce their profits by enabling more aggressive price shopping and plan switching

~~~

OpenSecrets reported that during the 2009–2010 Obamacare debates, the healthcare industry spent a record $270 million on lobbying in a single year and shaping the law to their liking (for instance, ACA ended up not having a public option, and it maintained private insurer roles). What's rarely mentioned is that AHIP secretly funneled $86.2 million to the U.S. Chamber of Commerce in 2009 to finance ads and campaigns attacking health reform proposals, even as it publicly claimed to support reform. This behind-the-scenes maneuvering helped ensure the final legislation would channel millions of new customers to private plans via insurance exchanges while eliminating the public option.

Another illustration, as noted previously, is how a group of lawmakers recently calling for action against UnitedHealth Group's size faces a steep uphill battle. UnitedHealth Group, being a behemoth, has deep lobbying pockets and influence. Over 2019–2024, UHG reportedly spent over $500,000 in Connecticut alone to block a state-level public option that threatened its business. Nationally, UnitedHealth Group has been one of the top political spenders among insurers, contributing $4.47 million in campaign donations in the 2024 cycle alone. The company's political influence is further amplified by its hiring practices. In 2023, approximately 51 out of 62 UnitedHealth lobbyists were former government officials, exemplifying the "revolving door" between government and industry that strengthens its influence network. Nationally, they and their competitors contribute generously to campaign funds of key committee members. This often means that regulatory proposals (like breaking up the company or limiting certain practices) might not get a fair hearing.

Lobbying isn't just about stopping things. It's also about setting the agenda. For example, insurance lobbyists have pushed for MA, the private plan part of Medicare, to be strengthened and grown. MA has indeed boomed, partly due to favorable rates and rules that lobbying has secured. When Congress created Medicare Part D (prescription drug coverage) and expanded Medicare Advantage in 2003, insurers and pharmaceutical companies deployed nearly 1,000 lobbyists (almost 10 per U.S. Senator) spending approximately $141 million on lobbying that year alone. This massive effort secured provisions requiring the new Part D benefit to be delivered via private insurers and prohibiting Medicare from negotiating drug prices. Critics say some MA plans have high denial rates or cherry-pick healthier patients, yet attempts to tighten oversight on those plans meet resistance due to the industry's influence.

An analysis found that insurers and related groups filed 22.6% of all new federal lobbying registrations in early 2020, illustrating how heavily they were lobbying especially during pandemic policymaking (when things like telehealth reimbursement, surprise billing, etc., were on the table).

At the state level, insurance commissioners and legislatures also face lobbying whenever they try to implement consumer protections. Health insurers maintain significant influence in state capitals through donations to gubernatorial campaigns and state legislators who oversee insurance committees. This state-level activity has repeatedly blocked single-payer initiatives. In Colorado, a single-payer state constitutional amendment called ColoradoCare was defeated after insurers helped fund a well-resourced opposition campaign. Similar scenarios have played out in California, where the insurance industry spent millions to defeat both a 1994 single-payer initiative (Proposition 186) and a 2014 proposition that would have required state approval for insurance rate hikes.

~~~

Working with families through CareYaya and Counterforce Health, I've heard countless stories about the human cost of this political inertia. The Robinsons spent 18 months fighting their insurer to cover their daughter's specialized therapy for her rare genetic condition. "Every time there's a big push for insurance reform in our state legislature," Mr. Robinson told me, "It seems to disappear into committee and never come back out. Later we read about insurance company donations to key lawmakers. It's like they've bought the right to ignore our daughter's needs."

The result of all this lobbying is often policy inertia or half-measures. Changes that could strongly protect patients, like banning most prior authorizations or allowing people to sue insurers for harmful denials, have not happened, in part because insurers argue these would increase costs or destabilize markets. And they often have the ear of policymakers who worry about budget impacts or who receive industry support.

It's worth noting the public is somewhat aware of this dynamic. The notion that "insurance companies and pharma have politicians in their pocket" is a common refrain, contributing to cynicism. In polls, large majorities of Americans across parties support things like letting Medicare negotiate drug prices (which pharma lobbied against for decades) or capping insulin costs, and when those don't happen quickly, people point to lobbying.

This cynicism is well-founded. The pattern of health insurance companies using political donations to shape policy dates back to the early 20th century. When President Harry Truman proposed universal public health insurance in 1945, the insurance industry supported the American Medical Association's record-breaking $1.5 million lobbying campaign to defeat it by branding it as "socialized medicine." The result? Truman's universal plan was blocked in Congress. This playbook of using substantial political investments to defeat reforms that threaten insurance industry profits has been repeated throughout American history.

Lobbying can however be weakened by strong all-public pressure. The furor following certain high-profile cases (like outrageous drug price hikes or the UnitedHealthcare CEO shooting) can sometimes overcome lobbying.

For example, the outrage over surprise billing eventually forced a law through in 2020 despite hospital and physician staffing firm lobbying. So, change is possible, but it often requires a groundswell to counteract the well-funded lobbyists. Reflecting on the Mangione case leads us to wonder about its legacy. Will it create enough public pressure to overcome lobbying inertia on issues like claim denials? Possibly in some areas. For instance, there's momentum on prior authorization reform (even CMS is proposing new rules to curb it in MA). Insurers are, of course, contesting those rules, trying to preserve flexibility. The outcome will depend on how much political capital leaders are willing to spend and how sustained the public outcry is.

Political gridlock and corporate lobbying have maintained insurance industry control over healthcare policies for a long time. Breaking the logjam likely requires persistent public engagement, savvy political strategy, and sometimes compromise. But as costs keep rising and more people are hurt by denials, the pressure is mounting. Some lawmakers are openly saying what was once unspeakable, echoing sentiments like those from Physicians for a National Health Program: "There will be no health care for all Americans until our leaders are willing to take on an insurance industry that showers them with cash." It remains to be seen if the coming years will see that willingness materialize.

HOW THIS BOOK WILL ARM YOU TO FIGHT BACK

This book is both a diagnosis and a prescription. In the chapters ahead, you'll learn exactly how the system works against you and how to fight back. We'll help you understand the healthcare system's structure, decode insurance

terminology, and provide practical tips for appealing denials. Beyond individual actions, we'll examine successful models of community organizing around healthcare issues and show how your personal experience can contribute to broader reform efforts.

The healthcare industry spends billions on lobbyists, lawyers, and PR firms to maintain their power. They've erected a seemingly insurmountable wall of complexity between you and your healthcare, hoping you'll give up before scaling it. But they've overlooked something crucial: when patients share knowledge and organize, their power crumbles.

This is the first book to directly address our current moment: the rise in wrongful insurance denials, the explosion of algorithmic claim rejections, the private equity playbook invading every corner of care, and the desperate scramble many families face to simply get the services they're already paying for. Others have covered the high cost of care or the policy failures of American healthcare, but this book is built to be used, not just read. It's an insider's map of the system's traps and an activist's toolkit for getting out of them.

My understanding of this crisis is deeply personal, shaped first by my own battles with insurance companies during my wife's cancer treatment, then by the countless heartbreaking stories I've heard from families seeking affordable care through CareYaya, and now by the determined patients who come to Counterforce Health, where we equip them with AI-powered tools to fight back against wrongful insurance rejections.

The American healthcare nightmare won't end overnight, but armed with the right tools and united in purpose, we can protect ourselves while building a more just system for all. Every time you successfully challenge a denial or negotiate a bill, you're not just winning your own battle. You're weakening the system's ability to exploit others. Our weapons are knowledge, solidarity, and persistent advocacy. Join us as we take back control from a system that has forgotten its purpose: healing, not profit.

PART I:
The Patient Trap

1

THE DENIAL INDUSTRY

> *"The greatest evil is not now done in those sordid 'dens of crime' that Dickens loved to paint...But it is conceived and ordered (moved, seconded, carried, and minuted) in clean, carpeted, warmed, and well-lighted offices, by quiet men with white collars and cut fingernails and smooth-shaven cheeks who do not need to raise their voices."*
>
> — *C.S. Lewis*

On a rainy Tuesday afternoon, Sarah sat at her kitchen table staring at an envelope from her insurance company. A third-grade teacher from Charlotte, Sarah had been diagnosed with stage 3 brain cancer six months earlier. The treatment was grueling—surgery, radiation, and now chemotherapy—but she'd been responding well. Her oncologist was cautiously optimistic.

Then the letter arrived.

"We regret to inform you that your claim for $47,326 for chemotherapy treatment has been denied. This service was determined to be not medically necessary according to our clinical guidelines."

Not medically necessary? Sarah read those words again, disbelief turning to rage. Her hands shaking, she flipped to the second page, searching for explanations among a sea of codes, subclauses, and references to policy sections. Buried at the bottom, she found a paragraph about her "right to appeal." There was a 180-day deadline and instructions to include "all relevant medical documentation."

Sarah called her insurance company immediately. After a seemingly interminable 47-minute wait she breathed a sigh of relief, only to be told by a customer service representative that her chemotherapy hadn't followed the "standard protocol" for her "specific condition classification." When Sarah asked what that meant, the representative couldn't explain. She'd need to have her doctor call the medical review department.

"But my oncologist prescribed this," Sarah said. "He's been treating brain cancer for 20 years!"

"I understand your frustration," came the practiced response. "But our medical review team has determined this treatment doesn't meet our criteria for coverage."

Sarah's story is tragically common. I've seen thousands of families devastated not just by illness, but by a system that abandons them at their most vulnerable moment. The cold, confusing letter Sarah received lies at the heart of America's healthcare crisis.

Insurance claim denials are neither rare accidents nor occasional mistakes. Instead, they are the product of a carefully engineered system, what I call the Denial Industry. This chapter will take you behind the curtain to see how this industry operates and how its mechanisms affect real people like Sarah.

CONFUSION BY DESIGN

Insurance denial letters and Explanations of Benefits (EOBs) represent a masterclass in obfuscation. They employ what linguists might call "strategic ambiguity," or language purposefully designed to be difficult to understand.

Consider this actual language from a denial letter received by one of our care recipients: "Based on the information provided, the requested service does not meet plan criteria for coverage determination as outlined in section 4.7.3(b) of your benefits handbook. This determination was made in accordance with generally accepted standards of medical practice."

What does that actually mean? Nothing specific enough to be actionable. The "information provided" could be anything. The reference to "section 4.7.3(b)" directs you to fine print you probably can't easily access. And "generally accepted standards of medical practice" sounds authoritative while saying nothing concrete.

This vagueness isn't accidental but strategic. The denial letter is designed to make you feel like the decision is final, based on sound medical judgment, and not worth fighting. In reality, many denials are automatically generated, based on arbitrary internal guidelines, and absolutely worth appealing.

With palpable exasperation, one ICU physician described her son's denial letters as "mostly pages of gobbledygook" that made no sense. That's a medical professional saying this. Imagine how incomprehensible these documents are to the average person.

Most denial letters include alphanumeric "reason codes" that supposedly explain why your claim was rejected. You might see something like "Denial code X478: Service not covered under plan benefits" or "Code B231: Documentation insufficient to support medical necessity."

These codes are technically "explained" in a key, but that explanation is often another layer of jargon. All too frequently the codes themselves conceal the true reason for denial behind generic language.

Mark, an IT manager whose mother needed post-stroke rehabilitation, showed me a denial that listed code "PA457" which the key defined as "Service requires prior authorization." But Mark had obtained prior authorization. In fact, he had the reference number to prove it. When he called, he discovered the real issue: the insurer claimed the facility was out-of-network, despite their hospital case manager's assurance it was approved.

"It's like they're speaking a different language on purpose," Mark told me. "And translators cost $400 an hour, if you can find one."

Some explanations for denials are so absurd they deserve special recognition:

- A Los Angeles man received a denial for a heart procedure stating he had requested spinal injections that were "not medically needed." However, he had never requested spinal treatment.
- A denial letter addressed to a newborn in the NICU claimed the infant was feeding and breathing on his own, making day four of intensive care unnecessary. The baby was on a ventilator and receiving nutrition intravenously.
- One member of the CareYaya community received a denial for her father's home oxygen, with the reason given that "the patient has not demonstrated low oxygen saturation while walking." Her father was bedridden and physically unable to walk.

These aren't simple errors. They reflect a system designed to say "no" first and ask questions later if at all.

COMMON DENIAL REASONS AND THEIR HIDDEN MEANINGS

While denial letters provide a vast array of reasons why your claim won't be paid, certain justifications appear with remarkable frequency. Learning to decode these common denial reasons is the first step in fighting back.

"Not Medically Necessary"

This is perhaps the most common and frustrating denial. It suggests your doctor, the medical professional who actually examined you, prescribed treatment you don't really need.

What it actually means: "We don't want to pay for this treatment."

Insurers maintain internal, proprietary guidelines for what they consider "necessary" care. These guidelines are often far more restrictive than standard medical practice. A landmark legal case against United Behavioral Health (UBH) found the company used overly strict guidelines not aligned with accepted standards, resulting in the wrongful denial of mental health and substance abuse treatment for tens of thousands of patients.

One pediatric gastroenterologist noted that his patients' MRE scans were routinely denied as "not necessary" in favor of older CT scans, even though MREs were the safer, recommended option for children. This was clearly a cost-driven decision rather than a medical one.

When you appeal such denials, they are often reversed. For instance, in Cigna's MA plans, 80% of appealed "not necessary" denials were overturned. This suggests the initial determination was incorrect by the insurer's own standards.

"Experimental/Investigational"

This denial implies the treatment is unproven or experimental, despite often being standard care at major medical centers.

What it actually means: "This treatment is too expensive, so we're claiming it's unproven."

Proton beam therapy for cancer is a prime example. Despite evidence of its efficacy for certain tumors, many insurers long refused coverage by classifying it as experimental. That's why internal policies at some companies automatically trigger denials for proton therapy, requiring patients to undergo a lengthy fight

to prove its necessity.

One major insurer (Aetna) was sued in a class action for systematically denying proton therapy; it ultimately agreed to a multi-million dollar settlement over these practices.

"Service Not Covered by Policy (Exclusion)"

This denial points to a contractual exclusion in your policy.

What it actually means: "We specifically wrote the policy to avoid paying for this."

Health plans exclude certain categories of care outright such as fertility treatments, weight loss surgery, or alternative therapies. The problem is that patients often don't realize something is excluded until they need it. These exclusions are cost-saving measures buried in the fine print.

Elena Gomez, a 35-year-old with endometriosis, discovered her insurance explicitly excluded the laparoscopic surgery her gynecologist recommended as the standard treatment. "They covered medications that barely helped and made me sick, but excluded the one procedure that could actually fix the problem," she told me. "It's like they designed the policy to ensure maximum suffering."

"Lack of Prior Authorization/Referral"

This denial cites failure to obtain pre-approval before receiving services.

What it actually means: "You didn't complete our bureaucratic obstacle course."

Prior authorization requirements have exploded in recent years, with insurers claiming they control costs and prevent unnecessary care. However, research shows they primarily create administrative barriers that delay necessary treatment.

In marketplace plans from 2021, about 8% of all denials were issued for no prior authorization or referral. Insurers have been accused of deliberately making the prior authorization process difficult, hoping patients don't get approval in time, thereby justifying a denial.

A neurologist I once spoke with described spending over 20 hours per week on prior authorization requests. "The forms are different for every insurer, the requirements constantly change, and they often 'lose' our submissions," she said. "It's not about improving care. it's about wearing us down until we give up."

"Out-of-Network Provider/Service"

This denial indicates you saw a provider not in your insurer's network.

What it actually means: "We've limited our network to control costs, and you stepped outside it."

Network restrictions have tightened dramatically, often without patients realizing it. Even at in-network hospitals, you may be treated by out-of-network specialists (like anesthesiologists or radiologists), leading to surprise bills.

Laws against "surprise billing" have started addressing some of these scenarios, but insurers still routinely deny non-emergency out-of-network care, even when no in-network specialist is available for your condition.

"Technical/Administrative Denials"

These include coding errors, duplicate claims, or incomplete information.

What it actually means: "We found a technicality to avoid payment."

A large portion of denials fall into miscellaneous categories that are often coding errors or incomplete information. While some are legitimate errors that can be corrected, insurers benefit when claims get dropped or delayed in the shuffle.

THE AUTOMATED REJECTION FACTORY

In 2021, Dr. Nick van Terheyden underwent a blood test to investigate the persistent bone pain he suspected was due to a vitamin D deficiency. The test confirmed it, but his insurer, Cigna, denied the $350 claim, deeming it "not medically necessary." A physician himself, Dr. van Terheyden was stunned: "This was a clinical decision being second-guessed by someone with no knowledge of me."

Only later, through a *ProPublica* investigation did Dr. van Terheyden discover his claim was likely denied via Cigna's PXDX algorithm, without a doctor ever looking at his file. The denial even contained a catch-22 rationale, stating the test was unnecessary since there was no prior evidence of deficiency.

In other words, the denial relied on circular logic, since the only way to find a deficiency is to perform the test.

Welcome to the age of algorithmic denial, where software, not medical professionals, determines whether your care will be covered.

Cigna's PXDX

In recent years, health insurers have increasingly turned to automation and AI algorithms to process (and deny) claims on a massive scale. Instead of assessing each claim individually, software flags those that meet certain criteria for automatic denial.

The poster child for this approach is Cigna's "PXDX" system (short for "procedure-to-diagnosis"), which was exposed by an investigative report in 2023. PXDX is essentially an algorithm that allowed Cigna's medical directors to batch-process denials without reviewing patient files.

The system compares submitted claims against a list of predetermined denial "rules." If a claim's reported diagnosis doesn't strictly warrant the procedure per Cigna's with list, it is flagged. A Cigna doctor then rejects dozens of claims in seconds with a few clicks with no need to open each patient's chart. As one

former Cigna medical director described: "We literally click and submit." According to internal records, a single Cigna doctor denied 121,000 claims in the first two months of 2022 using this method, averaging only 1.2 seconds per claim review.

Let that sink in. 1.2 seconds per claim. That's physically impossible for a human to thoughtfully evaluate a medical case.

United's Mental Health Algorithm

UnitedHealth's Optum unit reportedly developed an algorithm (part of a program called "ALERT") to flag mental health therapy claims deemed "excessive," leading to denials or administrative hurdles for patients seeking ongoing therapy.

Internal emails revealed there was "no real clinical rationale" behind these limitations. They were purely financial decisions disguised as medical review. In New York alone, United had to reprocess claims for 34,000 therapy sessions they unjustly denied via this algorithm.

As one former UnitedHealthcare "care advocate" said, he felt like "a cog in the wheel of insurance greed."

The Human Cost of Algorithmic Denial

The automation targets mostly low-cost, routine claims—often things like blood tests, screenings, or minor procedures that cost a few hundred dollars each. By denying these en masse, insurers save money in two ways: they avoid paying the claims and reduce labor costs since doctors don't have to spend time on each file.

Robert "Skeeter" Salim, a prominent attorney, had his advanced throat cancer treatment (proton therapy) denied by Blue Cross as "investigational." Internal appeals were handled by external review companies that simply copied and pasted the insurer's guidelines to uphold the denial. Essentially, an algorithmic guideline, not Salim's medical needs, dictated the outcome at each stage.

These systems push costs onto patients and providers unless they fight back. Insurers know that only a small fraction of people will appeal. In fact, internal documents showed Cigna expected only about 5% of people to appeal denials from PXDX.

As one former industry executive put it bluntly: "Why not just deny them all and see which ones come back on appeal? From a cost perspective, it makes sense."

INSIDE INSURER DENIAL DEPARTMENTS

Behind every claim denial (even automated ones) is an organization of people following policies and incentives. The internal culture and practices of insurance companies' claims and utilization review departments are shaped by performance metrics that often reward denials.

Within claims departments, employees have targets like closing a certain number of cases per day or ensuring the department's payout stays under a certain budget. There is often an inherent bias: approving a costly claim can draw scrutiny ("Why did you okay that $100,000 treatment?"), whereas denying it typically does not result in immediate internal criticism.

One of our CareYaya family caregivers, Jennifer, previously worked as a claims processor at a major insurer. She described a point system where adjusters received better scores for processing claims quickly, with bonuses tied to department-wide savings targets.

"There was no explicit instruction to deny claims," Jennifer told me. "But the metrics made it clear. If our department approved too many expensive claims, everyone's numbers looked bad. The path of least resistance was to find a reason to deny anything complicated."

Nurse Reviewers

Most insurers employ teams of nurse reviewers whose job is to evaluate claims or prior authorization requests flagged by the system. As the first live humans involved in the review process, they operate under immense pressure.

Dr. Debby Day described how nurses at Cigna would prepare denials for doctors to sign off. She characterized their work as "increasingly sloppy," with many cases that should have been approved getting denied upfront. These nurses were likely stretched thin or following rigid guidelines, leading to inappropriate denials.

The process creates moral distress for healthcare professionals who entered medicine to heal. As one former nurse reviewer told me at a conference: "I started having panic attacks. I knew I was hurting patients, but if I approved too many claims, my performance reviews suffered. Eventually, I had to quit. I couldn't look at myself in the mirror anymore."

The Corporate Culture

The corporate ethos can be gleaned from job titles and internal slogans. It's telling that one insurer employed nurses with the literal title "denial nurse." Their job was primarily to process denials, not approvals or patient advocacy.

Not all insurers are equally aggressive. The insurers that deny only a small percentage of claims (under 5-10%) might have an internal culture more focused on paying what's due and only challenging truly inappropriate claims. The variation among companies suggests that the tone is set at the top.

APPEALS INFRASTRUCTURE

When an insurance claim is denied, patients nominally have the right to appeal. In theory, this process exists to correct mistakes and ensure proper coverage. In practice, it's a complex, discouraging system that few patients successfully navigate.

There is no single, unified appeals process in the U.S. since it can vary by plan type and jurisdiction. A patient with an employer-sponsored self-funded plan (governed by ERISA) will have a different process than someone with an individual market plan under state law, or a MA plan, or Medicaid. Studies by KFF found that about 69% of insured adults who experienced a denial did not even know their plan had an appeals process or that they had the right to challenge a denial.

Veteran health journalist, Cheryl Clark, who attempted to map out the appeals pathways described it as a "mind-boggling labyrinth." She found that depending on what type of insurance a person has, the deadlines, steps, and even where to send an appeal differ dramatically.

Nearly everyone she interviewed, from doctors to lawyers to patient advocates, said that creating an easy, universal guide to appeals was "almost impossible."

The Burden of Effort

Even for those who know they can appeal, the burden is high. The patient (or their doctor on their behalf) must gather supporting medical documentation, write a formal appeal letter or fill out forms, and often get letters of medical necessity from providers. It can require hours of phone calls and paperwork.

For someone already dealing with illness or injury, this administrative battle can be overwhelming. In fact, the very patients most likely to face denials, those with serious health conditions, are often least able to take on an appeals fight. In addition to suffering from intense pain, they may be fatigued or cognitively impaired by illness or medications.

Karen, who used CareYaya while battling stage 4 lung cancer, described her attempts to appeal a denial while undergoing chemotherapy: "I couldn't even sit up for more than an hour at a time. I was vomiting daily from treatment. And they expected me to compile medical records, write letters, and make hour-long phone calls? It was literally impossible in my condition."

The Numbers Don't Lie

The statistics on appeals are shocking but revealing:
- In ACA marketplace plans, of the over 48 million denied in-network claims in 2021, consumers filed only 90,599 appeals. That's an appeal rate of just 0.2% (approximately one in 500 denied claims).
- Cigna's internal estimate for its PXDX denials projected only 5% of those quick denials would ever be appealed.
- Across all types of private health insurance, roughly 85% of denied claims go unappealed.

And yet, when patients do appeal, they often win:
- According to ACA marketplace data, when consumers appealed, about 41% of internal appeals led to the insurer reversing the denial.
- In MA plans, enrollees who appealed prior authorization denials won 80% of those appeals.

That means up to four out of five times, the insurer's denial was found to be unwarranted when an independent reviewer looked at it, a striking confirmation that insurers err or overreach frequently.

STATISTICAL ANALYSIS: HOW OFTEN AND WHO IS AFFECTED

Data on health insurance claim denials reveals the scale of the issue and variations across insurers, procedures, and patient groups.

In 2021, marketplace insurers reported receiving 291.6 million in-network claims and denying 48.3 million of them, an average denial rate of 16.6%. In other words, about 1 in 6 claims for in-network services was denied.

There was wide variation among insurers. Some plans denied less than 5% of claims, while at the other extreme, one insurer denied 49% of in-network claims in 2021. In 2020, a plan even hit an astonishing 80% denial rate.

Outside the marketplace, KFF's 2023 consumer survey found 18% of insured adults said they had a medical claim denied in the past year. Denials were more commonly reported by those with private insurance (21% of employer plan enrollees, 20% of individual marketplace enrollees) than those on public programs like Medicare (10%) or Medicaid (12%).

This suggests that private insurers, particularly those covering working-age people, deny claims at higher rates than government coverage does.

Who Gets Denied More?

Certain demographics experience more denials than others. The KFF survey found those who use a lot of health services (i.e., visited their provider over 10 times per year) had higher rates of denial—about 27% of people in the top utilization group. In contrast, only 14% of those who visited their provider less than 3 times a year experienced a denial.

This means the most ill or weakest patients face the most fights with their insurance, precisely when they're least equipped to battle bureaucracy.

Children also face unique challenges. Pediatric specialists often complain that insurance criteria are built around adult care norms, leading to inappropriate denials for children. One pediatric gastroenterologist's account noted how children with Crohn's disease were denied modern treatments because insurers only recognized adult FDA approvals.

Which Services Get Denied Most?

Denial rates vary by the type of service. Certain categories consistently see frequent denials:

- **Mental Health Services:** Mental health claims are often denied at higher rates, usually citing "medical necessity." A joint report by federal and state regulators in 2022 found many insurers failing to comply with mental health parity, effectively denying mental health care at levels that would not occur for analogous medical care.
- **Advanced Therapies:** New gene therapies or biologics (costing hundreds of thousands) see denials under "investigational" or "out of network" reasons.
- **Durable Medical Equipment and Rehabilitation:** These often get partial denials (e.g., approving only 10 physical therapy visits when 20 were requested).
- **Testing and Imaging:** Routine labs can be denied as unnecessary, and expensive imaging (MRIs, CTs) can be denied if the insurer prefers a cheaper alternative.

Denial Trends Over Time

Statistically, denials have been on the rise in recent years. Insurance claim denials have risen 16% from 2018 to 2024. From 2022 and 2023, commercial and MA claims denials increased an average of 20.2% and 55.7%. Elisabeth Rosenthal's 2023 investigation notes that millions of Americans are now encountering denials for claims that "once might have been paid immediately."

Insurers, armed with algorithms and stricter policies, are denying more as a cost-containment strategy, especially after the ACA mandated minimum Medical Loss Ratios (requiring 80-85% of premiums to go toward claims). Insurers can still increase profits by reducing the numerator (claims paid)—hence an incentive to deny more claims.

THE PSYCHOLOGICAL IMPACT

Getting a denial from an insurance company can trigger a cascade of negative emotions and health consequences for patients. Many describe the experience as deeply frustrating—they did everything right by paying premiums, visiting in-network providers, and following their doctor's recommendations, only to face rejection from their insurer. This betrayal of the basic insurance contract often leads to feelings of anxiety, anger, and profound helplessness.

The psychological impact extends beyond mere frustration. Patients facing serious diagnoses experience genuine fear when treatments are denied. A cancer patient refused a specific chemotherapy regimen might view this as their best chance at remission being taken away. For those with chronic conditions, the repeated battles create a "wear-down" effect that some describe as more traumatic than dealing with the illness itself. Many patients report feeling defeated or depressed by these ongoing insurance struggles.

The financial devastation resulting from denials significantly compounds this psychological distress. When insurers refuse to pay, patients can suddenly face bills ranging from tens of dollars to hundreds of thousands, creating immediate panic and long-term anxiety. Medical debt in the U.S. is already widespread, with the Commonwealth Fund reporting almost one-third of working-age adults struggling with medical or dental debt, and claim denials represent a major pipeline into such financial hardship.

The consequences extend beyond emotional and financial distress to tangible health deterioration. A vicious cycle forms where denials lead to delayed care, which worsens health conditions, potentially requiring more intensive treatments that might face further denials. Indeed, the Commonwealth Fund found that nearly 60% of people who experienced a coverage denial had their care delayed as a result, forcing many to forgo necessary treatment entirely.

Perhaps unsurprisingly, consumers who experience denials report significantly less confidence in their insurance coverage and greater difficulty understanding their benefits. This uncertainty creates an additional mental burden as patients begin second-guessing every medical decision, constantly wondering "will this be denied?" It's a psychological weight that no patient should have to carry while focusing on their health.

INDUSTRY SECRETS

The "delay, deny, defend" strategy has become so entrenched in modern insurance operations that even former insurance executives discuss it candidly. This three-word formula, which became tragically relevant in the Mangione case, captures the essence of how insurers systematically obstruct legitimate claims as a profit-maximization strategy.

When police recovered arrived on scene after the attack on UnitedHealthcare CEO Brian Thompson, they found that each of the three spent cartridges had been meticulously engraved with words: "deny," "defend," and "depose." These were deliberate references to what Mangione had experienced and to Jay Feinman's influential book *Delay, Deny, Defend: Why Insurance Companies Don't Pay Claims and What You Can Do About It*.

Feinman shares how what appears to consumers as bureaucratic incompetence or isolated incidents of poor service is actually a calculated business strategy. Behind the statistics and policies, there is a growing body of insider accounts and whistleblower revelations that expose how some insurers manipulate systems and prioritize profit over patients.

Delay: Strategic Stalling Tactics

Insurance companies systematically delay processing or payment as long as possible. They create procedural hurdles that exhaust and frustrate claimants. Documents are "lost," communications go unanswered, and simple requests require mountains of paperwork. These aren't just annoyances but deliberate friction points designed to wear patients down.

Some life and long-term care insurers literally would stall until the policyholder died. As noted by one regulator, "They'll do anything to avoid paying, because if they wait long enough, they know the policyholders will die."

Deny: Systematic Rejection Mechanisms

Even after delays, many valid claims receive automatic denials. Insurers know statistically that a significant percentage of patients will simply give up after an initial denial rather than navigate a complex appeals process. For seriously ill patients already dealing with physical suffering, the energy required to fight an insurance company can be simply too much.

Speed and Productivity Pressure

One of the most damning insights comes from Dr. Debby Day, who served as a Cigna medical director for over 15 years. In 2023, she became a whistleblower, revealing that her superiors increasingly emphasized speed over accuracy when evaluating claims and prior authorization requests. According to Dr. Day, Cigna "tracks every minute" a staff doctor spends on each case. There was a dashboard tracking each doctor's decision times, fostering a factory-like environment

In late 2020, she was bluntly told to work faster or be fired. She was expected to process cases at a rate that, in her view, compromised proper review. The company mantra was clear and chilling: "Deny, deny, deny. That's how you hit your numbers." Dr. Day observed colleagues complying with directives to speed up and deny more—many medical directors would just "click and close" cases quickly to keep up with quotas. Even life-saving treatments like surgeries or chemotherapy could be on the line; nonetheless, the pressure was to find a reason to say no if it helped meet the metrics.

Narrow Medical Criteria

Whistleblowers in mental health parity cases have also provided inside views. In the Wit v. UBH trial, internal emails and testimonies from clinicians within UBH (United Behavioral Health) showed how guidelines were doctored to limit care.

One key finding was that UBH's internal policies were guided by utilization managers rather than by current clinical science, leading to systematic under-approval of care. Essentially, UBH secretly substituted its own narrow definition of "medical necessity" in place of generally accepted standards, resulting in denials for thousands who actually needed care.

That's an industry secret: many insurers have internal criteria that are much stricter than what independent medical experts would consider appropriate. They do not advertise this fact; patients and providers only find out when care gets denied.

Algorithmic Denial Systems

Another insider perspective came from former Cigna officials interviewed in the PXDX investigation. One former Cigna medical director admitted, "The

PXDX stuff is not reviewed by a doc or nurse or anything like that," basically confirming that the algorithm bypassed normal review, something Cigna never told regulators or customers.

Another former executive defended the practice from a business angle, illustrating the mindset: He said he understood the economics and that the system "has undoubtedly saved billions" for Cigna, implying that in corporate strategy terms, it's a success.

Financial Incentives for Denial

Incentive structures have been a dirty secret. Health Net (a California insurer) was found to have paid bonuses to employees specifically for canceling coverage of sick policyholders to dodge big claims. After being caught, they were fined.

Insurers have since gotten savvier. Incentives might be subtler (e.g., department performance goals), but whistleblowers like Dr. Day make it clear that job security itself is wielded as an incentive: do as we say (deny more) or we'll find someone who will.

Defend: Aggressive Opposition to Claims

For those persistent patients who continue pursuing their claims, insurers deploy sophisticated legal and bureaucratic defenses that make resolution prohibitively expensive or time-consuming. They never admit fault, force the patient to prove the claim is payable, or take legal action.

After decades of relatively straightforward claims processing, insurers discovered that systematically challenging claims, even legitimate ones, could significantly boost their bottom line. The combination of delay tactics, systematic denials, and aggressive defense creates a nearly impenetrable barrier for many patients seeking the care they're entitled to under their policies.

THE ROAD AHEAD

Throughout this chapter, we've examined the machinery of denial. The picture is grim: a sophisticated system designed to maximize profit by minimizing payment for care.

But there is hope.

When Robert "Skeeter" Salim, the attorney denied proton therapy for his cancer, faced Blue Cross's rejection, he didn't accept it. He paid out of pocket for the treatment, then took Blue Cross to court. His legal knowledge gave him an advantage most patients don't have, but his story shows that the system can be beaten.

Sarah, the teacher I introduced at the beginning of this chapter, eventually won her appeal with help from a patient advocate and her oncologist's detailed documentation. Her chemotherapy was covered after a three-month battle, but she shouldn't have had to fight in the first place.

In the coming chapters, we'll explore the financial machinery that makes denial profitable (Ch. 2), hear more voices from the battlefield (Ch. 4), and most importantly, learn concrete strategies for fighting back (Ch. 7-9).

For now, remember these key takeaways:

1. Claim denials are not random errors. They're part of a systematic process designed to boost profits by denying care.
2. The confusing language in denial letters is deliberately engineered to discourage appeals.
3. Common denial reasons like "not medically necessary" or "experimental" often mask financial decisions, not medical ones.
4. Automated systems like Cigna's PXDX deny claims at inhuman speeds without proper review.
5. The appeals process is complex by design, yet those who persist often win.
6. The psychological and financial toll of denials creates a secondary health crisis for patients.

7. Whistleblowers have confirmed what many suspected: some insurers explicitly incentivize denials.

As we'll see in the next chapter, these denial systems are just one gear in a larger profit-making machine. To truly understand why your care gets denied, we need to follow the money.

The healthcare system may seem impenetrable, but it's made up of human decisions that can be challenged and changed.

2

PROFITS OVER PATIENTS

"It is difficult to get a man to understand something when his salary depends upon his not understanding it."
— *Upton Sinclair*

When Wendy, a 42-year-old librarian from North Carolina, came to us seeking help for her mother's dementia care, she brought a stack of insurance statements. Spreading them across my desk, she pointed to her monthly premium: $1,487.

"I've paid this for three years without a major claim," she said. "That's over $53,000. Now that Mom needs help, they're denying everything. Where did all that money go?"

This question lies at the heart of America's healthcare crisis. The answer reveals why our healthcare system fails so many Americans, and why insurance companies consistently rank among America's most profitable industries despite declining customer satisfaction.

Let's follow Wendy's premium dollar through the labyrinth of corporate health insurance to understand why so little reaches actual patient care.

For every dollar Wendy pays, approximately 80-85 cents eventually goes to medical claims—hospital care, doctor visits, and prescriptions. The industry calls this the "medical loss ratio" (MLR), a telling term that reveals how insurers view their core function. When they pay for your healthcare, they consider it a "loss."

The remaining 15-20 cents breaks down into administrative expenses (around 13-14 cents) and profit (roughly 1-4 cents). At first glance, these profit margins might seem modest. Insurance industry representatives frequently highlight these single-digit percentages in congressional testimony and media interviews to defend their business practices.

But this framing obscures the bigger picture. While profit margins may be relatively small per premium dollar, the absolute sums are astronomical. UnitedHealth Group, America's largest health insurer, reported net earnings exceeding $20 billion in 2023. That's more than the GDP of nearly 80 countries.

The focus on percentage profit margins is deliberate misdirection. It's like a grocery store claiming they only make pennies per item while omitting that they sell billions of items.

UnitedHealth returned over $16 billion to shareholders through stock buybacks and dividends in 2023 alone. This wealth transfer from premium-paying families to shareholders represents enough money to provide comprehensive healthcare for millions of currently uninsured Americans.

Wendy's case illustrates how this system works in practice. After three years of paying premiums without major claims, her insurer collected over $53,000 from her family. When her mother finally needed substantial care, the company deployed the sophisticated denial apparatus we examined in Chapter 1: challenging the medical necessity of memory care services, requiring endless documentation, and ultimately approving only a fraction of what her physician recommended.

"They made tens of thousands from us while we were healthy," Wendy told me, "then fought us for every dollar once we needed care."

This dynamic of collecting maximum premiums while minimizing payouts is the fundamental business model of private health insurance. To understand why our healthcare system fails so many Americans, we need to examine not just how much profit insurers make, but how they make it.

ADMINISTRATIVE BLOAT

When Michael, a restaurant owner in Atlanta, contacted us about care options for his father following a stroke, his first question wasn't about caregiving techniques or rehabilitation services. It was simpler and more desperate: "How do I get past the insurance company's phone tree to speak to an actual human being?"

Michael had spent 17 hours over three days trying to get a straight answer about coverage for his father's rehabilitation. Each call meant navigating an intricate automated system, explaining his situation repeatedly to different representatives, and ultimately receiving contradictory information.

"I'm running a business while trying to care for my dad," he said, "and I've wasted nearly half a work week just trying to understand what's covered."

Michael's experience is a window into one of the most troubling aspects of American healthcare: administrative bloat. While insurers typically claim that 13-14% of premiums go to administration, independent research paints a far more disturbing picture of system-wide administrative waste.

A landmark study published in the *Annals of Internal Medicine* found that bureaucracy consumed approximately 34% of total U.S. healthcare spending. That's over $800 billion annually. This represents a staggering increase from about 31% in 1999, demonstrating that administrative costs grow faster than medical expenses.

For perspective, Canada's single-payer system spends about 17% on administration, or half the U.S. rate. In per-person terms, Americans pay approximately $844 per person annually on insurance overhead, compared to just $146 per person in Canada. The difference isn't because American administrators are less efficient. It's because our system is designed to maximize complexity rather than care. This complexity manifests in multiple ways:

First, the multi-payer landscape forces providers to maintain massive billing departments. A typical American hospital employs more billing specialists than beds. These workers aren't providing care but rather navigating the labyrinthine requirements of dozens of insurance plans, each with different rules, codes, and documentation demands.

Secondly, insurers themselves maintain enormous administrative infrastructures dedicated to reviewing claims, processing paperwork, and critically, finding reasons to deny coverage. United Healthcare, for instance, employs over 350,000 people, relatively few of whom are directly involved in patient care.

Thirdly, the marketing and sales apparatus is enormous. MA plans alone spend billions annually on television advertising, broker commissions, and direct marketing. These costs, ultimately paid by premiums and taxpayers, don't contribute a penny to actual healthcare.

Fourthly, the lobbying machine is relentless. The insurance industry spent nearly $158 million on lobbying in 2023 —funds used to fight against regulations that might limit their profit mechanisms or expand public insurance options that could threaten their business model.

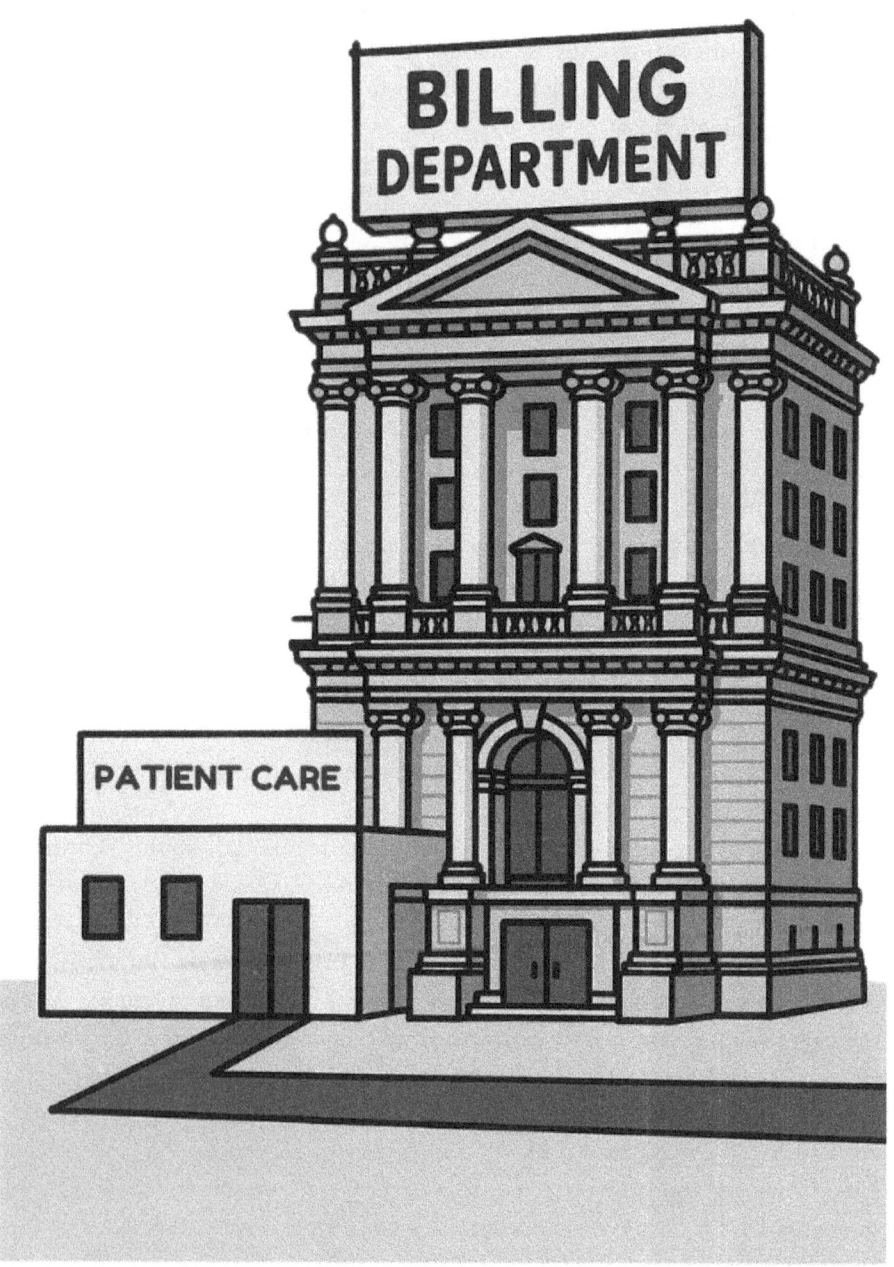

NOW EMPLOYING MORE BILLING SPECIALISTS THAN BEDS!

Michael eventually got his answer after contacting his state insurance commissioner's office, but his experience illuminates a critical truth: administrative bloat isn't a bug in our system, but rather an established feature. The complexity serves as a defensive moat protecting insurance profits.

INCENTIVIZING DENIAL

In February 2023, I was invited to participate in a healthcare innovation roundtable at a major university. During lunch, I found myself seated next to a recent retiree who had served as an executive at one of America's largest health insurers.

After some small talk, I asked him the question that had long puzzled me: "How do insurance executives reconcile their mission statements about improving healthcare with business practices that often seem designed to deny it?"

He looked around, then leaned in. "It's simple," he said. "We were compensated based on the 'medical loss ratio.' The less we paid for care, the bigger our bonuses."

This candid admission offers a window into one of the most troubling aspects of health insurance: executive compensation packages that directly reward limiting patient care.

The numbers are staggering. In 2023, UnitedHealth Group CEO Andrew Witty received $23.5 million in total compensation. CVS Health (which owns Aetna) CEO Karen Lynch earned $21.6 million. Cigna's CEO David Cordani earned $21 million. These packages typically include base salary, performance bonuses, and substantial stock awards.

For perspective, these CEOs earn more in a single day than most American families make in a year. More troublingly, their performance metrics often include controlling the "medical loss ratio," meaning they personally profit from ensuring less money goes to actual healthcare.

This compensation system permeates throughout insurance company hierarchies. Regional managers, medical directors, and even claim reviewers often have performance metrics tied to limiting payouts.

This perverse incentive structure reveals a fundamental truth about American health insurance: the system rewards executives for limiting care, not improving it. As long as compensation packages tie executive wealth to denying claims, patients will continue to suffer while insurance CEOs become increasingly wealthy.

WALL STREET'S HEALTHCARE TAKEOVER

In April 2023, UnitedHealth Group announced its first-quarter earnings. Despite inflation and post-pandemic healthcare challenges affecting most Americans, the insurance giant reported a $5.6 billion profit, exceeding Wall Street expectations. The company's stock price jumped 6% that day, adding billions to its market capitalization.

During the earnings call, not a single analyst asked about patient outcomes, care quality, or customer satisfaction. Instead, questions focused relentlessly on the medical loss ratio, profit margins, and future earnings projections.

This scene repeats quarterly across the health insurance industry, illustrating a fundamental reality of American healthcare: Wall Street's interests consistently trump patient needs.

"Most Americans don't realize that health insurers answer primarily to shareholders, not policyholders," explained one of our CareYaya physician advisors. "Decisions about coverage, networks, and claims are ultimately driven by stock prices, not health outcomes."

For publicly traded insurers like UnitedHealth, Cigna, and Humana, shareholder expectations dictate corporate strategy. Investors demand consistent profit growth and regular dividend increases. At the same time, they punish companies whose medical loss ratios increase even temporarily regardless of the underlying healthcare reasons.

This shareholder primacy manifests in several ways:

First, insurers engage in massive stock buybacks and dividend payments that redirect premium dollars to investors rather than healthcare. As mentioned previously, UnitedHealth alone returned over $16 billion to shareholders in 2023 through buybacks and dividends —funds that could have reduced premiums or expanded coverage.

Second, quarterly earnings pressure leads to short-term thinking. Insurance executives know that missing Wall Street's profit expectations by even a small margin can crash their stock price and potentially cost them their jobs. This creates intense pressure to maintain tight control over medical spending, especially near the end of reporting periods.

Third, the financial industry actively tracks and compares medical loss ratios across insurers. Companies with higher MLRs (meaning they spend more on actual healthcare) are often downgraded by analysts, regardless of patient outcomes or satisfaction.

"It's a perverse system where spending money on patient care is actively punished by the market," noted Stephanie Rose, a former insurance company actuary who now works in healthcare policy. "The ideal customer from Wall Street's perspective is someone who pays premiums faithfully but never needs care."

I witnessed this dynamic when helping the Williams family navigate their father's stroke recovery. Their insurer initially approved eight weeks of rehabilitation therapy. However, as the quarter's end approached, the company suddenly reversed course, claiming further therapy wasn't "medically necessary" despite the physician's strong recommendation.

When I investigated, a sympathetic insurance company employee confided: "It's end-of-quarter cleanup. We're under pressure to improve the medical loss ratio before earnings are reported."

The Williams family eventually secured the needed therapy through an appeals process we'll explore in Chapter 7, but only after crucial weeks were lost. Their experience highlights how Wall Street's quarterly calendar can directly impact patient care decisions.

This shareholder-first approach extends beyond daily operations into long-term strategic planning. Insurance companies regularly acquire competitors, vertical integration targets, and technology firms, moves designed primarily to enhance market power and financial returns rather than improve healthcare delivery.

For instance, UnitedHealth's Optum division has purchased thousands of physician practices, surgery centers, and home health agencies. While the company touts integration benefits, the primary motivation is capturing profit across more segments of the healthcare value chain.

When Wall Street dictates healthcare decisions, patients inevitably suffer. Financial markets reward companies that minimize care while maximizing premiums. That fundamental misalignment explains much of what's broken in American healthcare.

MEDICAL LOSS RATIO MANIPULATION

When the ACA passed in 2010, healthcare advocates celebrated its "80/20 rule" as a victory for consumers. The provision requires insurers to spend at least 80% of premium dollars (85% for large group plans) on medical care or quality improvement activities rather than overhead and profit.

Theoretically, this Medical Loss Ratio (MLR) requirement should limit insurance company profits and administrative bloat. In practice, insurers have developed sophisticated strategies to circumvent its intent while complying with its technical requirements.

"The MLR rule was like putting a cap on a water balloon," explained Diane Reynolds, a healthcare compliance attorney. "Insurers just squeezed the balloon elsewhere to maintain their profits."

Through my work with families navigating insurance challenges, I've witnessed several MLR manipulation tactics firsthand:

First, insurers have mastered the art of reclassifying administrative expenses as "quality improvement activities" that count toward the medical spending requirement. Federal regulators found some companies "gaming the system by misallocating expenses... while minimizing reported administrative expenses and profits."

For example, a Florida family we worked with was enrolled in a plan that trumpeted its "nurse care coordinator" program as a quality improvement initiative. In reality, these coordinators functioned primarily as gatekeepers, rarely contacting patients but routinely questioning physician orders and recommending less expensive treatments.

Secondly, when insurers project they'll exceed the allowed overhead ratio, they sometimes deliberately increase provider payments temporarily to boost the "medical" side of the equation rather than reducing premiums.

An NBER study found that after the ACA's implementation, some insurers responded to the MLR rule by increasing claims spending by 7–11% rather than lowering premiums. This tactic allows them to meet the ratio requirement without actually reducing overhead or profits.

Thirdly, insurers manipulate report timing and classification to meet MLR requirements. By averaging results over three years or across different market segments, they can offset low-MLR periods with higher ones, creating the appearance of compliance while maximizing retained revenue.

Perhaps most cynically, some insurers have adapted by simply raising premiums faster than medical costs are increasing. If both the numerator (medical spending) and denominator (total premiums) grow proportionally, the MLR ratio stays constant, allowing insurers to increase total dollars retained while technically complying with the percentage requirement.

The real-world impact of these manipulations became clear to me when helping the Garcia family appeal coverage denials for their son's developmental therapy. Their insurer had restructured its provider payment system in a way that technically increased spending on claims (improving its MLR) while reducing the services available to patients.

"They're paying providers more per service but authorizing fewer services overall," Mrs. Garcia told me. "It looks good on their MLR report but means less actual care for my son."

Regulators are aware of these tactics. In 2022, CMS proposed tightening definitions of "quality improvement" expenses to prevent questionable accounting. However, the insurance industry consistently deploys its considerable lobbying resources to resist such reforms.

The MLR requirement has returned over $2 billion to consumers through rebates in 2020 alone, but the persistence of record insurance profits demonstrates how effectively companies have adapted to protect their bottom line regardless of regulatory constraints.

"The 80/20 rule is a perfect example of how the industry responds to regulation," Reynolds told me. "They find ways to comply technically while undermining the intent. Until we address the profit motive at the core of our system, such rules will always be circumvented."

PRIVATE EQUITY'S PLAYBOOK

When residents of Clearmont (a pseudonym for a real community) learned that their local community hospital had been acquired by Platinum Capital Partners, a major private equity firm, the announcement came with reassuring promises: "enhanced services," "operational efficiencies," and "continued commitment to patient care."

Eighteen months later, the emergency department's waiting times had doubled, a third of the nursing staff had been laid off, and the hospital had stopped accepting several major insurance plans. Meanwhile, Platinum Capital reported a "successful operational restructuring" to its investors, highlighting a 27% increase in EBITDA (earnings before interest, taxes, depreciation, and amortization).

This pattern of private equity acquisition followed by aggressive cost-cutting and service reduction has become increasingly common across America's healthcare landscape.

Private equity's involvement in healthcare began in earnest in the early 2000s, but it accelerated dramatically following the 2008 financial crisis, when low interest rates and a search for stable returns pushed firms toward recession-resistant sectors. Healthcare fit the bill. Initial acquisitions focused on niche specialties like dermatology, radiology, and urgent care. After the ACA expanded insurance coverage in 2010, private equity moved aggressively into core services, including hospitals, emergency medicine, and nursing homes. As of 2024, PE firms own an estimated 30% of for-profit hospitals in the U.S.

While large insurers themselves are typically public companies, private equity firms have aggressively expanded into adjacent healthcare sectors, often with devastating consequences for patients. Over the past decade, private equity has invested $1 trillion in U.S. healthcare. Their playbook is remarkably consistent. Acquire a healthcare entity, implement aggressive cost reductions, show improved short-term profitability, then flip the company within 3-7 years, often after loading it with debt.

This short-term profit focus fundamentally conflicts with healthcare's inherently long-term nature. Private equity firms typically aim for annual returns of 20-30%, far exceeding reasonable margins in patient-centered healthcare. Achieving such returns almost inevitably requires cutting corners on care.

In physician practices, private equity ownership often leads to production pressure: shorter appointments, more required procedures, and aggressive upcoding to maximize billing. One primary care doctor told me his patient load increased from 18 to 28 patients daily after PE acquisition, reducing average visit time from 20 minutes to just 12.

"It's assembly-line medicine," he confided. "I can't possibly provide proper care in those timeframes, but the metrics are all about revenue, not outcomes."

Meanwhile, in nursing homes, PE ownership correlates with staffing reductions, quality declines, and higher mortality rates. A landmark NBER study found that PE-owned nursing facilities were associated with a 10% increase in mortality compared to non-PE facilities.

I saw this impact directly when helping the Alverez family find care for their grandmother after her PE-owned nursing home cut staff ratios below what her condition required. "They kept saying they were 'optimizing staffing efficiency,'" Mrs. Alverez told me. "But that meant no one answered her call button for hours."

~~~

In insurance-adjacent companies like utilization management firms, private equity's influence is particularly pernicious. These companies that insurers hire to review and often deny claims operate in relative obscurity while dramatically impacting patient care.

Even health IT companies that process claims are PE targets. After acquisition, these firms often implement aggressive "payment integrity" systems that automatically flag and delay provider payments "optimizing float time" (financial jargon for holding onto money longer) at patients' and providers' expense.

"Private equity brings Wall Street's worst impulses into healthcare," noted a healthcare finance expert I spoke to. "They view patients as revenue streams to be maximized and expenses to be minimized within a 3-5 year window. Actual health outcomes are irrelevant to their model."

The consequences extend beyond individual facilities. Private equity's extractive practices can destabilize entire regional healthcare systems. When PE-owned entities cherry-pick profitable services and patient populations while abandoning unprofitable ones, safety-net providers face increased burdens with fewer resources.

Most troublingly, private equity operates with minimal transparency or oversight. Many acquisitions fall below regulatory thresholds that trigger antitrust review. Once acquired, previously public information about quality metrics and financial performance often disappears behind private reporting structures. The public sees local healthcare deteriorating but rarely connects it to the private equity acquisition that preceded it. PE firms prefer to extract value quietly before moving on to the next target.

The Clearmont hospital story had a sadly predictable conclusion. Three years after acquisition, Platinum Capital sold the struggling facility to a larger health system at a substantial profit, having extracted tens of millions through management fees, real estate sales, and operational cuts. The new owner immediately announced further "restructuring" to address the now-struggling hospital's financial challenges.

As one hospital board member who resigned in protest told me: "They stripped everything valuable, loaded us with debt, and then sold the husk. And somehow, they made a fortune doing it."

THE PUBLIC-PRIVATE DISCONNECT: HOW FOR-PROFIT INSURERS MANAGE GOVERNMENT PROGRAMS

When Rebecca enrolled her mother in what the insurance agent described as "Premium Medicare Coverage," she believed she was securing comprehensive care from the government's flagship health program. The glossy brochure highlighted "all of Original Medicare's benefits and more!" with "no monthly premium!"

Six months later, her mother needed spinal surgery. That's when Rebecca discovered the reality behind the marketing: she hadn't enrolled in traditional Medicare but in a private MA plan that denied her mother's surgery as "not medically necessary" despite her neurologist's urgent recommendation.

"I thought Medicare was Medicare," Rebecca told me when seeking CareYaya and Counterforce Health's help navigating her mother's care needs. "I had no idea private insurance companies could override Medicare's coverage standards and deny care that traditional Medicare would have covered without question."

Rebecca's experience illustrates one of the most consequential trends in American healthcare: the aggressive expansion of for-profit insurers into government healthcare programs. What was once a relatively small piece of the insurance market has become the industry's primary growth engine and profit center.

Today, private insurers administer coverage for more than half of Medicare beneficiaries (through MA plans), most Medicaid enrollees (via Medicaid managed care organizations), and millions of Americans purchasing subsidized coverage on the ACA marketplaces.

This public-private partnership was ostensibly designed to leverage private sector efficiency while maintaining public program benefits. In practice, however, it has created a system where taxpayer dollars increasingly fund insurance company profits rather than patient care.

The numbers tell a troubling story. Traditional Medicare operates with approximately 2% overhead, while MA plans take 12% or more for administration and profit. This six-fold difference represents billions in taxpayer dollars diverted from care to corporate coffers.

Researchers calculated this administrative bloat costs about $1,155 more per MA enrollee annually compared to traditional Medicare —money not spent on patient care but on marketing, executive salaries, and shareholder returns.

Beyond higher overhead, private insurers managing government programs employ several strategies to extract maximum profit from taxpayer funds:

First, they exploit risk-adjustment mechanisms intended to compensate for covering sicker patients. MA plans receive higher payments for enrollees with more documented health conditions. This has led to aggressive "upcoding," or exaggerating diagnosis severity to increase payments.

Second, private plans implement utilization management tools like prior authorization and step therapy requirements that often don't exist in traditional government programs. A 2022 HHS Inspector General report found MA plans wrongly denied 13% of prior authorization requests and 18% of payment claims that met Medicare coverage rules.

Third, private insurers managing government programs often maintain narrow provider networks, thereby limiting patients' choices while advertising "comprehensive coverage." When Rebecca's mother needed surgery, she discovered that the nearest in-network neurosurgeon was 87 miles away, with a three-month waiting list.

Fourth, insurers aggressively market these plans to healthier seniors while subtly discouraging enrollment by those with complex conditions, a practice known as "cherry-picking." Meanwhile, patients with more serious conditions or ailments who enroll often face so many hurdles that they switch back to traditional Medicare, a phenomenon researchers refer to as "lemon-dropping."

The financial impact is striking. Despite claims of "efficiency," insurers extracting profit from government programs comes at enormous cost to taxpayers. The Congressional Budget Office estimates that MA plans cost approximately 4% more than traditional Medicare for comparable beneficiaries.

MA has yielded particularly high margins for insurers. Recent analysis shows insurer gross margins per enrollee in MA (approximately $1,900) are about double those in employer plans. Not coincidentally, UnitedHealth, Humana, and CVS/Aetna have all dramatically expanded their MA businesses. Government programs were supposed to protect Americans from insurance company abuses. Instead, we've invited those same companies to manage the programs, bringing their profit-maximizing tactics along with them.

For patients like Rebecca's mother, this public-private disconnect creates dangerous confusion. Most beneficiaries don't understand the fundamental differences between traditional Medicare and private MA. These differences become apparent only when serious healthcare needs arise.

After weeks of appeals, Rebecca's mother finally received approval for her surgery, but only after her condition had deteriorated significantly. "By the time they approved it, she needed a more extensive procedure and longer recovery," Rebecca told me. "All to save the insurance company money on a plan that was supposed to be Medicare."

FUTURE PROFIT STRATEGIES

In 2023, I attended a healthcare investment conference where insurance executives discussed emerging "revenue optimization strategies." While the public-facing panels featured predictable talking points about "patient-centered care" and "value-based solutions," the private sessions revealed a more candid roadmap for future profit extraction.

As healthcare costs rise and public scrutiny intensifies, insurers are developing sophisticated new approaches to maintain and grow their profits. Understanding these emerging strategies is crucial for patients and advocates seeking to navigate the evolving landscape.

AI-Driven Denial Systems

Perhaps the most troubling development is the rapidly increasing use of artificial intelligence and algorithms to automate claim denials. Unlike human reviewers who might exercise judgment or compassion, these systems apply denial criteria with ruthless efficiency.

A striking example emerged in a *ProPublica* investigation of Cigna's PXDX algorithm, which allowed the company's doctors to deny over 300,000 claims in just two months, averaging an impossible 1.2 seconds per "review." The system automatically rejected claims that didn't precisely match Cigna's coverage criteria, and medical directors simply mass-approved these automated denials.

"AI doesn't get tired, doesn't feel sympathy, and can't be swayed by a heartfelt appeal," explained Dr. Michaels, a former insurance medical director. "From a profit perspective, it's the perfect claims adjudicator."

While insurers publicly frame these systems as tools to "identify fraud" or "ensure appropriate care," the financial incentives clearly favor maximizing denials. Every rejected claim represents immediate savings that flow directly to the bottom line.

The Counterforce Health team recently assisted a family whose cancer treatment claim was denied by what the insurer later admitted was an "automated clinical review system." The algorithm had flagged the treatment as "experimental" despite it being the standard of care for that specific cancer type. It took three appeals and intervention from the state insurance commissioner to override the AI's determination.

We're entering an era where algorithms, not doctors, increasingly determine what care patients receive. These algorithms are designed by companies whose financial interests directly conflict with paying claims.

Vertical Integration and Data Monetization

Another emerging profit strategy involves insurers expanding across the healthcare value chain to capture revenue at multiple points. UnitedHealth's Optum division exemplifies this approach, having acquired thousands of physician practices, urgent care centers, surgery facilities, and even home health agencies.

This vertical integration allows insurers to profit not just from premium collection but from care delivery, pharmacy benefits, data analytics, and more. When an insurance company owns the entire care journey, it can extract margin at each step while controlling referral patterns and utilization.

Particularly valuable is patient data. Insurers hold vast troves of claims information that can be monetized through analytics services, decision support tools, or de-identified data sales to pharmaceutical companies and researchers.

UnitedHealth's Optum Insight arm sells analytical software and consulting services to hospitals, pharmaceutical companies, and other payers. After acquiring the health-tech firm Change Healthcare, Optum's data analytics revenues jumped 35% year-over-year.

Subscription Models and Benefits Segmentation

Insurers are also exploring subscription-based healthcare models that bypass traditional insurance regulation. These include flat-fee primary care, concierge membership programs, and specialized service packages offered outside standard health plans.

"The subscription approach is brilliant from a business perspective," noted one healthcare economist "It creates predictable recurring revenue while potentially falling outside medical loss ratio requirements since it's not technically "insurance."

Alongside this trend is growing benefits segmentation, or the practice of offering basic coverage to meet legal requirements while selling various "enhanced" services as add-ons. By unbundling comprehensive coverage into a la carte options, insurers can maintain high margins on supplemental products while technically complying with ACA requirements for base plans.

I recently counseled a family who discovered their insurance plan covered hospital care but required a separate "outpatient services rider" for specialist visits and a "pharmacy supplement" for prescription coverage. Together, these add-ons nearly doubled their monthly premium while creating confusion about what services were actually covered.

Regulatory Capture and Public Option Positioning

Perhaps the most consequential long-term strategy involves aggressive lobbying and positioning around potential healthcare reforms. The insurance industry consistently ranks among the highest-spending lobbying sectors, investing over $150 million annually at the federal level alone.

These efforts focus on preserving profitable arrangements like MA while shaping any potential reforms to include roles (and profits) for private insurers. Industry representatives now regularly express conditional support for "public options" or coverage expansions, but only if private insurers administer these programs.

Preparing for Resistance

As these profit strategies inevitably generate patient frustration and advocacy pushback, insurers are developing countermeasures like investing in sophisticated public relations, "patient satisfaction" metrics that don't reflect actual care quality, and artificial intelligence tools to predict and manage customer dissatisfaction.

One presenter at the investment conference described a "propensity to appeal" algorithm that identifies which denied patients are most likely to fight back, allowing the company to strategically overturn certain denials while maintaining most rejections.

"The goal isn't maximizing denials but optimizing them," he explained. "We want to deny as many claims as possible without triggering regulatory action or excessive appeals."

For patients, this evolving landscape presents new challenges but also opportunities. Understanding these emerging profit strategies is the first step toward effectively challenging them, a topic we'll explore further in Part III.

A SYSTEM DESIGNED FOR PROFIT, NOT PATIENTS

Health insurance in America operates according to a simple, ruthless equation: Maximize premium collection while minimizing care delivery. Every aspect of the industry, from executive compensation to Wall Street expectations, from administrative complexity to AI-driven denials, serves this fundamental goal.

The profit mechanisms we've explored in this chapter explain why so many Americans with "good insurance" still find themselves fighting for care, drowning in paperwork, and facing financial ruin when serious illness strikes. The system isn't failing accidentally; it's succeeding at its actual purpose of generating returns for executives and shareholders.

This reality is why incremental reforms have consistently fallen short. Regulations like the ACA's Medical Loss Ratio requirement are quickly circumvented through creative accounting and strategic adaptations. As long as profit remains the system's primary driver, patients will remain secondary considerations.

The insurance industry has invested billions in constructing a labyrinth designed to exhaust and defeat patients. But that labyrinth has vulnerabilities—points where determined individuals and organized communities can successfully challenge denials, demand appropriate care, and ultimately transform the system itself.

As insurers develop new profit strategies using artificial intelligence, vertical integration, and data monetization, patients and advocates must develop equally sophisticated countermeasures. The balance of power has tilted dramatically toward insurance companies, but it can be reclaimed through knowledge, persistence, and collective action.

In the next chapter, we'll examine how this profit-centered system became entrenched in American healthcare—and why approaches that work successfully in other countries have been systematically blocked here. By understanding both the mechanisms of profit extraction and their historical development, we'll be better equipped to envision and create a more just alternative.

The healthcare system we deserve is possible. But achieving it requires first understanding precisely how the current system converts our premiums, tax dollars, and medical suffering into corporate profit. Armed with that knowledge, we can begin the work of taking our healthcare back.

3

THE GREAT AMERICAN HEALTH SCAM

> *"The American healthcare system is neither healthy, caring, nor a system."*
>
> — *Walter Cronkite*

As the CEO of CareYaya, I've had a front-row seat to America's healthcare dysfunction. Although our original mission was simply to help families find affordable, quality care we inadvertently became chroniclers of a broken system.

Sad stories poured in on a daily basis. There was a husband of an Alzheimer's patient who thought his "comprehensive" insurance would cover home care, only to discover it covered virtually nothing. There was a daughter of a stroke survivor whose expensive insurance wouldn't pay for a rehabilitation facility. No less fortunate was a retired couple who worked hard, saved diligently, purchased the best Medicare supplemental plan they could afford only to face bankruptcy because of care denials and crushing out-of-pocket costs.

After listening to thousands of these stories, a disturbing pattern emerged that couldn't be merely attributed to inefficiency or honest mistakes.

That's when we discovered that the American healthcare system isn't just broken but rigged.

AMERICAN EXCEPTIONALISM: PAYING MORE, GETTING LESS

In any other industry, American exceptionalism would mean standing head and shoulders above our global peers. But in healthcare, the reality is quite different. The fact is that we've achieved a perverse form of exceptionalism by spending vastly more than any other nation while achieving worse outcomes.

The numbers tell a damning story. The United States devotes 17.8% of its entire GDP to healthcare, nearly double the average for comparable developed

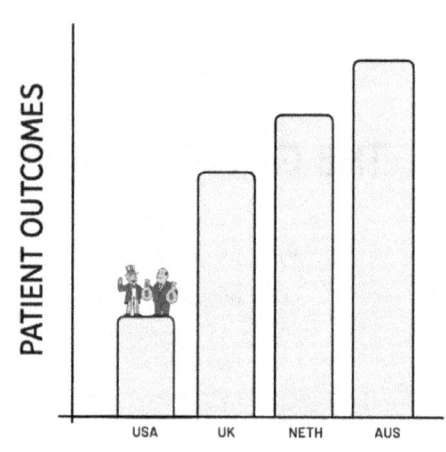

nations. On a per-person basis, we spend nearly twice as much as Germany (the next highest spender) and four times more than South Korea. With such a level of investment, we should expect much better results, right? The reality is very different. Sadly, Americans get less. We live shorter lives, with our life expectancy pegged at 78 years, falling four years below the average for developed nations. We suffer higher rates of preventable death, meaning more Americans die from causes that timely care could have addressed. The statistics are even more grim for vulnerable populations: our infant mortality rate stands 5.4 per 1,000 births compared to just 1.6 in Norway, while our maternal mortality rate is three times higher than peer countries.

The American healthcare paradox becomes even more disturbing when we consider access. Despite our astronomical spending, Americans see doctors less frequently than people in other wealthy nations. One-third of Americans report skipping needed medical care due to cost, a phenomenon virtually unheard of in other developed countries. I encounter this reality daily through CareYaya's work: families delaying necessary interventions or rationing medications to save money, even with insurance. As such, this problem doesn't just indicate poor performance but more damningly, systemic failure. We've built the world's most expensive healthcare system that somehow delivers less care to fewer people with worse results.

How did we get here? The answer lies in understanding that our system wasn't designed to maximize health but instead revenue for stakeholders, with countless mechanisms working against patients' interests.

International Comparisons

To truly understand the stakes and alternatives, it's useful to compare the American healthcare system with those in other nations. These comparisons can serve as both inspiration and a benchmark for what is possible.

In countries with universal health coverage—whether a single-payer model, a national health service, or tightly regulated multi-payer system—the concept of going bankrupt from medical bills is virtually nil. For example, in Canada, the healthcare system is single-payer for most medical services. Canadians do not pay anything out-of-pocket when they visit a doctor or hospital because treatment is funded through taxes. So, if a Canadian is hospitalized for an emergency surgery, they aren't worrying about deductibles or network coverage.

Prescription drugs and some services like dental might require separate coverage or modest copays, but for core health needs, there's a safety net. The result? No one in Canada loses their home or declares bankruptcy when they get sick, unlike in the U.S.

Similarly, in the United Kingdom, the National Health Service (NHS) provides healthcare to all residents largely free at point of use because it is funded by taxes. As such, Britons who need chemotherapy or appendectomies don't receive bills for treatment. Prescription drugs have low flat fees (and many people are exempt from even those, like seniors and low-income individuals) just as there are also out-of-pocket caps for long-term care prescriptions. Because the NHS's principle is that care is based on need, not ability to pay, nightmares of claim denials or surprise bills simply aren't part of the British health landscape.

Other European countries have multi-payer systems which include a mix of non-profit insurers, sickness funds, etc., all of which are tightly regulated with out-of-pocket spending capped. Some have statutory health insurance for all where people often pay premiums as a percentage of income (like a tax), and in return, nearly all medically necessary care is covered.

For instance, copayments are small in France where out-of-pocket costs are capped, after which the government picks up 100%. (Note that a doctor visit copay is equivalent to a few dollars, but even that is often reimbursed by supplemental coverage that most have.) Financial ruin from health costs is therefore relatively rare in France and Germany. The American idea of crowdfunding basic treatment would be considered nothing short of absurd. Likewise, consider Japan: It has a system of public health insurance where everyone is covered either through work or a community plan. Although patients pay coinsurance (generally 30% of the cost) for services, there is a monthly out-of-pocket maximum tied to income, beyond which the patient pays nothing. This cap might be a few hundred equivalent dollars for low-income folks or slightly higher for those with higher incomes, but it's manageable. So, if a Japanese person has a major surgery, their out-of-pocket total might be a few hundred dollars, not tens of thousands.

It's not surprising then that immigrant families express shock at the American system after experiencing healthcare elsewhere. I've met a number of these through CareYaya, such as Sophia, who moved from Germany to the U.S. for work. She expressed disbelief when her husband needed gallbladder surgery. "In Germany, we would have just gone to the hospital, had the procedure, and maybe paid €10 per day for the hospital stay" she told me. "Here, with a 'good' insurance plan through my employer, we still had to pay $4,800 out-of-pocket. I called my mother in Germany, and she thought I was joking." The raw confusion in Sophia's voice as she recounted this experience stays with me. I had no good answer to her question "Why would anyone design a system this way?" The contrast with healthcare systems implemented by other nations is stark and damning.

Even countries without single-payer have mechanisms to protect. Moreover, while Australia has a public Medicare for all for core care as well as optional private insurance for elective or private hospital care where citizens might pay some charges for elective items, catastrophic costs are absorbed by the system.

As we examine healthcare systems around the world, it should be clear that universal coverage isn't just about having insurance, but rather it's about ensuring that health services don't cause financial hardship. The World Health Organization defines universal health coverage as enabling everyone to get the services they need without suffering financial hardship. Most developed countries have achieved or nearly achieved that. The U.S., plainly, has not.

Despite our excellent medical technology and skilled providers, we have little financial protection when it comes to healthcare. As a result, Americans express a mixture of admiration and envy for friends or relatives abroad who don't have to think twice about going to the doctor. Conversely, foreigners are often shocked by stories of Americans rationing insulin or avoiding ambulance calls due to cost.

One might wonder: do these countries simply spend a lot more publicly? As mentioned earlier, many spend less overall per capita than the U.S. but have better outcomes. So, whereas the U.S. spends roughly twice what countries like Canada, the UK, or Japan spend per person on healthcare, our results aren't better–not to mention the financial burdens which follow. In short, American patients carry a much larger financial burden than those in other countries. This suggests that there are inefficiencies and profit extractions in the U.S. system (administrative costs, higher prices) that, if controlled, could fund broader coverage without bankrupting individuals.

International comparisons also indicate that when everyone is in one risk pool or guaranteed coverage, insurers or systems have less incentive to deny necessary care. In those systems, the focus might be on public health and making sure people actually get care (since preventing illness can save money for the system).

On the other hand, the operations of US health insurers appear perverse by comparison. If an insurer denies an expensive treatment, that insurer saves money (at least in the short term), even if it harms the patient. In a single-payer or national system, if a treatment is truly beneficial, the system wants the patient to get it because it's responsible for that patient either way, (Conversely, if the patient gets worse, the system pays more later). This realignment of incentives in other countries often results in more patient-centered decisions.

Of course, no system is perfect. Some countries struggle with underfunding or slower adoption of new therapies; patients in those systems may end up going abroad or paying privately if they want something outside guidelines. But what stands out is the near absence of personal financial calamity due to medical expenses in other advanced countries. Health troubles that frequently spiral into money troubles are a uniquely American phenomenon.

International case studies are often used to bolster arguments for universal healthcare in U.S. policy debates. Advocates point to those countries and say, "Look, it's working elsewhere. People aren't losing homes over chemo in France or Germany. Why can't we do that?" Opponents might dwell on the possibility of higher taxes or wait times elsewhere. Yet, surveys of citizens in those countries generally show higher satisfaction with access and less worry about costs compared to Americans. As it is, Americans already face long wait times in the current system, while these universal healthcare countries actually maintain lower overall costs despite their higher taxes.

Looking abroad shows that preventing financial ruin due to health costs is not only possible but standard in most wealthy nations. These countries have structured their systems to ensure that getting sick or injured doesn't also mean going broke. For Americans, such examples serve as both a contrast (highlighting the harshness of our current system) and a hopeful vision (that maybe we could adapt some of those protections here).

ADMINISTRATIVE COMPLEXITY: PROFITING FROM CHAOS

When Lilyan, a retired dentist in Charlotte, called me last year to find caregiving help for her husband with Parkinson's, her voice cracked with exhaustion. But she wasn't worn down from the physical demands of caregiving so much as the paperwork.

"I spend 20 hours a week just dealing with insurance," she complained. "Submitting claims, responding to denials, searching for in-network providers, deciphering explanation of benefits statements that explain nothing. It's a full-time job, and I'm drowning in it."

Lilyan isn't alone. By design, American healthcare inundates us with paperwork. We spend around $2,500 per person annually on healthcare administrative costs that provide zero clinical value. That's nearly $496 billion per year with roughly 15% of all health spending going to billing clerks, claims processors, insurance middlemen, and administrative overhead.

This administrative bloat isn't an unfortunate side effect. It's a profit center. For insurers, complexity creates opportunity. Every denied claim, every coding error, every overlooked submission deadline represents money saved. As one physician told me, "Insurers have figured out that it's cheaper to hire an army of people to find reasons to say 'no' than to actually pay for care."

The statistics support this observation. American physician practices spend four times more on billing-related costs than their Canadian counterparts—about $83,000 per doctor annually in the U.S. versus $22,000 in Ontario. Why? Because our physicians must navigate dozens of different insurers, each with their own forms, rules, and procedures, while Canadian doctors submit standardized claims to a single payer.

Not surprisingly, this complexity has spawned entire industries that profit from it. Insurance companies employ legions of staff to process claims, and more to the point, to deny them when possible. Specialized firms contract with insurers and state Medicaid programs to find reasons to reject or reduce payments. In turn, these denials directly improve insurers' bottom lines.

The most telling statistic: there are now roughly ten administrators for every physician in the U.S., a dramatic shift since the 1970s. This explosion of paperwork warriors doesn't improve care. It simply creates an arms race where every denial requires providers to hire their own billing specialists to fight back, driving costs up for everyone except the insurers.

We've seen countless families give up fighting denied claims simply because the process is too exhausting. One family I worked with last winter had a legitimate claim for home care services denied three times despite meeting all criteria. When I asked why they weren't appealing further, the wife sighed, "I just don't have the energy to fight anymore. They've worn me down." That surrender is a win for the insurer's profit margins.

Even understanding basic terms can be an obstacle. Three-quarters of consumers report being confused by medical bills and insurance "explanations." This confusion isn't accidental but rather intended to bewilder patients such that they will be less likely to contest a charge or successfully navigate the system.

When I talk with pre-health students working through CareYaya, they're often shocked by this reality. They entered healthcare to help people, only to discover they'll spend much of their careers navigating administrative systems designed to limit care rather than deliver it.

Given the massive waste, you might expect broad support for simplifying health administration. But vested interests vigorously resist change since every layer of complexity represents someone's job or profit center. Cutting out middlemen would save an estimated $265 billion but also disrupt lucrative business models.

A 2022 investigation found U.S. hospitals and clinics spent $25.7 billion in one year just contesting insurers' claim denials amounting to nearly $57 in extra administrative costs per claim. That "waste" from the provider perspective is, from the insurer perspective, money saved by not paying. The fact that providers contest only a fraction of denials shows how profitable these strategies can be.

This administrative morass isn't just inefficient but ultimately harmful. Lilyan's situation illustrates the human cost: while she battled paperwork, her husband's care suffered. She had less time and energy for actually supporting him, all because our system prioritizes administrative hurdles over patient wellbeing.

EMPLOYMENT-BASED INSURANCE

When Tom, a software developer from the Bay Area, reached out to CareYaya about care options for his mother, his situation reflected a quintessentially American problem. At 54, he'd been diagnosed with a treatable but serious chronic condition. His doctor recommended a treatment plan, and his employer's insurance would cover it. But there was just one problem: he hated his job.

"I feel trapped," he explained. "I've wanted to start my own business for years, but now I'm chained to this job I can't stand because I need the insurance. Without it, my condition would bankrupt me."

Tom is experiencing "job lock," one of the many consequences of America's peculiar approach to health coverage. Most Americans don't realize our employer-based insurance system wasn't carefully planned. It was a historical accident that became a double-edged sword.

The practice dates back to World War II, when the federal government-imposed wage freezes to control inflation. Companies couldn't attract workers by offering higher pay, so they began offering benefits, notably health insurance, as a workaround. In 1943, the War Labor Board ruled that these fringe benefits didn't count as wages, and in 1954 the IRS cemented this by making employer health insurance contributions tax-deductible.

This effectively subsidized employer-based health plans through the tax code, spurring explosive growth. The number of Americans with job-based health insurance jumped from just 21 million in 1940 to 142 million by 1950. For mid-century businesses, it was a win-win—they could recruit workers with attractive benefits that were both modest in cost and tax-free.

By the 1960s, employer-sponsored insurance (ESI) had become the de facto way most non-elderly Americans got coverage, which explains why broader national health insurance efforts stalled. Even today, job-based plans cover the largest share of Americans at approximately 60.4% of the non-elderly population.

This accident of history now profoundly shapes American lives and often not for the better.

For people like Tom, job lock is a lived reality. Workers with employer insurance are significantly less likely to change jobs compared to those without, even when controlling for other factors. This reduces labor mobility and overall economic productivity, since people can't freely move to where they'd be most effective. Even after the ACA created individual marketplaces and banned preexisting condition exclusions, research shows job lock remains substantial.

I've collected dozens of stories like Tom's where people feel forced to tolerate toxic work environments, delay retirement, or abandon entrepreneurial dreams solely because they can't risk losing their health coverage.

Perhaps most inefficient is how employer-based insurance fragments the population into thousands of small risk pools—one for each employer or group. This is inherently less efficient than one big risk pool. A small firm with a few sick employees can see its premiums skyrocket, whereas a national pool spreads risk broadly.

It also means insurance options depend on employer size, industry, and negotiating power, which naturally thereby introduces a substantial variation unrelated to health needs. A software engineer at a big tech company might have a platinum plan with low out-of-pocket costs, while a retail worker at a small shop pays more for a skimpy plan that covers less.

The linking of health care to employment made some sense in the 1950s when costs were low, and most families had a long-term job with one employer. But today, with our gig economy, frequent job changes, and sky-high medical bills, the model increasingly fails. The employment-based approach creates inequity as the tax exclusion for employer health benefits disproportionately benefits higher-income workers, who are in higher tax brackets and tend to have more generous health plans. Meanwhile, lower-wage workers at companies that don't offer insurance derive little tax benefit and often struggle to afford individual coverage. The growth of contract work means many workers hustle without any benefits, forced to patch together individual insurance if they can afford it.

THE COBRA TRAP

Recently, Allison, a 37-year-old marketing specialist from North Carolina, contacted CareYaya and Counterforce Health in a panic. Her husband had just been laid off from his job, the job that provided health insurance for their family of four, including their daughter with asthma. They had received their COBRA election notice, offering to continue their coverage for "just" $1,687 per month.

"That's more than our mortgage," Allison told me, her voice tight with anxiety. "His unemployment is $1,800 a month. We'd have $113 left for everything else. How is that even possible?"

Allison's family was falling into what I call the "COBRA trap." COBRA (the Consolidated Omnibus Budget Reconciliation Act of 1985) gives workers who lose their jobs the right to continue their employer's health plan for up to 18 months in most cases. Sounds good, right? The problem: you must pay the full premium—both your share and your former employer's share—plus a small administrative fee.

For most families, that cost is crushing. A study by Families USA found that the average COBRA premium for a family plan equaled 84% of the average monthly unemployment check. One analysis found that in nine states, the entire unemployment check wouldn't even cover the COBRA premium. In Alaska for example, family COBRA premiums were 132% of the state's average UI income.

In other words, an unemployed Alaskan would have to spend all their jobless benefits and then some just to pay for health insurance, leaving nothing for food, rent, or other necessities. Nationally, COBRA for a single person costs around $7,000 per year, and for a family about $20,000—untenable sums when you have no paycheck.

My conversation with Allison exposed this brutal reality. When I asked if they were considering COBRA, she laughed bitterly. "With what money? We have some savings, but it would be gone in months. Then what?"

It's no surprise that many laid-off workers forego COBRA entirely and join the ranks of the uninsured. Even during the 2008–2009 recession, sign-ups with COBRA were low until the government intervened. As part of the 2009 stimulus, the federal government temporarily subsidized 65% of COBRA premiums. With that subsidy, about 34% of eligible people opted for COBRA.

The vast majority who declined COBRA cited cost as the main factor, with 80% of non-enrollees complaining it was still too expensive, despite the subsidy. This underscores that without hefty subsidies, COBRA is out of reach for most people during job transitions.

The result is that many people experience dangerous coverage gaps when uninsured between jobs. In the best case, this creates anxiety as one hopes not to get sick or injured during the gap. In the worst case, people delay needed care or stop medications, sometimes with dire consequences.

Through CareYaya, I've witnessed these consequences firsthand. One family we worked with included a father with diabetes who lost his job and couldn't afford COBRA. He rationed his insulin during his uninsured period, checking his blood sugar less frequently to save on test strips. By the time he found new employment with benefits three months later, his condition had deteriorated significantly, requiring hospitalization.

For those who do attempt COBRA, the financial strain can be enormous. I've collected dozens of stories from families draining savings or running up credit card debt to pay COBRA premiums. Imagine a cancer patient who loses her job due to illness: she might feel compelled to elect COBRA to keep her oncologist and treatment going, but that could mean $1,500+ monthly when she has no income.

COBRA's burden falls heaviest during life transitions that are already stressful: job loss, divorce (when a spouse may lose coverage), or other qualifying events. It's essentially a trap: when you most need continuity of coverage, you're least able to pay for it.

Many Americans don't realize how much their employer contributes to their health insurance until they see the COBRA bill. Sticker shock is common; one family I worked with had been paying $420 monthly through payroll deductions, only to discover their COBRA premium would be $1,860. That's because the difference had been hidden as the employer portion.

Even policymakers recognize flaws in COBRA. In 2021, during the wake of the COVID-19 pandemic, Congress temporarily covered 100% of COBRA premiums for a few months to prevent massive losses of coverage. These patches highlight that the underlying system is broken.

The COVID-19 pandemic brutally exposed the vulnerability of tying healthcare to employment. When unemployment spiked, KFF estimated that nearly 27 million people risked becoming uninsured due to job loss during the initial wave. One study concluded about 7.7 million workers lost jobs that provided health insurance, affecting an additional 6.9 million dependents who were on those plans. By mid-2020, roughly 14 million of those who lost employer coverage became uninsured, despite ACA safety nets.

Even outside of large-scale layoffs, everyday job transitions pose risks. If you switch jobs, typically there's a waiting period (maybe 60-90 days) before new benefits kick in. That gap can leave you uninsured unless you pay for COBRA in the interim. For someone living paycheck to paycheck, costly sums might not be feasible; so they roll the dice uninsured for a couple of months.

COBRA was intended as a safety net but functions somewhat like a placebo. It offers the promise of seamless coverage, but the cost makes it unusable for most people. The trap tightens most around those who can least afford a lapse in insurance, namely, those with serious health conditions or expensive treatments who face an agonizing choice: pay an exorbitant premium with money they don't have or go without care and risk their health.

For Allison's family, the COBRA trap meant going without insurance until her husband found new employment three months later. Their daughter's asthma went undertreated during that time, a common story and one more way the system is rigged against families at their most vulnerable moments.

There's a growing chorus for delinking health coverage from jobs—whether through a public option available to anyone, a Medicare buy-in or universal single-payer. The idea is that losing your job shouldn't mean gambling with your life or your finances.

NETWORK MANIPULATION

When Roberto, a 62-year-old professor in San Francisco, called us last year, he was frustrated to the point of rage. His insurance plan that he'd carefully selected for its supposedly broad coverage had denied his request to see a particular neurologist for his worsening migraines.

"I did my research. This doctor is the migraine specialist in our region," he told me. "But my insurer says she's out-of-network. There are supposedly five in-network neurologists in my area. I've called all of them. Three aren't taking new patients, one doesn't specialize in migraines, and the fifth can't see me for four months."

Roberto had discovered what millions of Americans learn the hard way: a provider network is not so much a helpful resource but a carefully curated control mechanism. Insurance companies don't just manage money; they also manage which doctors and hospitals you can see. By controlling the network, they control your care.

A provider network is the roster of doctors, clinics, labs, and hospitals that have contracted with an insurance plan to provide services at negotiated rates. Insurers often advertise broad provider choice, but in practice many plans use "narrow networks" that limit the providers available as a strategy to control costs and, sometimes, to cherry-pick healthier patients.

How narrow is "narrow?" Quite narrow, it turns out. A comprehensive study by the KFF found that MA plan networks included less than half (46%) of all local physicians, on average. Another KFF analysis of marketplace (ACA) plans found a similar pattern: enrollees had access to only about 40% of physicians in their area through their plan's network.

In that study, nearly a quarter of enrollees were in plans that included 25% or fewer of local doctors. Some of the narrowest networks occurred even in big cities. For instance, in Chicago, certain marketplace plans had only 14% of area doctors in-network.

These statistics expose the reality that when you sign up for many insurance plans, you are implicitly agreeing to not see a large majority of providers in your community without paying extra.

Network manipulation has multiple purposes for insurers. By curating who is "in-network," insurers gain leverage. Fewer in-network providers means the insurer can negotiate lower fees (steering volume to selected providers) and exclude those who demand higher rates.

But narrow networks can also serve as a form of "indirect risk selection." In plain terms, a way to discourage sicker people from choosing the plan. For example, a plan that leaves the premier cancer hospital or most top oncologists out-of-network is unattractive to someone with cancer (who might then choose a different plan), thereby keeping that costly patient out of the insurer's risk pool.

Regulators consider this a problematic practice ("cream skimming"), but it can be hard to prove intent. Still, the law requires networks to cover a sufficient range of services without "unreasonable delay," a vague standard that, in practice, hasn't prevented plans from limiting their networks in many areas.

Some regulators have pushed back. South Dakota voters approved an "any willing provider" law in 2014, forcing insurers to accept any provider who meets their terms. This effectively bans narrow networks by ensuring all providers can join. While that increases choice, insurers argue it takes away their bargaining power to lower prices.

Despite these limitations, insurance marketing materials often boast about "large networks" or show smiling patients with their trusted doctors. They rarely mention that a given plan might exclude your doctor or the nearest hospital. A review of MA TV ads found they almost never mentioned limitations like networks or prior authorizations, instead hyping extra benefits and low costs.

Consumers like Roberto may only discover the narrowness of a network after they sign up and start looking for doctors. And as noted earlier, many people don't understand terms like "out-of-network" until faced with a bill.

There is an argument that narrow networks can have some positive effect: for example, steering patients to "high-value" providers and weeding out low-quality ones. Insurers might say they exclude providers who charge too much or have poor outcomes. In theory, this could improve efficiency.

However, the evidence is mixed, and from the patient perspective, lack of choice is usually a negative. A plan might deem a hospital too expensive and exclude it, but that hospital could be the one with the best specialists for a certain condition. If you're the patient with that condition, you'd regard the network as unreasonably restrictive.

In practice, insurers often prioritize cost over quality when forming networks. One Yale study noted that network formation is a strategic bargaining process—insurers include providers who will accept lower rates and exclude those who won't. Quality metrics are improving, but they are not the primary driver of network breadth in most cases.

Moreover, narrow networks can sharply limit mental health services, where finding any available provider is challenging. Indeed, analyses of MA found access to psychiatrists was more restricted than any other specialty. MA plans included only 23% of local psychiatrists on average.

This is a sobering figure given the mental health crisis; it suggests many patients will struggle to find an in-network therapist or psychiatrist, even though the plan claims to cover mental health.

For Roberto, the narrow network meant a four-month wait to see a neurologist who wasn't his first choice. During that time, his migraines worsened, impacting his work and quality of life.

His experience illustrates how network manipulation is a subtle way insurers "rig" the system: they promise coverage but circumscribe where you can actually use it. It saves them money, but at the potential expense of convenience and even health.

THE PHANTOM PROVIDER DIRECTORY

Related to narrow networks is an even more deceitful practice that has come to light in recent years: ghost networks. A ghost network refers to an insurance plan's provider directory that is filled with names and locations of providers who, in reality, aren't actually available to patients under that plan.

They might be retired, not accepting new patients, not in the network, or dead ends for other reasons. The directory gives the illusion of a robust network ("Look at all these doctors you can go to!"), but when patients call those providers, they hit a wall.

Last year, one of the families we serve in Winston-Salem spent weeks trying to find a therapist for their teenager struggling with depression and anxiety. The mother methodically worked through her insurer's directory of supposedly in-network therapists.

The results? Four numbers were disconnected. Six providers said they weren't accepting new patients. Eleven weren't actually accepting that insurance despite being listed. Three had 3+ month waiting lists. Only three were potentially viable options, and one of those required a 45-minute drive each way.

"I feel like I'm being gaslighted," she told me. "My insurance card says I have mental health coverage. The directory shows dozens of providers. But when I actually try to use it, there's nothing there."

Their experience isn't unusual. Investigations have found ghost networks to be shockingly prevalent. In New York, the state attorney general conducted a secret shopper survey across 13 major health plans' directories for mental health providers. The result: 86% of the listed in-network mental health providers were effectively ghosts. That means only one in seven directory listings actually led to a possible appointment! Similar studies elsewhere echo this. In an Arizona review, callers could not schedule appointments with two out of every five providers listed in popular plans.

Although mental health is where the problem is often the worst, other specialties show significant directory inaccuracies too.

The consequences are deeply frustrating and sometimes dangerous. Patients seeking care, say for depression or a child's autism, diligently go through their insurer's directory and call provider after provider only to hear "Sorry, not taking new patients," "That doctor hasn't been at this clinic for two years," or "We're not in-network with that insurance." It can take dozens of calls to find just one viable option. Many give up or delay care as a result.

Ghost networks effectively deny patients access to care that the plan is supposed to cover, forcing them either to go out-of-network (and pay out-of-pocket) or not get help. For mental health, this is especially pernicious. Untreated mental illness can worsen or become crisis-level while someone is navigating a phony list of providers.

As New York Attorney General Letitia James put it, ghost networks can force people to choose between "paying out-of-pocket, which is not possible for many, or forgoing treatment altogether."

Why do ghost networks exist? It often comes down to lack of accountability and a bit of deliberate neglect. Maintaining accurate directories is work. Providers change status frequently. Insurers may not prioritize updating the information or may intentionally list more names to make their network look better.

There's also an incentive to list providers even if only a small fraction of them are actually accessible because it satisfies network adequacy requirements on paper and makes the plan look competitive in marketing. Some experts claim ghost listings can be a tactic to pad networks without actually paying for more providers. If a provider left the network, an insurer might drag its feet in removing them from the directory.

Legally, insurers are required to keep directories up to date. The ACA and MA have regulations mandating accurate provider lists. However, enforcement has been lax. *ProPublica* found that most state insurance commissions have

issued few if any fines for directory inaccuracies.

For instance, New York passed a law in 2016 against ghost networks, but since then, regulators have issued only one fine of $7,500 to a plan, even after hundreds of consumer complaints. Industry-wide, *ProPublica* noted that all fines combined across states amounted to a tiny fraction of 1% of insurers' profits—merely a "cost of doing business" that does not compel change.

In response to public outcry, the Senate Finance Committee held a hearing on ghost networks in 2023. Lawmakers from both parties have called for tougher oversight, and some class-action lawsuits are in the works on behalf of patients misled by false directories.

For our Winston-Salem family, the ghost network meant their teen's depression went untreated for months longer than necessary. They eventually found a therapist, but only after paying out-of-pocket for an out-of-network provider, thereby adding financial stress to an already fraught situation.

Ghost networks allow insurance companies to claim broad coverage while actually limiting access. It's a bait-and-switch that benefits the insurer (which satisfies regulators and attracts customers with the promise of a big network) while harming the patient (who finds that promise empty when they need care).

The phenomenon is now so well-documented that it's impossible to dismiss as a fluke. It reveals a deeper truth: the health system's complexity can be exploited to give the appearance of coverage that isn't real. Just as fine print can void an insurance policy's value, ghost provider listings can void a network's value.

PRICE OPACITY

Imagine going to a restaurant where there are no prices on the menu, and you won't know the cost of your meal until a month later when a bill arrives in the mail. That, in a nutshell, is how U.S. healthcare pricing operates.

Clear, upfront pricing is virtually absent in most of our health systems. Instead, patients face a convoluted game of blindfolded darts with charges varying wildly from one provider to another while discounts are negotiated secretly. Sometimes, even the providers themselves often can't tell you what something will cost ahead of time.

How The System Maintains Price Opacity

This price opacity serves the financial interests of hospitals and insurers, keeping consumers in the dark prevents price shopping and head-to-head competition, but it has devastating consequences for Americans' finances. Several factors maintain this opacity:

Confidential Negotiated Rates: Most Americans have insurance that negotiates prices with providers. These negotiated rates are typically kept confidential, treated as proprietary information by insurers and hospitals (sometimes even labeled "trade secrets"). A hospital might have five different prices for a knee MRI: one for Medicare, one for BlueCross, one for Aetna, one for uninsured patients (full "chargemaster" rate), etc. But as a patient, you would have no easy way of knowing which price applies to you ahead of time.

Providers argue that publishing their contracted rates could undermine their bargaining or even lead to tacit collusion (all hospitals seeing competitors' prices might raise prices). Whether or not those arguments hold water, the effect is that prices remain hidden until after services are rendered.

Inflated Chargemasters: Hospitals maintain a master list of charges (the "chargemaster"), often wildly inflated relative to actual costs or what insurance pays. These charges are starting points for negotiation and for out-of-network billing. But patients rarely ever see a simple fee schedule for services.

Even basic questions like "How much will this blood test cost?" can be met with confusion or refusal to estimate. The complexity of medical billing, with thousands of billing codes, multiple payers, and different patient-specific variables, makes it far too easy for providers to say, "we can't know your exact cost upfront."

While there is some truth to that (emergencies and complications can arise), the lack of standardized pricing or even price ranges is unique to healthcare. Consumers have been conditioned not to expect price transparency in this realm.

Industry Resistance to Transparency: Whenever regulators push for more price transparency, industry groups push back. For example, when the federal government ordered hospitals to post their prices for various procedures (effective 2021), compliance was initially spotty. Early reports found that less than half of hospitals fully complied with the price transparency rule. One advocacy report in 2023 found only 34.5% of 2,000 hospitals surveyed were in full compliance.

Types of Hidden Costs

High Out-of-Pocket Expenses: Most insurance plans have an annual deductible (the amount you pay before insurance pays at all) and cost-sharing requirements (like paying 20% of the cost of a service). Plans also have an out-of-pocket maximum cap per year, but those caps can be high - up to $8,700 for an individual and $17,400 for a family in employer plans.

Surprise Medical Bills: These occur typically when you unknowingly receive care from an out-of-network provider. In a classic scenario, you might go to an in-network hospital for a surgery, but the anesthesiologist or a consulting specialist isn't in your insurance network, so you get a separate bill that your insurance won't fully cover. Patients have been hit with surprise bills for everything from ambulance rides and emergency room doctors to pathology tests. Some surprise bills have been exorbitant, like $500 for a doctor's five-minute consultation in the ER or tens of thousands for an assistant surgeon you didn't even realize was on your case. A 2024 study by the Commonwealth Fund found that 45% of insured, working-age adults received a surprise medical bill or were charged for something they believed their plan would cover at no cost in the past year

Coverage Loopholes: Often, the devil is in the details: maybe a screening is covered only every five years, but you got it after four years. Maybe you get a mammogram covered 100% by insurance as preventive care, but if the radiologist sees something and orders a diagnostic ultrasound, you end up with an expensive bill because the follow-up imaging it's no longer "preventive."

Medication Costs and Formularies: Insurance might not outright deny a drug, but it might put it on a high tier with big copays or require you to try cheaper drugs first (step therapy). Patients often discover that the brand-name drug that works best for them costs significantly more in copays than alternatives.

Medical Devices and Supplies: CPAP machines, insulin pumps, and other devices might have separate cost-sharing or rental fees that are not obvious upfront.

Routine Procedure Extras: Even routine things can have hidden costs. Childbirth, for instance, is generally covered by insurance, but many families get stuck with thousands in bills afterwards due to things like hospital fees, newborn care costs, or an epidural administered by an out-of-network anesthesiologist.

The consequences for consumers are severe. Without transparency, providers can charge vastly different prices for the same service, and patients have little recourse. One hospital might charge $20,000 for a routine childbirth, another $10,000, another $5,000. These differences often aren't linked to quality. In the dark, patients can't "shop around" effectively, so high-cost providers feel little pressure. Such variation was famously highlighted in a 2013 *TIME* exposé "Bitter Pill" by Steven Brill, which showed extreme examples like a hospital charging $77 for a box of gauze pads and $4,000 for a stress test that Medicare would pay $550 for. These hidden prices contribute to the U.S. paying much more per procedure than other countries.

Congress addressed some of this with the No Surprises Act (2022), which now protects patients from many out-of-network surprise bills in emergencies and at in-network facilities. However, surprise bills can still occur in other contexts (e.g., ground ambulance rides remain unregulated).

The ultimate consequence of unclear (and high) prices is medical debt. As of 2021, an estimated $88 billion in medical bills was in collections on Americans' credit reports. The Consumer Financial Protection Bureau found medical bills to be the most common debt item on credit records.

If price opacity isn't the sole cause, it's nonetheless a major one. If prices were known and standardized, at least patients could make informed decisions or shop for better deals. Currently, it's like playing roulette.

Another consequence is less tangible but important: the lack of transparent pricing erodes trust in the healthcare system. Patients feel gouged or tricked when they get an outrageous bill. These experiences lead people to view hospitals and insurers as adversaries, not allies.

When people treat healthcare like a scam to guard against (e.g., avoiding ambulance calls because of cost fears), that's a public health problem too.

The push for price transparency is growing. Federal rules now require hospitals to post machine-readable price lists and consumer-friendly shoppable service lists. Insurers must post all their negotiated rates.

Tech companies and researchers are parsing these to create price comparison tools. In some markets, employers are steering workers to lower-cost providers (e.g., through "reference pricing" or incentivizing shopping).

Early results show transparency alone won't dramatically cut costs. Many consumers still don't or can't shop around, especially in emergencies. But it's a start. At least with data out there, egregious overpricing can be spotlighted.

Nevertheless, the culture of opacity won't change overnight since entrenched interests will continue to find ways to obfuscate. Some hospitals have argued in court that their prices are trade secrets and shouldn't be forced into the open. The lack of price transparency is a cornerstone of how the U.S. health system is rigged against consumers. It keeps patients powerless and dependent, unable to exert consumer pressure to discipline prices. It allows wild price discrimination and perpetuates a "black box" where only the insiders know the rules. Until prices are upfront and comparable, there is no true market in healthcare. It's a rigged game where the house (hospitals, pharma, insurers) always wins, and the patient often loses financially.

MEDICARE ADVANTAGE: MARKETING HYPE VS. PATIENT EXPERIENCE

For Americans over 65, Medicare is a universal entitlement, but even here, the system has been partly privatized in a way that shortchanges patients. MA plans are private insurance plans that administer Medicare benefits, and they have exploded in popularity (over half of Medicare beneficiaries are now in MA).

These plans are heavily marketed as an all-in-one, often lower-cost alternative to original government-run Medicare. They advertise extras like dental coverage, hearing aids, gym memberships, and caps on out-of-pocket spending.

However, behind the glossy marketing lies a reality of restricted networks, prior authorization hurdles, and denied care that has begun to raise alarms. The contrast between what's promised and what's delivered in MA is a prime example of how the system may be "rigged" by savvy corporate players.

At CareYaya, we work with many seniors navigating Medicare choices. One couple contacted us after experiencing what they called a "bait and switch" with their MA plan.

"The ads made it seem perfect," the husband told me. "Zero-dollar premium, dental and vision included, even a gym membership. What they didn't mention was that when my wife needed specialized cancer care, we'd have to fight for every approval and travel 70 miles to find an in-network specialist. Traditional Medicare would have let us go to the cancer center 15 minutes from our house."

Each fall during Medicare open enrollment, seniors are inundated with TV ads, mailers, and phone calls touting MA plans. Celebrity spokesmen enthusiastically promote plans that offer "$0 premiums! $0 copays! Dental and vision included! Even money back in your Social Security check!"

These ads paint MA as a no-brainer: more benefits than traditional Medicare, for little to no cost. And indeed, many MA plans have low or zero monthly premiums. The marketing tends to show active, healthy seniors hiking or playing tennis, suggesting a happy, hassle-free experience. What the ads don't mention are the limitations. Only 4% of MA TV ads referenced plan limitations like networks or need for referrals.

This has led to some seniors feeling misled. In fact, complaints about misleading MA marketing have spiked in recent years, with reports of brokers or ads implying things like "you'll get all the same access as Medicare plus more," which isn't always true. Congress has held hearings on aggressive and deceptive MA marketing, noting seniors are often "inundated with aggressive tactics and false information."

When a beneficiary enrolls in an MA plan, they typically agree to use the plan's network of providers and follow its rules. This is a fundamental difference: Original Medicare allows one to see any doctor or hospital nationwide that accepts Medicare (which is the vast majority). MA ties you to a network (usually local) and often requires referrals to see specialists and prior authorization for expensive procedures.

Just like under-65 insurance, many MA plans have narrow networks of doctors. A comprehensive study found MA plan networks include only 46% of local physicians on average. About one-third of MA enrollees are in plans with narrow physician networks (covering under 30% of doctors).

This means if you value keeping your choice of doctors, MA can actually restrict your choices. For example, if you split time between two states, Original Medicare travels with you but an MA HMO plan might not cover non-emergency care outside its home region. If your favorite specialist or hospital isn't contracted with the MA plan, you either pay a lot more or can't see them. Many seniors don't realize this until they face a serious illness and find that the renowned cancer center or specific surgeon they want is out-of-network.

Perhaps the biggest friction point is that MA plans commonly require prior authorization for many services, meaning you and your doctor must get the plan's approval before the service is covered. This could be for MRIs, specialist visits, home health care, hospital stays beyond a certain number of days, etc.

The plans claim this is to ensure cost-effective, appropriate care, but patients often experience it as a hurdle or delay in getting care. A 2022 federal investigation by the HHS Inspector General found that MA plans wrongly deny many requests that should be approved. Specifically, they found 13% of prior authorization denials in MA were for services that met Medicare's coverage rules and should have been approved under traditional Medicare. In other words, if those patients had been in Original Medicare, they would have gotten the service, but their MA plan initially said no.

The OIG also found about 18% of payment denials were wrong, meaning providers were not paid for care that was indeed covered, likely deterring those providers from treating MA patients. While many of these denials get overturned on appeal, the appeals process itself is cumbersome that only a small fraction of patients appeal.

According to KFF, only about 11% of denied prior authorization requests in MA were appealed in 2021, but when appealed, 75% were decided in favor of the patient (the plan's denial was reversed). That suggests a lot of inappropriate denials are never appealed and thus never remedied.

Even beyond outright denials, the need to get approval can cause dangerous delays or make doctors alter their recommended treatment to something easier to approve. The OIG report warned that MA denials can "delay or prevent medically necessary care" and create hassle for providers. Some doctors have admitted they sometimes don't even bother trying to get certain things authorized because they expect a refusal from the plan. Instead, they go with a second-best option, a subtle form of care limitation that is hard to measure but real.

While many seniors are happy with their MA plans when they are relatively healthy (enjoying the lower costs and extra benefits), problems often surface when they succumb to serious illness or disease. Consider the story of Jenn Coffey, a 51-year-old breast cancer patient in New Hampshire who enrolled in a MA plan (administered by UnitedHealthcare) after she became disabled and eligible for Medicare.

She soon found that "so many times... the response was, 'They won't cover.'" Despite her doctors' recommendations, her plan second-guessed or outright denied numerous services for her cancer recovery and a painful secondary condition.

The constant battles and denials took such a toll that Jenn, a former EMT who understood healthcare, felt "there was no more hope" and even considered stopping all treatment and signing a DNR (do-not-resuscitate order) because the fight with the insurer was too exhausting. "I never thought about not having access," she said, until MA taught her that access to care was not a given.

Her case is extreme, but it highlights how for-profit insurers in MA have an incentive to deny or limit care, since they get a fixed payment. Every dollar not spent on a patient's care is profit (within regulatory medical loss ratio limits).

She's not alone. Government audits have found "widespread and persistent problems" with inappropriate denials in MA. A Senate report in 2023 concluded that beneficiaries in MA are denied care that would be covered in Original Medicare, pointing to a fundamental problem.

Even the former head of Medicare, Dr. Donald Berwick, has expressed concern that some MA plans make their profits by getting patients to skimp on care and by aggressive upcoding (making patients look sicker on paper to get higher payments, even as they deny some services).

Tellingly, a not insignificant number of seniors switch out of MA and back to traditional Medicare each year, especially those who develop serious health conditions. However, a trap here is that if they missed their initial Medigap enrollment window, they might not be able to get a Medicare supplemental

(Medigap) policy without underwriting, meaning returning to traditional Medicare could expose them to high 20% coinsurance costs.

This lock-in aspect makes the initial choice of MA vs. Original Medicare very consequential, and some seniors regret choosing MA once they experience its limits.

Meanwhile, the marketing rolls on. MA plans have high satisfaction rates in surveys when asking about general care, and indeed they often do well on preventive services. Many seniors do enjoy the vision and dental benefits (though those are often quite limited in scope).

Because of these positives and heavy marketing, enrollment grows yearly, and the plans reap large payments from the government (over $400 billion a year now). They are very profitable for insurers, partly because of coding practices that yield higher payments for sicker-looking populations and partly by managing utilization tightly.

MA ads won't tell you any of the downsides as they rarely mention that prior authorizations can delay your care, or that your favorite doctor might not be in-network. They focus on "free" extras and potential savings.

There is a growing chorus of experts warning that if MA becomes the dominant form of Medicare, we must institute stronger oversight to ensure seniors aren't denied needed care. The Senate Finance Committee and Medicare Payment Advisory Commission (MedPAC) have both flagged issues with MA, from coding inflation to network adequacy and denial rates.

MA demonstrates the tension between private insurance incentives and patient-centered care. It's marketed as a better deal than traditional Medicare—and for some, it can be, as long as you don't need costly care or out-of-network specialists.

But the fine print (networks, authorizations) and the evidence of care denials reveal that the system can be rigged in favor of the insurer's finances. Patients may not realize the trade-offs until they're in a vulnerable health situation.

The big picture is that a program intended to give consumers choice and extra benefits has also given insurers power to dictate care in ways Medicare (the public program) never did. As one health advocate bluntly stated, "When MA insurers inappropriately deny doctor-recommended care, patients suffer," and often they don't even know what they're missing until it's too late.

UNRIGGING THE SYSTEM

From the international level down to individual patient experiences, these facets of the U.S. health system illustrate a common theme of misaligned incentives and structural bias against the consumer. American healthcare is exceptional—exceptionally costly, complex, and often inequitable—because it has been engineered that way by those who profit within it.

Administrative bloat, tied-to-job insurance, gaps like COBRA, manipulated provider networks, phantom directories, hidden prices, and privatized Medicare plans all serve certain business or institutional interests. They help maximize revenue or minimize payouts for companies, but they leave patients footing the bill, navigating confusing hurdles, or going without care.

Real-world stories and data make it clear that these aren't just benign inefficiencies; they cause genuine harm, whether it's a bankrupt family, an untreated illness, or a life lost to a denied service.

Understanding how the system is rigged is the first step toward unrigging it. Each of these issues is complex, but not intractable. Other countries have achieved universal coverage, price transparency, and simpler administration.

At CareYaya, we see both the broken system and glimmers of hope. Every day, our pre-health students witness firsthand how families struggle with our convoluted system. Many enter their healthcare education determined to create change.

Policy solutions and reforms (some already attempted, some yet to be tried) could address each scam exposed in this chapter. The challenge is overcoming the powerful status quo interests and inertia.

The hope is that shining a light on these problems—with facts and stories—will build the will to rewrite the rules of the game in favor of patients, not profits. Only then can we transform "American exceptionalism" in healthcare from a cautionary tale into something to be proud of.

PART II:
The Human Cost

4

VOICES FROM THE BATTLEFIELD

"The true measure of any society can be found in how it treats its most vulnerable members."

— *Mahatma Gandhi*

The doctor looked exhausted as she pulled me aside in the hallway. "I've been treating Mr. Daley for nearly six years," she kept her voice low. "His cancer was responding to treatment. We had a plan. And now..." She looked at the denial letter in her hand. "This should be a medical decision, not a bureaucratic one."

I was visiting this community hospital as part of CareYaya's outreach efforts, but I will never forget what I witnessed that day. The doctor was holding a letter stating that her patient's life-extending therapy was "not medically necessary" as determined by someone who had never examined him nor reviewed his full medical record.

Mr. Daley, a 62-year-old retired mechanic with comprehensive employer insurance through his wife's job, had just been informed he needed to "fail" on an older, less effective chemotherapy before his insurer would cover the targeted therapy his oncologist had prescribed. The likely result? Disease progression that could close his window for the more effective treatment altogether.

Through my work at CareYaya, I've heard hundreds of variations of this story not just from older adults needing care, but from their adult children, from our caregivers working second jobs to pay medical bills, and from healthcare providers watching their patients suffer. Each represents a personal battle against a system that works impressively well for shareholders and executives but fails Americans when they're at their most vulnerable.

This chapter isn't about abstract policy or distant statistics. It's about real people facing the devastating reality of America's broken health insurance system. Their stories reveal patterns of failure so consistent that they can't be dismissed as anomalies. They expose the gap between what we're promised and what countless Americans actually experience when illness strikes.

CANCER CARE DENIED: LIFE-AND-DEATH DECISIONS MADE BY NON-PHYSICIANS

Jessica came to us seeking caregiving help for her father, Manuel, a 67-year-old retired postal worker with stage 3 lymphoma. During our onboarding process, she broke down.

"The doctor says there's a treatment with a good chance of putting Dad's cancer into remission," she explained. "But the insurance company won't approve it."

Manuel's case isn't unusual. In fact, it follows a pattern we've seen repeatedly with cancer patients facing critical treatment decisions. Despite having what appeared to be excellent insurance through his retirement plan, Manuel found himself caught in an insurance company's web of definitions, protocols, and financial calculations that had little to do with his medical needs.

Across America, cancer patients regularly face denials for treatments their doctors believe offer the best chance for survival. In a particularly egregious case documented by *ProPublica*, 50-year-old Forrest VanPatten was denied coverage for CAR-T cell therapy, an innovative treatment that reengineers a patient's own immune cells to fight cancer, after standard chemotherapy failed to curb his aggressive lymphoma. Despite Michigan law requiring insurers to cover clinically proven cancer drugs, his insurer, Priority Health, refused to approve the treatment. Internal emails later revealed the denial was driven almost entirely by cost. VanPatten would die in February 2020 before his third and final appeal was reviewed.

The consequences extend beyond the binary of approved or denied. A 2024 study at a major cancer center found that among patients initially denied radiation therapy, 10% had to accept lower radiation doses than prescribed due to insurer requirements, a dangerous change linked to decreased tumor control and survival. More than a quarter had to switch to less advanced radiation techniques, potentially increasing side effects and reducing effectiveness.

Stacy, whose mother receives CareYaya assistance while undergoing breast cancer treatment, described the psychological toll of fighting these battles. "Mom should be focused on healing, not spending hours on the phone with insurance," she said. "Every denial letter sends her into a panic. She's literally fighting for her life on two fronts."

The patterns become clear when you see enough cases: expensive but effective treatments face the highest scrutiny; denials often cite obscure policy exclusions; and the appeals process is designed to exhaust patients who are already depleted from fighting disease. It's a calculated approach that prioritizes the quarterly balance sheet over human life.

THE CHRONIC ILLNESS MAZE

"I've been on the same medication for seven years," Todd told me during a CareYaya consultation for his elderly father. "Every January, I have to prove all over again that I still have multiple sclerosis."

Todd's experience highlights a fundamental mismatch: our health insurance system is structured around annual enrollment periods and short-term cost calculations, even though chronic illnesses persist for years or lifetimes. This creates a perpetual obstacle course for the approximately 60% of American adults managing at least one chronic condition.

Consider Christopher McNaughton, a college student with severe ulcerative colitis documented by *ProPublica*. After years of trial and error, his doctors finally found a medication regimen that kept his debilitating inflammatory bowel disease in check. Nonetheless, his insurer, UnitedHealthcare, abruptly decided it wouldn't pay. In a recorded call, a UnitedHealthcare representative admitted any appeal would be futile, since they would "still gonna say no" regardless. When McNaughton filed an appeal anyway, the company misrepresented his physician's statements to justify the rejection.

This Kafkaesque nightmare is familiar to millions with conditions like diabetes, autoimmune disorders, or heart failure. Insurance companies effectively force chronically ill patients to continuously re-justify treatments that are working, thereby creating dangerous gaps in care and mountains of paperwork.

"The amount of administrative work is ridiculous," explained Emily, who helps her 83-year-old father with Parkinson's navigate his MA plan through UnitedHealthcare. "Dad needs physical therapy to maintain mobility, but every ten sessions, we have to stop, get a new prescription, submit for authorization, and wait. During those gaps, he declines. Then we start over. It's maddening."

Chronically ill patients also face "step therapy" requirements (trying cheaper drugs first before insurers will cover more effective ones) and frequent coverage changes as formularies and preferred drug lists shift. Gina, a CareYaya care recipient with rheumatoid arthritis, described having to "fail" on three different medications, each taking months to prove ineffective while her condition worsened, before her insurer would cover the original drug her rheumatologist had initially prescribed.

"By the time I got the right medication, I had permanent joint damage," she told me. "That damage was preventable. It happened because someone at an insurance company thought they knew better than my specialist."

For many, the burden becomes so overwhelming they simply give up. The AMA survey revealed 78% of physicians report that patients "abandon recommended treatments" because of authorization struggles and insurance red tape. This isn't merely inconvenient: it's dangerous because interruptions in therapy for conditions like epilepsy, heart failure, or bipolar disorder can trigger life-threatening crises.

The mental and emotional toll is equally devastating. Managing a chronic disease is challenging enough; managing the insurance battle simultaneously can be overwhelming. Many patients describe spending more time fighting for coverage than on actual self-care—a cruel irony that worsens their health outcomes.

MIDDLE-CLASS MEDICAL BANKRUPTCY

"We did everything right," Nick told me, his voice tight with anger. "Good jobs, health insurance, savings account. Then my wife got cancer, and within 18 months, we lost it all."

It's not just the poor or uninsured who are ravaged by medical costs. Nick and Susan represent America's vulnerable middle class: too wealthy for Medicaid, too young for Medicare, and completely exposed to the financial devastation that serious illness can bring despite having job stability and insurance. Middle-class life in America typically comes with fixed costs (mortgage, car, student loans, etc.) and not a ton of liquid savings. A major medical event adds massive new costs and potentially reduces income (if the sick person or caregiver can't work as much). As of 2022, only 63% of American adults could afford a $400 emergency. It's a perfect storm that can engulf a family in debt quickly.

Nick and Susan's echoes research findings that medical problems such as sky-high bills, lost income from illness, or both are a leading cause of personal bankruptcy in the United States. In the early 1980s, only about 8% of U.S. families filing bankruptcy cited healthcare expenses as a contributing factor. But by the mid-2010s, roughly two-thirds of personal bankruptcies involved medical issues, equivalent to about 530,000 American families filing for bankruptcy each year because of illness or medical bills. Once you account for spouses and children, that's well over a million people annually experiencing medical bankruptcy.

This reality has become so common that some economists warn medical expenses are a key driver pushing middle-class families into lower economic strata. Case studies and statistics bear this out. For instance, a study in the American Journal of Public Health found that among those who declared medical bankruptcy, the majority had been middle-class earners and three-quarters had health insurance at the onset of illness. They weren't destitute or uninsured to start with but rather ordinary homeowners, professionals, and working families who happened to get sick.

How does this happen, even to insured families? Often, it's a combination of high cost-sharing and coverage gaps. Many insurance plans come with hefty deductibles and coinsurance. A family might face a $5,000 or $10,000 deductible, amounts that are difficult to meet, especially if illness already disrupts their income.

When Alexandra's husband was diagnosed with stage 4 colon cancer at 42, they thought their employer-provided insurance would protect them. What they discovered was that protection had fine print.

"Our plan covered 80% after the deductible," Alexandra explained. "That sounds good until you realize 20% of a $300,000 cancer treatment is still $60,000. And that's not counting the deductible, out-of-network charges, experimental treatments, and everything insurance just refused to cover."

Two years later, despite her husband's employer-provided insurance, they had depleted their savings, maxed out credit cards, withdrawn retirement funds (with penalties), and still owed over $100,000 in medical debt. When he died, Alexandra filed for bankruptcy, joining the ranks of Americans for whom illness means financial death as well.

Take the story of the Coy family in Colorado as another example. In 2021, Andrea Coy's infant son contracted a severe pneumonia that necessitated an airlift by helicopter from a local hospital to a specialized children's hospital. The air ambulance was out-of-network, leading to a massive $65,000 bill for the short flight. Their insurer (UnitedHealthcare) covered only about $28,000 of it.

Andrea tried every avenue, from calling insurance to negotiating with the ambulance company to seeking aid and managed to get the balance down to $5,000. Even then, she was left with that bill plus $12,000 in out-of-pocket costs for the hospitalization itself. This middle-class family suddenly had nearly $17,000 of unexpected medical costs.

Medical debt can also accumulate quietly. It's not always one catastrophic event; sometimes it's chronic illness expenses over years. Copays for specialist visits, monthly drug costs, medical equipment rentals, and therapy sessions can steadily drain savings. Many people wind up putting expenses on credit cards or take out second mortgages until one day they realize they've fallen into an impossible hole.

Medical bills of even a few thousand can force tough choices: do we drain Junior's college fund? Skip mortgage payments? It becomes a juggling act, often with no good outcomes financially. We also see middle-class families strategically downscaling or altering life plans due to medical cost fears. Some delay having a second child or any children because they worry about hospital costs associated with childbirth and pediatric care. Others keep working past retirement age not because they want to, but to maintain employer health benefits until they hit Medicare age.

These are quality-of-life hits that might not show up as bankruptcies but indicate financial strain from healthcare. Importantly, this middle-class squeeze has social ripple effects. The frustration and fear in the middle class around healthcare costs have become a potent political force.

If the middle class loses faith that the system will protect them in their time of need, pressure for systemic change will grow. That's why, when discussing health reform, you often hear not just moral arguments for the poor, but very pragmatic arguments aimed at the middle class: "This could happen to you. One medical crisis and you could lose everything, even with insurance." It's a warning that unfortunately resonates widely in America today.

CROWDFUNDED HEALTHCARE

When Lisa told me her family had raised $18,000 through GoFundMe for her mother's cancer treatment, I initially thought this was good news until she explained the campaign's goal was $150,000.

"We're trying everything," she said. "Bake sales, church fundraisers, even asking Mom's former students to donate. But it's not enough. And every day we wait, her condition gets worse."

In twenty-first century America, millions find themselves turning to a modern digital safety net: crowdfunding their healthcare. Websites like GoFundMe now host hundreds of thousands of campaigns for medical needs, where patients plead for donations to pay medical bills or fund treatments.

GoFundMe's leaders have noted that while they never intended the platform to become a healthcare funding source, medical expenses have become the most common category of fundraiser on the site. Internal estimates suggest roughly one-third of all GoFundMe fundraisers are for healthcare costs. As of the early 2020s, more than 250,000 health-related campaigns are started each year, collectively raising over $650 million annually.

While these numbers are large, they pale in comparison to the need. A comprehensive study in the American Journal of Public Health found that only about 12% of medical campaigns met their goal, and 16% received no donations at all. In other words, nearly 88% of campaigns fail to reach their target, often collecting only a fraction of the cost of care.

"It's like a popularity contest for survival," observed Dr. Clark, a primary care physician I spoke with at a healthcare conference. "Patients with photogenic stories, cute kids, or large social networks do better. What about everyone else?"

Research confirms this observation. Campaigns in wealthier, well-networked communities raise more money, while those from poorer areas or addressing less "marketable" illnesses raise less. One study noted that campaigns raised substantially less money in areas with higher medical debt, higher uninsurance rates, and lower incomes. In essence, crowdfunding is "best positioned to help populations that need it least."

I've observed this firsthand. When Peter, a retired firefighter with an aggressive brain tumor, launched a GoFundMe for an immunotherapy treatment denied by his insurer, his former fire department rallied around him. As local news covered his story, donations poured in; he ultimately raised enough for treatment. But for every success like Peter's, there are dozens of equally deserving patients whose campaigns languish unnoticed.

Despite these limitations, turning to GoFundMe has rapidly become normalized. As such, hospital social workers and patient advocates sometimes recommend crowdfunding when patients can't afford care.

The implications are troubling. As one journalist noted, paying for care via GoFundMe is being "normalized as part of the health system, like getting blood work done or waiting on hold for an appointment." Need a heart transplant?

You need to crowdfund in order to get on the waiting list in some cases. The fact that access to life-saving care might hinge on a viral fundraiser is perhaps the most damning indictment of all.

John, whose daughter needed specialized therapy not covered by insurance, told me how crowdfunding affected him psychologically: "I felt like I was begging. I spent hours crafting the perfect story, choosing the right photo, sharing it everywhere. It was humiliating, but what choice did I have? Let my daughter suffer?"

MENTAL HEALTH BARRIERS

"My insurance says they cover mental health, but when I tried to find a therapist for my depression, not a single provider on their list was accepting new patients," shared Monica, a CareYaya caregiver attending nursing school. "The few who were didn't actually take my insurance despite being listed. I finally found someone who would see me, but she's out-of-network. Each session costs $150 out-of-pocket."

Monica's experience is painfully common. Despite laws requiring parity (equal coverage) for mental health, Americans seeking psychological or psychiatric treatment often hit unique and daunting barriers. Provider shortages are rampant especially for psychiatrists and child therapists. As of March 2023, about 160 million Americans live in areas with mental health professional shortages, with over 8,000 additional providers needed to fill the gap.

This scarcity is compounded by insurance networks that don't include enough mental health providers. In a National Alliance on Mental Illness survey, 55% of people looking for a new psychiatrist couldn't find one accepting new patients, while 56% couldn't find one who took their insurance. The result: over 1 in 4 patients (28%) had to go out-of-network for mental health therapy, versus only 7% who went out-of-network for other medical specialists.

Going out-of-network means higher out-of-pocket costs. Patients were much more likely to face bills over $200 for mental health visits than for primary care visits. These extra costs lead many to delay or forgo therapy altogether.

Brandon, whose elderly mother receives CareYaya services while he manages her care, described the impact of insurance barriers on his own mental health: "Caregiving is incredibly stressful. My doctor recommended therapy, but my insurance only covers 10 sessions per year. My therapist said my anxiety issues would require at least 6 months of weekly sessions to address properly.

So what am I supposed to do for the other 42 weeks?"

The consequences of these barriers are severe. Despite enormous unmet need, less than half of adults with mental illness receive treatment. In 2021, only 47.2% of U.S. adults with any mental illness received treatment, and even among those with serious mental illness, only about 65% received care. For youth, the gap is also large (only around half of children with diagnosable mental health conditions get treatment). These shortcomings leave millions suffering without help.

The Mental Health Parity and Addiction Equity Act (2008) and the ACA were supposed to eliminate unequal coverage limits for mental health and substance use treatment. However, enforcement has been weak. Insurers have found subtle ways to skirt parity requirements—such as maintaining narrower networks for mental health providers or using more stringent managed-care techniques on mental health claims.

"The laws look good on paper," noted Dr. Wong, a psychiatrist I consulted about our caregivers' mental health program. "But in practice, insurance companies have a thousand ways to make mental health care harder to access. They'll approve medications but not therapy. They'll cover generalists but not specialists for complex conditions. They'll authorize a handful of sessions when evidence shows more are needed."

For serious conditions like eating disorders, bipolar disorder, or substance use disorders, these barriers can be life-threatening. Families report insurers refusing to cover residential treatment or discharging patients from psychiatric hospitals against doctors' advice because the company deems further days "not necessary."

As Jason, a father seeking care options for his teenage daughter with severe depression, told me: "If my daughter had cancer, the insurance would cover whatever treatment she needed. But because her illness affects her brain instead of another organ, we have to fight for every appointment, every medication adjustment, every day of treatment. How is that parity?"

RURAL HEALTHCARE DESERTS

The phone call from Martha, who used to book care through CareYaya, highlighted a healthcare crisis that numbers alone can't capture.

"The closest hospital is 47 miles away now," she explained. "When my husband had his heart attack last year, the ambulance took nearly an hour to reach us. Then another hour to get to the hospital. The doctor said if we'd gotten there sooner..."

Her voice trailed off, but the implication was clear. In America's rural areas, hospitals and clinics have been shutting down at alarming rates, creating "healthcare deserts" where residents struggle to find basic medical services. These geographic disparities mean that for millions of rural Americans access to necessary treatment is literally a matter of distance, compounding the challenges of insurance coverage.

The statistics are alarming. From 2010 through 2021, 136 rural hospitals closed across the United States, and by 2023 the total since 2010 had risen to over 150. Each closure leaves a community without an emergency room, obstetric services for pregnant women, and local inpatient beds.

Beyond the hospitals that have already closed, hundreds more rural hospitals are in jeopardy. A recent report found that over 700 rural hospitals (about 31% of all rural hospitals nationwide) are at risk of shutting down due to financial losses. This includes 360 rural hospitals (16% of the total) at immediate risk of closure because of their dire finances.

For Martha's family, like many others, the rural hospital closure has made their insurance coverage almost irrelevant. "We have Medicare," Martha told me, "but what good is coverage if there's nowhere to use it? My husband needs regular cardiology check-ups, but that means a full-day trip now."

When a rural hospital closes, the effect ripples throughout a community. Emergency care is the most immediate loss. For time-sensitive conditions like strokes, heart attacks, or traumatic injuries, increased travel time can mean the difference between life and death. Studies have found mixed evidence on health outcomes, but some research shows increased mortality for time-sensitive conditions after rural hospital closures.

Obstetric services have been disappearing as well: over half of rural counties now have no hospital-based obstetrics. One report noted 60% of Pennsylvania's rural hospitals have no labor and delivery services. This has led to rising rates of emergency deliveries and complications for rural mothers.

When CareYaya expanded into some rural counties last year, we witnessed firsthand how distance creates healthcare inequality. Bob, an 84-year-old with congestive heart failure, described a taxing 156-mile round trip for specialist appointments: "By the time I get there, I'm exhausted. The doctor rushes through our visit because they're overbooked. Then I turn around and drive back. It takes three days to recover from the trip itself."

Insurance plays a role in these healthcare deserts in a few ways. First, insurance networks may not account for the lack of providers; a rural resident might technically have an "in-network" hospital 100 miles away, but the closer out-of-network hospital (if one remains) would trigger huge bills.

Second, the financial viability issues of rural hospitals are partly linked to payer mix. Rural hospitals serve older, poorer populations (more Medicare and Medicaid, which reimburse at lower rates than private insurance). They also often get paid less by private insurers who negotiate rates based on volume and competition, which rural hospitals lack.

"We're in a coverage dead zone," explained Nancy, a rural home health nurse. "People here have insurance cards in their wallets, but nowhere that accepts them nearby. So they delay care until it's an emergency. Then they get transported to the urban medical center, rack up huge bills, and return home with no follow-up resources. It's a terrible cycle."

For rural Americans, having health insurance can create a false sense of security. Coverage means little without accessible providers, creating yet another way the system fails vulnerable populations.

PREVENTABLE TRAGEDIES

Some stories remain with you forever. Samantha came to us seeking help after her father suffered a massive stroke. When I met with her to discuss care options, she was still processing her grief and anger over how it happened.

"Dad had been having these episodes. His speech would slur, his arm would go weak, but it would pass quickly," she explained. "The doctor said they were mini-strokes, warning signs. He wanted to admit Dad for tests and start him on blood thinners right away."

But her father's insurance required prior authorization for the hospital admission. While they waited for approval, which took four days, he suffered a devastating stroke that left him partially paralyzed and unable to speak.

"The doctor told us directly this was preventable" Samantha said, tears streaming down her face. "A four-day delay. That's all it took to destroy his life."

Perhaps the most heartbreaking aspect of insurance failures is when they directly result in preventable injury or death. These are the tragedies that didn't have to happen. Patients who might have lived or recovered if not for an insurance denial or delay. Investigations and anecdotes have revealed numerous cases where bureaucratic decisions in insurance offices had fatal consequences on the ground.

What allows these tragedies to happen? For one, patients rarely appeal denials, or don't know how. Astonishingly, data show that only about 1 in 500 denied claims is ever appealed. Insurers bank on this inertia, assuming most people will pay or drop the matter rather than endure a convoluted appeals process.

Another issue is fragmented accountability. When an insurer's decision leads to harm, legal recourse is limited. Employer-sponsored health plans are governed by ERISA, a federal law that largely preempts state malpractice or bad-faith lawsuits against insurers. Families like Nataline Sarkisyan's (mentioned in the Introduction) have found they cannot sue for damages even when an insurer's denial proved fatal.

Dr. Martin, a cardiologist I once spoke to, described the emotional toll these cases take on medical professions: "We spend years learning how to save lives, only to watch patients decline or die while waiting for some anonymous person at an insurance company to approve what we know they need. It's morally devastating."

Even routine denials that eventually get overturned can have permanent consequences. When Richard's insurer denied coverage for his wound care treatments after a diabetic foot ulcer, the resulting two-week delay allowed the infection to spread. By the time approval came through, the damage was irreversible, ultimately leading to amputation.

"I asked the surgeon directly if earlier treatment would have saved my foot," Richard told me during his CareYaya onboarding. "He just looked at me and said, 'Almost certainly.' That's something I live with every day. Knowing this was preventable."

What's clear is that the current oversight and consumer protection mechanisms are inadequate to prevent these tragedies. Regulators often step in only after media attention or patterns of complaints. Internally, insurers may have utilitarian protocols that accept a certain number of "false negatives" (denying valid care) as a trade-off for cost savings, without individual accountability for those decisions.

CHILDREN CAUGHT IN THE SYSTEM

"They sent the denial letter addressed to my seven-month-old," Natalie told me, disbelief still evident in her voice months later. "It said, 'Dear Tyler, we are writing to inform you that your request for the specialized formula prescribed by your doctor has been denied as not medically necessary.'"

Tyler was born with a severe metabolic disorder that prevented him from digesting standard infant formula. His specialized formula, which cost over $800 monthly, was medically prescribed but repeatedly denied by insurance as "nutritional" rather than "medical," despite documentation from three specialists.

"We went into debt keeping him alive while fighting the insurance company," Natalie explained. "How do you put a price on your child's life?"

When illness strikes a child, the last thing a parent should have to worry about is fighting an insurance company. Yet families of sick children often face some of the most maddening insurance challenges. Children with congenital conditions, rare diseases, or cancer require highly specialized care, exactly the kind of care that insurers are most likely to scrutinize or deny due to its expense.

One illustrative case is that of Liam Doxsee, an 8-year-old boy from Illinois born with severe combined immunodeficiency (SCID), a rare "bubble boy" disease where the immune system doesn't function. Liam needed a life-saving surgery from a uniquely qualified pediatric surgeon. But the family's insurance denied the surgery because the surgeon also practiced plastic surgery, and the insurer categorized the procedure as cosmetic due to a billing code technicality.

"It's not a butt lift, it's a pediatric, time-sensitive emergency surgery that he really needs," Liam's mother protested. Still, the insurer wouldn't budge initially. The family had to organize a fundraiser to raise the out-of-pocket price tag while appealing.

Children with rare diseases often encounter insurance roadblocks when new, expensive treatments emerge. For instance, a revolutionary gene therapy for spinal muscular atrophy (SMA) can prevent a fatal or disabling outcome in babies, but it costs $2.1 million for a single dose. Stories have surfaced of insurers dragging their feet on approving this therapy (brand name Zolgensma), or limiting it to certain ages or criteria, despite clear evidence that earlier treatment is better.

Another issue is that insurance policies reset annually, while a child's illness is continuous. Each year, families may have to re-obtain prior authorizations for the same medications or therapies their child has been on. Similarly, a parent's job change can force a child with complex needs into a whole new insurance network with new rules, jeopardizing carefully calibrated care.

The administrative burden on parents is tremendous. Parents of kids with special healthcare needs often describe themselves as case managers. They coordinate among pediatricians, specialists, pharmacies, medical equipment suppliers, and the insurance plan, all of which entails hours of calls and paperwork on a weekly basis.

It's worth noting that many children with serious health needs are covered by public insurance like Medicaid or CHIP, which generally have broad benefits and no cost-sharing. However, middle-class families often don't qualify for Medicaid, so they rely on private insurance that might have high co-pays or limited networks.

Some parents find they have to "spend down" their assets or reduce work hours to get their child onto state disability Medicaid waivers, thus essentially impoverishing themselves to secure stable coverage for the child. This speaks to a broader policy failure: the lack of seamless, affordable coverage for every child with serious illness.

THE SYSTEM IS BROKEN, BUT THERE'S HOPE

These case studies and data points paint a stark picture: the American health insurance system, in its current form, often fails to protect patients when they need it most. From cancer patients denied proven treatments, to chronically ill people stymied by red tape, to families pushed into debt, to mental health and rural coverage gaps, the problems are deep and wide-ranging. What they all share is a common thread of systemic failure.

Through our work, we see both the devastation these failures cause and the resilience of those fighting back. We've witnessed families successfully appeal denials after arming themselves with knowledge. We've seen communities rally around neighbors in need. And we've observed healthcare providers going above and beyond to help patients navigate the system.

These stories of people are not just tales of suffering but calls to action. Each represents thousands of similar experiences happening daily across America. Their collective voice demands something better.

In the chapters ahead, we'll explore how the healthcare system looks from the perspective of doctors trapped in the same bureaucratic nightmare and hear confessions from insurance industry insiders. Then we'll turn to solutions—specific strategies to fight back against denials, tools to navigate the system, and broader reforms that could transform American healthcare.

For now, know this: you are not alone in your healthcare struggles. The system may be broken, but there are pathways through it, around it, and ultimately to change it. The first step is understanding exactly how it fails, which is what these brave individuals have shown us. Their stories matter not just as cautionary tales, but as the foundation for building something better.

5

DOCTOR IN HANDCUFFS

"Kafka would have been right at home in the American healthcare system."

— Dr. Atul Gawande

D r. Ness had been practicing family medicine for twenty-three years when I met her through CareYaya. At 52, after building a thriving practice that once served three generations of families in her community, Dr. Ness was leaving medicine. She was now offering her services to us.

"I didn't sign up to be a data entry clerk," she told me as we discussed her career change. "I went to medical school to help people. Now I spend more time fighting with insurance companies than I do with my patients."

Her voice cracked slightly as she described her breaking point: "Last month, I had a patient with clear signs of multiple sclerosis. The MRI she needed was denied three times. By the time we got approval, she'd lost feeling in both legs. That's when I knew I couldn't do this anymore."

Dr. Ness isn't alone. Countless physicians get caught in a prior authorization prison. One doctor described it as practicing medicine with "invisible handcuffs," meaning they are technically free to make decisions, but practically constrained at every turn by forces outside their control.

This isn't just a physician problem. When doctors can't practice medicine according to their training and judgment, patients suffer. The story you're about to read reveals the other side of America's broken healthcare system where the same corporate forces that deny patients care are systematically handcuffing the professionals we trust to heal us.

PRIOR AUTHORIZATION PRISON

The irony isn't lost on physicians: after completing four years of medical school, three to seven years of residency training, passing multiple board examinations, and accumulating hundreds of thousands of dollars in educational debt, they must routinely beg for permission to provide basic care.

"Prior authorization" sounds innocuous enough, seemingly connoting a simple check to ensure appropriate care. In reality, it has become one of the most frustrating and dangerous barriers between physicians and patients.

According to the American Medical Association's 2024 survey, an overwhelming 94% of physicians report that prior authorization delays necessary patient care. Even more alarming, nearly one in four doctors reported that prior authorization requirements led directly to a serious adverse event for a patient in their care, including hospitalization, permanent disability, or even death.

The volume is crushing. Physicians complete an average of 43 prior authorization requests weekly, consuming nearly two full business days of staff time. More than a third of doctors have had to hire staff dedicated exclusively to processing prior authorizations. The millions of hours annually diverted from patient care to paperwork serves only to satisfy protocols created by insurance companies, not medical societies.

A primary care physician who regularly refers patients to CareYaya shared a revelation that came to him during a peer-to-peer call: "I realized I was arguing with another doctor who agreed with me clinically but was constrained by the insurance company's policies. He basically whispered, 'I have to deny this, but resubmit with these specific terms.' It was like we were engaged in some elaborate dance around what we both knew was the right treatment."

The system pits doctors not just against insurers but against time itself. For every hour physicians spend with patients, they typically spend nearly two additional hours on electronic health records and desk work. This administrative avalanche often spills over into evenings and weekends, creating what doctors ruefully call "pajama time," or hours spent documenting after their children are in bed.

Insurers defend prior authorization as a cost-control mechanism, but 87% of physicians report that these requirements actually increase overall healthcare resource utilization. Delayed care leads to complications. Denied medications lead to emergency room visits. The obsession with controlling costs on the front end often creates much higher expenses down the line, not to mention unnecessary suffering.

THE PHYSICIAN BURNOUT EPIDEMIC

"I cry in my car almost every day after work," a young primary care physician told me last year. "I love my patients, but I hate what medicine has become."

The statistics on physician burnout tell a devastating story. By 2021, burnout rates among U.S. physicians reached a record high of 62.8%. Think about that. Nearly two-thirds of America's doctors experience emotional exhaustion, depersonalization, and a reduced sense of accomplishment.

The human consequences are dire. Physicians have among the highest suicide rates of any profession, with an estimated 300-400 doctors dying by suicide annually, more than double the rate of the general population. That's the equivalent of an entire medical school's worth of doctors lost each year.

Administrative burdens are the primary culprit. In a 2022 physician survey, an overwhelming 98% identified onerous administrative tasks as significantly contributing to burnout. Prior authorization requirements topped the list, with 95% reporting these insurance hurdles significantly increased their burnout levels.

Dr. Ness described the relentless pressure: "I was spending hours each night finishing charts because my 'productive' day was filled with patient visits scheduled every 15 minutes. The electronic health record systems are designed for billing, not patient care. I felt like a data entry clerk with a medical degree."

The time allocation is shocking. During a typical day, physicians spend nearly half their time (49%) on electronic health records and desk work, while only 27% of their time is spent in direct patient care. For every hour a doctor spends with patients, they spend almost two additional hours on paperwork.

When we think about healthcare reform, we must recognize that physician well-being isn't just about a doctor's quality of life but about patient safety and public health as well. Burnout has been linked to increased medical errors, lower patient satisfaction, and higher staff turnover. Not surprisingly, a burned-out physician simply cannot provide the same quality of care as one who is professionally fulfilled and emotionally healthy. As more physicians reduce hours, retire early, or leave practice altogether, we face a worsening physician shortage that threatens access to care for millions of Americans.

As Dr. Ness put it: "Medicine is the only field where the people with the most training and responsibility have the least control over how they do their work. Imagine telling a pilot they need to get permission from an insurance company before making flight adjustments. It would be considered absurd, yet that's exactly what we ask of physicians."

CODING OVER CARE

Few people outside medicine understand how dramatically the need to generate billing codes shapes modern medical practice. What looks like a simple doctor's visit is now a complex dance of documentation designed primarily to justify billing rather than improve care.

"I spend more time making sure I've clicked all the right boxes than I do looking at my patient," a family physician told me. "It's backwards. The electronic health record should serve the doctor-patient relationship, not the other way around."

The problems begin with the fundamental structure of the system. American medicine runs on billing codes. Every encounter must be translated into standardized CPT (Current Procedural Terminology) and ICD (International Classification of Diseases) codes to generate revenue. This "coding over care" phenomenon distorts clinical practice in subtle but profound ways.

Take the problem of "note bloat." To bill at higher levels, physicians must document extensive reviews of systems and physical examinations, whether clinically relevant or not. The result is electronic health records filled with pages of template-generated text that buries the actual important information.

Dr. Foster, an internal medicine physician who advises CareYaya, explained how the system distorts care: "If I spend an hour with an elderly patient with multiple chronic conditions, carefully adjusting five medications and counseling them on managing their complex conditions, I might bill three 'value units.' If I spend 20 minutes doing a simple procedure, I can bill five units. The system literally incentivizes me to do things to patients rather than talk with them."

The reality is stark: a primary care doctor typically earns only about 1-2 RVUs (relative value units, the measure that determines payment) for a 20-minute office visit (roughly $50–$100) while a specialist performing an hour-long procedure can generate 10+ RVUs worth thousands of dollars. This payment disparity, established by Medicare's RVU system and followed by private insurers, systematically undervalues the cognitive work of diagnosing, counseling, and coordinating care.

Morgan, whose mother has multiple chronic conditions, shared her frustration with the assembly-line approach this creates: "Mom's doctor is clearly rushing through appointments to see enough patients. Last visit, when Mom tried to ask about a second concern, the doctor said, 'I'm sorry, we'll need to schedule another visit for that issue.' It's ridiculous. Mom's health isn't neatly divided into 15-minute problems."

The time pressure this creates has real clinical consequences. A 2023 study found that shorter primary care visits were significantly associated with more inappropriate antibiotic prescribing for respiratory infections. When doctors don't have time to properly evaluate and educate patients, they're more likely to reach for quick fixes like unnecessary antibiotics, thereby contributing to the growing crisis of antibiotic resistance.

"The system rewards volume over value," Dr. Foster told me. "I know doctors who see 40 patients a day. It's physically impossible to provide thoughtful care at that pace. But that's what they're pressured to do."

This volume-driven approach doesn't just dilute quality but often fails even on its own economic terms. As one commentary noted, "More is not always better" in healthcare. Rushed care leads to missed diagnoses, higher complication rates, and avoidable hospitalizations, all of which increase costs downstream.

The coding system also focuses perversely on documentation rather than action. As one physician put it, "In modern medicine, if it wasn't documented, it didn't happen. Even if it actually did happen and benefited the patient." This leads to the absurd situation where excellent care without proper documentation is considered lower quality (and reimbursed less) than mediocre care with perfect documentation.

WHEN WALL STREET MANAGES YOUR DOCTOR

"When I started practice 30 years ago, most doctors owned their practices," a doctor once told me during a planning session. "Now most of us are employees, and increasingly, our bosses have MBAs, not MDs."

The transformation has been swift and profound. As of 2024, over 77% of physicians are employed by hospitals, health systems, or other corporate entities. Between 2019 and 2023 alone, more than 44,000 physician practices were acquired by hospitals or corporations.

Even more telling, 2023 marked the first time that corporate owners (including private equity firms and insurers) owned more physician practices (30.1%) than hospitals did (28.4%). In total, nearly 60% of all physician practices are now owned by non-physicians.

This corporate takeover changes the fundamental nature of medical practice. When I speak with physicians employed by large systems or private equity-backed groups, I hear consistent concerns about loss of autonomy and growing pressure to meet financial targets rather than clinical goals.

The American College of Physicians found that most physicians view private equity's influence negatively, with only 10% regarding it in a positive light. Doctors directly employed by private equity-owned practices were significantly less likely to report high job satisfaction or autonomy compared to those in independent settings.

Dr. Martinez shared her experience after her primary care group was acquired by a private equity firm: "Almost overnight, our patient appointment slots were shortened from 20 minutes to 15. We were given productivity targets that essentially required us to see 25% more patients. When I objected that this would compromise care, I was told, 'The data shows this is achievable.' What data? Certainly not data on quality."

This mirrors what research has found, with nearly 60% of doctors reporting that after their practice was acquired by a corporate entity, their ability to make the best care decisions for patients worsened. More significantly, they felt quality of care declined.

The profit-driven ethos of corporate owners often conflicts with the patient-first ethos of medicine. Investor-owned practices may prioritize revenue-generating services, higher patient volumes, and cost-cutting measures over what physicians believe is best for patients.

Eric, whose father receives care through a recently acquired pulmonology practice, described the change: "Dad's been seeing the same lung specialist for years. After the practice was bought out, they moved his doctor to a different location, scheduled him with a nurse practitioner instead, and when he finally did see his doctor, the visit felt rushed. His doctor seemed stressed and apologized repeatedly about the new system."

The "corporate practice of medicine" is actually restricted by law in some states, which historically barred non-physicians from owning medical practices to ensure clinical decisions remained in medical hands. However, through various workarounds (like management service organizations that technically don't "own" the practice but control its operations), corporations have found ways to effectively control medicine despite these laws.

This corporate consolidation extends beyond just physician practices. Hospital mergers create giant health systems that employ thousands of doctors under standardized, often rigid policies geared toward consistency and cost control rather than individualized care.

"I felt like a widget in a factory," said Dr. Ness. "There were protocols for everything, and deviating from them, even when clinically appropriate, required layers of approval. They called it 'standardization of care,' but it was really standardization of process to maximize billing."

While integration can improve coordination in theory, it also introduces layers of administrative control. Many employed physicians must adhere to corporate formularies (limiting which medications they can prescribe), referral networks (restricting which specialists they can send patients to), and care protocols geared as much toward cost containment as quality.

The situation has led to what one doctor described as "moral injury," the distress that comes from knowing what's right for patients but being unable to provide it due to system constraints. When physicians are forced to practice in ways that conflict with their professional judgment and values, both they and their patients suffer.

The financial impacts are significant as well. Studies show that when physician practices are acquired by hospitals or health systems, prices for the same services typically increase by 14% or more. These higher costs are passed on to patients and payers without necessarily improving quality.

The corporatization of medicine represents one of the most profound shifts in healthcare delivery in generations, and one that has occurred with remarkably little public debate about its implications for patients and physicians alike.

PRODUCTIVITY METRICS

"Time is the currency of good medicine," a physician once told me. "When you strip that away and force doctors to practice at an assembly-line pace, you fundamentally change what medicine is."

Many physicians employed in today's healthcare systems work under strict productivity metrics like requirements for number of patients seen, RVUs billed, or procedures performed. While measuring productivity isn't new, its intensity has increased dramatically in the corporate era.

Doctors commonly face quotas such as seeing 20-30 patients per day or hitting specific RVU targets quarterly. These expectations effectively limit time per patient, contributing to what many physicians describe as "assembly-line medicine." In a traditional factory assembly line, workers must complete repetitive tasks under time pressure; similarly, many physicians now have only 10-15 minutes per patient, with little flexibility for complex cases.

A family physician writing in 2018 put it bluntly: "Sure, if pushed I can see ten patients an hour. But I don't want to, and no doctor should be forced to. When we rush, that's when mistakes happen, and things get overlooked." She mentioned how an abnormal mammogram that needed follow-up was missed because "no one had time to read the actual report" in the rush to see the next patient.

The risks of such hurried care are well-documented. Studies indicate that shorter visit lengths correlate with higher likelihood of errors and inappropriate prescriptions. One analysis found that for each additional minute a primary care visit lasts, the odds of an unnecessary antibiotic prescription drop by 0.11%. In other words, providing doctors with just a bit more time leads to more thoughtful, judicious care.

These time constraints are largely driven by revenue and staffing models. In fee-for-service practice, more patient visits equal more billing. Hospitals and clinics under financial strain (or private equity ownership expecting high returns) often double-book appointments or shorten slots to boost throughput.

The situation creates impossible expectations. A 2022 JAMA study estimated that to fully meet all preventive, chronic, and acute care guidelines for an average patient panel, a primary care physician would need to work 27 hours per day, an absurd expectation that highlights the gap between ideal care and what's feasible under current productivity pressures.

This assembly-line mentality erodes the doctor-patient relationship. Trust and communication suffer when visits feel rushed. A recent survey found patient trust in doctors and hospitals fell significantly from 2020 to 2023, which some experts attribute partly to the impersonal, hurried nature of modern care.

The American Medical Association published an article titled "It's time to stop treating doctors like assembly-line workers," arguing that physicians' skills are best used for nuanced problem-solving and patient counseling, not as speed clinicians seeing a new patient every 7-10 minutes.

Sadly, the system often measures the wrong things. As one physician leader observed, "We have exquisite metrics for productivity but weak measures for quality, relationships, and outcomes that actually matter to patients."

The results are predictable: physician burnout, patient dissatisfaction, and often poorer outcomes. Many doctors are voting with their feet, leaving high-volume practices for models that allow them more time with each patient.

PHYSICIAN RESISTANCE

But physicians aren't taking these changes lying down. In recent years, we've noticed a marked uptick in physician advocacy and collective action pushing back against corporate control and fighting to reclaim professional autonomy.

One of the most striking developments is the rise of physician unions, a concept that would have seemed almost unthinkable a generation ago. Historically, very few doctors unionized (less than 2% of unionization petitions filed from 2000-2022 were for attending physicians). But that's changing dramatically with physician-led unions accounting for 23% of all new union petitions filed in recent years.

Medical residents and fellows have led the charge, unionizing at institutions like Mass General Brigham, Stanford, and throughout the University of California system. Likewise, the Committee of Interns and Residents (CIR-SEIU) doubled its membership between 2021 and 2024, now representing over 37,000 trainee physicians.

But even attending physicians, traditionally considered management, have begun unionizing. In 2023, attending physicians at the Cambridge Health Alliance in Massachusetts voted to form a union, and similar efforts are underway nationwide.

The issues driving physician unionization mirror those we've discussed: excessive workload, burnout, lack of voice in decision-making, staffing shortages, and patient safety concerns. As one newly unionized doctor put it, "Unions give physicians some protection against hospitals and can push back when corporate owners make changes that undermine care."

Even the American Medical Association, which historically has never supported unions, now does so, endorsing physicians' right to collective bargaining and is working to expand those rights, especially as more doctors become employees.

Beyond labor organizing, physicians are also engaging in policy advocacy and public campaigns. Medical societies and coalitions of doctors have lobbied legislators for relief from onerous insurance practices. For instance, physician advocacy helped drive the introduction of the Improving Seniors' Timely Access to Care Act, a bipartisan bill to reform prior authorization in MA.

Some physician groups have filed lawsuits against corporate employers, alleging violations of corporate practice of medicine laws and arguing that profit-driven policies endangered patients. Others have used their voices in media and public forums to expose problems like undue pressure to upcode or limit costly services.

There is also a cultural shift: physicians are reasserting the core values of the profession and using their voices collectively. In online forums and op-eds, many doctors have rallied around the concept of treating burnout as "moral injury," arguing that the problem is not individual resilience but a broken system that forces ethical compromises.

I've seen this resistance firsthand. One physician who partners with us described attending a corporate meeting where managers unveiled new "productivity targets" that would require seeing patients every 12 minutes. "I stood up and simply said, 'This is unsafe. I won't do it.' Then I waited to be fired. Instead, three other doctors stood up too. They actually backed down, not because they cared about our concerns, but because they couldn't afford to lose four doctors at once."

This resistance is essential not just for physicians but for patients. When doctors advocate effectively for their ability to practice good medicine, patients benefit. As one physician leader put it, "We're not just fighting for better work conditions. We're fighting for the soul of medicine, for the right to put patients first."

ALTERNATIVE PRACTICE MODELS

Dr. Reeves was approaching her breaking point. After 12 years in a large health system where she faced increasingly tight schedules, mountains of paperwork, and constant battles with insurers, she was ready to quit medicine altogether. Then she discovered Direct Primary Care (DPC).

"I went from seeing 25-30 patients daily to about 10-12," she told me when I interviewed her. "I went from spending 70% of my time on administrative tasks to spending 80% of my time with patients. I'm practicing medicine again, not just processing people."

Dr. Reeves's story represents a growing trend. Frustrated by insurance hassles and corporate oversight, some physicians are voting with their feet by leaving traditional practice models to create new ways of delivering care. Two notable alternatives are DPC and concierge medicine, which significantly reduce or eliminate insurance middlemen, and a renewed interest in nonprofit and community-based clinics.

In DPC, doctors do not bill insurance at all. Instead, patients pay the physician a flat monthly membership fee (typically $50-100), and in return, the physician provides comprehensive primary care services, often including visits, telemedicine, basic labs, and generic medications at cost. By eliminating insurance billing, DPC physicians dramatically reduce paperwork and overhead and can keep patient panels smaller.

One family physician who switched to DPC recounted his journey: after seven years in a private insurance-based practice, he was burned out from administrative work. On the brink of quitting medicine, he discovered DPC and made the leap. Though financially challenging at first, it ultimately allowed him to focus more time on a smaller number of patients.

While DPC is still relatively small (around 3% of family physicians as of 2018), interest is high. Over 40% of family doctors not already in DPC said they were considering it as frustrations with insurance mounted. Studies show promising results: one analysis found DPC patients had 65% fewer ER visits and about 35-50% fewer hospitalizations compared to similar patient populations, along with higher satisfaction and better blood pressure control.

Closely related is concierge medicine, where practices typically bill insurance for visits while also charging patients an annual retainer fee for enhanced access and services. Patient panels are kept small (hundreds instead of thousands per doctor), allowing more time per patient.

In late 2023, all five physicians at a New York family practice (Linden Medical Group) resigned together to launch a new concierge clinic. Their sudden departure from the hospital-owned practice made local news. The head of the local medical society observed that heavy consolidation in the area's healthcare and administrative burden had created "unsustainable" conditions, driving some doctors to concierge models.

Candace, whose family switched to a concierge doctor last year, applauded the difference: "Our old doctor was wonderful but always rushed. Our new doctor spends 45 minutes with us when needed. When my husband had chest pain, she called the cardiologist personally while we were in the office. It costs more monthly, but we've actually saved money by avoiding unnecessary specialists and ER visits."

Concierge medicine has drawn criticism for potentially creating a two-tier system since physicians who go concierge often cut their patient load by 75-80%, meaning hundreds of patients per doctor must find new physicians. Those who can pay the fees get ample time and excellent access, but those who cannot may struggle to find a new primary care doctor.

Another segment of doctors has pursued work in nonprofit clinics, free clinics, and direct community care. Some mid-career physicians leave high-pressure jobs to work at Federally Qualified Health Centers or charity clinics serving uninsured and underserved populations.

A compelling example is that of Dr. Doug Curran and Dr. Ted Mettetal in

Texas. After decades in private practice in rural East Texas, they grew weary of seeing patients unable to afford care in a state with the nation's highest uninsured rate. In 2019, nearing retirement age, they decided to open a safety-net clinic for anyone, regardless of ability to pay. By 2020, they launched the East Texas Community Clinic, offering primary care on a free or pay-what-you-can basis. Within months, thousands of patients came seeking care who previously had nowhere to go.

Dr. Curran explained that years of practicing in the traditional system had shown him the fallout of coverage gaps, and that this new venture was as much an act of conscience as of medicine. He also took on advocacy, pressing state lawmakers to expand Medicaid while his clinic cared for those left behind.

These alternative models represent physicians carving out spaces where the needs of patients, not paperwork or profit, dictate the practice. While they aren't scalable to the entire system since they often rely on donations, out-of-pocket payments, or physician financial sacrifice, they serve as living case studies of different healthcare paradigms.

As Dr. Reeves put it: "I earn less now than I did in the health system. But I sleep better. I know my patients better. I remember why I went into medicine. That's worth more than the difference in salary."

TRAINING THE NEXT GENERATION

It's a Thursday afternoon, and I'm speaking with a group of medical students. What strikes me immediately is how their education differs considerably from that of physicians who trained even a decade ago.

"We had a whole course on health systems science," explains Anna, a third-year student. "We learned about insurance models, prior authorization processes, even how to read an explanation of benefits form. They're trying to prepare us for the business side of medicine, not just the science."

This represents a significant shift. Traditionally, medical school curricula focused almost exclusively on basic sciences and clinical diagnosis/treatment, with little training in health policy, economics, or systems management. Young doctors often graduated naïve to the business side of medicine.

That's changing. In the last decade, many U.S. medical schools have begun integrating "Health Systems Science" into their curricula alongside basic and clinical sciences. This education covers topics like healthcare policy, insurance and payment models, public health, quality improvement, population health, value-based care, and systems thinking.

Since 1999, the Accreditation Council for Graduate Medical Education has required "systems-based practice" as a core competency, pushing training programs to teach residents about the broader healthcare system. The American Medical Association even published a textbook on health systems science for medical students.

The rationale is clear. To be effective and resilient, future clinicians need to understand the context in which they practice, including the rapidly evolving organizational structures, reimbursement models, and care delivery systems that will shape their daily work.

"They're trying to give us a roadmap for navigating a broken system," says Matt, another medical student. "But there's a tension. They're simultaneously teaching us how to work within the system and encouraging us to think about how to fix it."

Despite these efforts, many students and new doctors still feel unprepared for corporate-driven healthcare realities. Surveys of residents often find they struggle with administrative tasks and practice management early in their careers. One qualitative study of final-year medical students found they were shocked by the billing and coding demands they encountered during clinical rotations.

Critics worry that focusing on resiliency training without fixing underlying system issues is simply preparing young doctors to tolerate the intolerable. This concern is fueling a notable trend among medical trainees: student activism.

Today's medical students and residents are more outspoken on healthcare system issues than perhaps any generation since the 1960s. They're organizing and advocating not only for social issues like health equity but also for structural health system reform. Students are lobbying their schools to allocate more attention to healthcare leadership and ethics in the context of corporatization. Some have pushed for a curriculum on medical economics, so they don't emerge as "helpless pawns" in employment contract negotiations or insurance battles.

Dr. Chase, who teaches medical students and works with CareYaya, sees hope in this new generation: "Today's students enter medicine with eyes wide open about the system's problems. They're idealistic enough to want change but pragmatic enough to learn the tools to navigate the system as it exists. Many are drawn to medicine specifically to be agents of change."

WHERE DO WE GO FROM HERE?

The handcuffing of America's physicians isn't just a problem for doctors but also a crisis for patients. When insurance bureaucrats override medical decisions, when corporate metrics prioritize volume over care, when billing requirements distort practice, patients suffer.

Yet there are reasons for hope. Physicians are pushing back, organizing, and creating alternative models. Medical students are entering the profession with both awareness of the problems and determination to solve them. Patients and doctors are increasingly recognizing they share common interests against corporate control of healthcare.

The solutions must be multifaceted. We need:
- Prior authorization reform that respects physician expertise and limits insurers' ability to override medical decisions arbitrarily.
- Administrative simplification to reduce the paperwork burden crushing physicians and diverting time from patient care.
- Payment reform that values cognitive work and relationship-building, not just procedures and volume.
- Protection for physician autonomy against corporate intrusion into medical decision-making.
- Support for alternative practice models that allow doctors to spend more time with patients and less time on paperwork.

Most importantly, we need to recognize that physicians and patients are natural allies in the fight against a system that too often prioritizes profit over health. When doctors can't practice according to their training and judgment, patients suffer. When patients can't access timely, appropriate care, physicians suffer the moral injury of watching preventable harm.

Together, physicians and patients represent a powerful force for healthcare reform. It's time we recognized our common interests and worked together to break the handcuffs constraining American medicine.

6

INSIDE THE INDUSTRY

"Nearly all men can stand adversity, but if you want to test a man's character, give him power."

— Abraham Lincoln

When Ashley first came to us at CareYaya, she was desperate. Her 72-year-old father had just been denied coverage for an experimental treatment that showed promise for his aggressive lymphoma. The insurance letter simply stated it was "not medically necessary" despite his oncologist's insistence that standard protocols had failed. Ashley's eyes welled with tears as she described spending hours on the phone, being transferred between departments, and getting nowhere.

"They just don't care if he lives or dies," she said bitterly.

What Ashley didn't know—indeed, what most patients don't know—is that the person who ultimately denied her father's claim might have gone home that night and cried too.

Through CareYaya and Counterforce Health's work with helping thousands of families navigate healthcare crises, we've encountered countless insurance nightmares. But we've also connected with an unexpected group: current and former insurance employees who reached out to share their experiences.

Their stories reveal something surprising: behind every frustrating denial letter is often a conflicted human being, someone caught between company profit mandates and their own conscience. The insurance representative who stonewalls you on the phone might secretly be looking for ways to help you. Similarly, the medical director who denies your treatment might be fighting depression from similar decisions.

This isn't to excuse the insurance industry's systematic extraction of profit from human suffering. But understanding the inner workings, the incentive structures, the psychological pressures, the quiet resistance, gives us powerful knowledge for fighting back.

THE CLAIMS ADJUSTER'S DILEMMA

Tracy worked as a claims adjuster at one of America's largest insurers for eight years. When I asked what finally drove her to leave, she didn't hesitate: "The quotas. There's this fiction that we're evaluating each claim on its merits, but that's not how it works. We had targets. They called them 'savings goals,' but everyone knew what they meant. Deny enough claims to save the company X dollars per month."

Tracy's experience isn't unusual. Claims adjusters across the industry face explicit or implicit expectations to maintain certain denial rates, regardless of claim legitimacy. This practice dates back decades but continues today in more sophisticated forms.

Dr. Linda Peeno, who worked as a medical reviewer for Humana in the 1980s, revealed in congressional testimony that during her job interview, she was specifically asked if she could "be tough" because she would be "expected to keep a 10 percent denial rate." In other words, one in ten claims had to be denied, regardless of medical necessity.

Today's quotas might not be as explicit, but the pressure remains intense. The math becomes painfully simple: approve too many claims, get flagged by management. As Tracy told me, "My supervisor would literally say, 'Your approval rate is too high this month. Find some more problems.'"

For adjusters with clinical backgrounds, this creates an excruciating conflict. They understand the medical necessity of the treatments they're evaluating, yet they're expected to find reasons to deny them.

"Every week I handled cases where I knew the patient needed the treatment," Tracy explained. "Sometimes I'd call their doctor, hoping they'd give me something I could use to justify approval. But if I approved too many expensive treatments, I'd be called into a meeting about my 'pattern.'"

This quota system forces adjusters into an impossible ethical position. One former Blue Cross adjuster told me about a review of a claim for a 7-year-old's emergency appendectomy that came to be automatically flagged. "The family had gone to an out-of-network hospital because their daughter was in agony, and it was the closest option. According to our guidelines, I was supposed to deny it or only pay a fraction. But I knew this could financially destroy that family over something completely beyond their control."

In that case, the adjuster found a technical loophole to approve the claim. But such small acts of resistance come with risk. Adjusters who don't meet their "savings targets" can face performance improvement plans, reduced bonuses, or even termination.

The psychological burden of this conflict is immense. "I'd be on the phone with a mother begging for her child's medicine while my computer screen showed the denial script I was supposed to read," Tracy recalled.

Although most insurance companies firmly deny the existence of explicit denial quotas, former employees consistently describe performance metrics tied

to money saved through denials. "The incentives are completely backward," Tracy said. "You're not rewarded for making accurate decisions, you're rewarded for saying no."

Some companies have modernized this approach through algorithms that automatically identify claims for denial, with adjusters essentially ratifying the computer's decision. This adds a layer of plausible deniability while maintaining the same financial outcomes.

A particularly distressing practice is what industry insiders call "retrospective review," or approving a treatment initially, then denying payment after it's completed, leaving the patient with the bill. "That was the worst," Tracy said. "People would get treatments thinking they were covered, then we'd find some reason later to deny it. Sometimes it was because the doctor didn't document something exactly right. Other times it was because we'd suddenly decide it wasn't medically necessary after all."

The claims adjuster's dilemma exposes an industry where human judgment has been subordinated to financial algorithms. For patients, this means that the person reviewing your claim isn't simply evaluating its medical necessity, they're weighing your care against their job security.

WHEN DOCTORS BECOME DENIAL ENFORCERS

Insurance companies employ physicians as medical directors to review certain claims, especially those involving medical necessity determinations or expensive procedures. In theory, these doctors ensure that only inappropriate or non-evidence-based treatments get denied. In practice, they often find themselves under intense pressure to prioritize cost savings over patient care.

Dr. Linda Peeno's story again provides historical context. As a medical director at Humana in the 1980s, one of her denials was for a life-saving heart transplant, a decision that saved the company roughly $500,000 and cost the patient his life.

"In the spring of 1987, as a physician, I denied a man a necessary operation that would have saved his life and thus caused his death," Peeno later confessed to Congress. "No person and no group has held me accountable for this, because, in fact, what I did was I saved the company a half a million dollars."

Little has changed in the decades since. In 2015, Dr. Jay Ken Iinuma, who served as an Aetna medical director, testified under oath that he "did not personally review patients' medical records" when approving or denying coverage, and that this was standard company protocol. Instead, nurses would provide summaries, and he would base decisions on that secondhand information. This revelation prompted a state investigation in California.

This culture creates a profound ethical conflict for physicians who become medical directors. Trained to prioritize patient welfare, they instead find themselves ratifying corporate policies that may harm patients. Some rationalize it as combating unnecessary care, but the financial incentives overwhelmingly favor denial.

For these physicians, the psychological burden of repeatedly denying care can be immense. Some develop what medical ethicists call "moral injury," the trauma that occurs when one is forced to act against deeply held ethical beliefs. Others compartmentalize, telling themselves they're simply applying guidelines rather than making individual judgments.

The medical director's dilemma underscores a fundamental conflict in our healthcare system: physicians employed by insurers find their professional ethics directly at odds with their employer's financial interests. And increasingly, as Cigna's 1.2-second reviews demonstrate, even the pretense of medical judgment is giving way to automated denials with a doctor's signature mechanically applied.

CUSTOMER SERVICE CONFESSIONS

When Sam's mother needed home healthcare after a stroke, their insurance initially denied coverage. Sam spent weeks on the phone with customer service, growing increasingly frustrated with representatives who seemed unable or unwilling to help. "It felt like they were reading from scripts designed to make me give up," Sam told me when they came to CareYaya seeking alternatives.

What Sam didn't realize is that those customer service representatives (CSRs) typically have almost no power to fix problems. They're often as frustrated as the callers they're speaking with.

"The most painful part of the job was wanting to help but not being able to," explained Jordan, who worked in insurance customer service for four years. "People would call crying, desperate for coverage for their sick child or parent, and all I could do was read the denial reason and direct them to the appeals process."

When patients or providers receive a claim denial, their first instinct is to call the insurance company's customer service line for an explanation or resolution. This puts frontline representatives in the difficult position of handling angry, anxious callers while having minimal authority to actually resolve issues.

Training for customer service roles tends to focus on protocols and scripts that prioritize efficiency and adherence to policy rather than problem-solving. Empathy is encouraged only up to a point. The rep might say "I'm sorry you're going through this," but they are not empowered to waive rules or approve exceptions.

Natalie Collins, a former UnitedHealthcare service representative, explained that during her training, "There was no instruction on how to actually pay the claim" that a customer was disputing; "the entire training was about different ways to deny the claim." She and fellow trainees spent their first weeks learning various tactics to stall callers or hand off their issues, rather than learning how to genuinely investigate and approve contested claims.

Supervisors would even stand behind the trainees listening to calls, coaching them on techniques to end the call quickly once it appeared the claim wouldn't be paid. Collins recalled that these supervisors sometimes "laughed at the misery" of the people on the other end of the line, a toxic culture that taught reps to view upset customers as obstacles rather than people to assist.

One explicit strategy taught was to use any procedural reason to close a case. If a caller didn't have some specific form or piece of information, the rep would instruct them to obtain it, effectively ending the call. If a claim was technically filed under the wrong code or had a minor error, that could be grounds to deny and force the patient to re-submit, adding delay and hassle.

"If we could find any reason to tell the customer 'we need more information,' that was considered a successful call," recalled Jordan. "The goal wasn't resolution. It was call volume and avoiding approvals."

Customer service metrics typically focus on call handle time and efficiency, not on customer satisfaction or problem resolution. Representatives who spend too long trying to help a particular caller may be flagged for "excessive call time" by supervisors.

Importantly, frontline staff are rarely authorized to overturn a denial themselves. If a doctor's office calls arguing that a claim was wrongly denied, the CSR can check if perhaps it was a billing error or missing information. But if the denial was intentional (e.g., deemed not covered or not medically necessary), the rep cannot simply approve it. At best, they can escalate the issue to a supervisor or a medical review team or guide the patient through the formal appeal process.

"The most heartbreaking calls were from elderly people who didn't

understand why their medication suddenly wasn't covered," Jordan said. "I'd try to explain the formulary had changed, but they'd say, 'But I need this medicine to live.' And all I could say was, 'I understand your frustration' and suggest alternatives that I knew were less effective."

Some customer service reps develop their own subtle resistance tactics. They might drop hints about the most effective appeal language or quietly suggest calling on a different day to reach a more sympathetic supervisor. But these small acts of compassion can put their jobs at risk.

For patients, understanding the limited power of customer service representatives is crucial. The person on the phone isn't ignoring your problem but most likely lacks the authority to solve it. This is by design, with insurers deliberately separating the "face" of the company (friendly CSRs) from the actual decision-makers (claims adjusters, medical directors, and algorithms).

The frustration this creates serves a purpose. As Jordan put it: "Every day, I'd watch people just give up. They'd say, 'Fine, I'll pay it myself' after getting transferred for the third time or told to submit yet another form. The system is designed to exhaust you."

The CSR's limited power creates a Kafkaesque experience for patients where they're talking to a human who expresses sympathy but can only redirect them back into the bureaucratic maze. This disconnect between human interaction and institutional response is a key mechanism by which insurers wear down legitimate appeals.

Recognizing these dynamics can help patients develop more effective strategies. Rather than expecting resolution from customer service, successful patients use these interactions strategically to gather documentation, understand the specific denial reason, and map the next steps in the appeals process. The customer service representative might want to help you, but the system they work within isn't designed to let them.

MARKETING VERSUS REALITY

We've all seen the insurance commercials: smiling families thanking their insurer for "being there when it matters most"; doctors and patients joyfully connecting through cutting-edge technology; silver-haired couples peacefully enjoying retirement without financial worries. These glossy images paint insurers as benevolent protectors, standing between families and financial ruin.

But inside the companies producing these ads, employees often experience a profound disconnect between marketing promises and operational reality.

"The marketing meetings were surreal," said Thomas, who worked in product development at a major insurer before leaving the industry. "We'd spend the morning analyzing which benefits to cut from a popular plan to improve margins, then spend the afternoon reviewing commercials showing how much we care about members' well-being. Nobody acknowledged the contradiction."

Wendell Potter, a former senior executive who headed public relations at Cigna for many years, has become one of the industry's sharpest critics after leaving. He has stated that he once "described for [U.S.] senators how insurers make promises they have no intention of keeping." According to Potter, confusing customers and even "dumping the sick" were standard practices concealed behind upbeat rhetoric.

"I'm ashamed that I let myself get caught up in deceitful and dishonest PR campaigns," Potter has said of his time crafting industry messaging. Those campaigns, he pointed out, "worked so well" that they kept profits high while "hundreds of thousands of our citizens have died, and millions of others have lost their homes and been forced into bankruptcy" due to medical bills.

Insurance companies invest heavily in both external marketing and internal employee engagement programs, often using similar messaging. They want their workforce to feel they are part of a noble mission, which can make employees more productive and loyal. But these efforts can backfire when employees see them as empty propaganda.

Marketing departments and lobbyists often run campaigns completely contrary to the company's internal actions. For instance, an insurer might publicly champion a program to help diabetics get care, while internally instructing adjusters to enforce caps more strictly on diabetes supplies. Or an insurer might join a PR blitz about how "patients are our priority" while simultaneously launching initiatives to purge unprofitable chronically ill members from its rolls through tactics like formulary changes or narrow networks.

Potter also exposed how insurers manipulate public opinion through "duplicitous and well-financed PR and lobbying campaigns" whenever legislation threatens to rein in their profits. Insurers might fund seemingly independent "front groups" that spread fear about proposals like a public health plan option or stricter regulations, all while the companies themselves claim innocence.

Employees in departments like communications, government affairs, or sales often know about these behind-the-scenes efforts. They might be asked to contribute to a trade association's study that "proves" why some reform would be bad, or to gather customer testimonials that support the insurer's stance. This can be disheartening for an employee who genuinely wants to help patients.

The marketing-versus-reality divide is a constant internal theme in insurance companies. Employees who are aware of it must either compartmentalize (telling themselves that marketing is "just business") or confront the truth that their work contributes to a deceptive narrative.

"The biggest lie is the choice narrative," Thomas told me. "We marketed 'freedom of choice' while systematically narrowing networks and adding barriers to care. We knew most people had very little actual choice. Either take what your employer offers or go uninsured. But our ads talked about empowered consumers making informed decisions in a competitive marketplace."

This dissonance doesn't just affect marketing staff. Customer service representatives have to feign belief in the "caring" brand while following scripts designed to minimize payouts. Claims adjusters see commercials touting their company's responsiveness while being evaluated on the number of claims they deny. Nurses working in case management advertise how they "coordinate care" while actually functioning as utilization reviewers looking for reasons to reduce services.

Industry defectors like Potter play a crucial role in exposing this gap. By speaking out, they help consumers understand that a slick ad campaign doesn't equate to ethical conduct. "When you see an insurance commercial talking about how they have your back," Potter has advised in interviews, "remember they're a publicly traded company with a fiduciary responsibility to maximize shareholder value, not to maximize your healthcare."

Understanding this marketing-reality gap is essential for patients navigating the system. The friendly, helpful image projected in advertising often bears little resemblance to the actual experience of filing claims or seeking pre-authorizations. Patients who expect the company to live up to its marketing promises may become discouraged when they encounter resistance. Those who recognize the disconnect are better prepared to advocate effectively for themselves.

PTSD AND MORAL INJURY AMONG INSURANCE WORKERS

I met Elise, a case manager at a major insurer for seven years, at a conference. During our conversation, she shared something that surprised me:

"I think I have PTSD from my insurance job," she said quietly. "I still have nightmares about the patients I couldn't help."

Working inside the health insurance industry can exact a serious emotional and psychological toll on employees. The term "moral injury," originally used to describe soldiers' trauma from actions that violate their moral beliefs, has been applied in recent years to healthcare professionals faced with systemic pressures that conflict with patient care.

Insurance workers, especially those with clinical backgrounds or those who deal directly with suffering patients, are increasingly recognizing their own version of moral injury. They experience profound distress when their job requires them to act in ways that harm patients or contradict their personal ethics. Over time, this can lead to burnout, depression, anxiety, and even PTSD-like symptoms.

Researchers note that many clinicians feel demoralized by a health care system that puts profits ahead of patients, and when they cannot help patients due to bureaucratic or financial barriers, moral distress occurs. The same phenomenon affects people on the insurance side as well. Every day, insurance employees witness or participate in decisions that negatively impact individuals' health: a chemotherapy denied here, a surgery delayed there, a claim payment so low the patient faces bankruptcy.

Dr. Debby Day who was mentioned earlier experienced this trauma. As Cigna pushed her to speed up denials, she struggled with the idea of sacrificing quality and fairness for the sake of metrics. Eventually, "the daily stress of being pushed to work faster coupled with the threat of being fired took a toll" on her mental health. She became insomniac and clinically depressed, teetering on the edge. "I actually sort of had a mental breakdown," Day recalled. She took a leave of absence for a few months in 2021 and sought help from a therapist. Upon returning to full duty, the same dynamics pushed her toward yet another breakdown again. To save her sanity, she ultimately retired early.

Dr. Linda Peeno experienced a different psychological journey but likewise suffered moral injury. The realization that she had "caused [a patient's] death" by denying treatment hit her like a moral crisis. This moment, knowing her medical decision, made under corporate directives, directly led to a man dying, haunted her for years. It catalyzed her into whistleblowing, but not before she went through intense soul-searching and remorse.

Even non-clinical staff can experience trauma. Customer service reps might constantly speak to people in dire straits, hearing stories of ill children, of treatments denied, of fear and grief, while being unable to help. Over time, absorbing all that emotional pain and feeling complicit in the system can lead to secondary traumatic stress.

Elise described taking calls from patients who had been denied care: "There was one woman with stage 4 breast cancer whose treatment was denied because of a network issue. She was sobbing, asking if we wanted her to die. My script said to tell her about her appeal rights, but what she needed was her treatment approved right away. I went home and cried for hours that night."

For those with medical backgrounds (nurses, doctors, therapists working at insurers), the moral injury can be acute. They know exactly what the patient clinically needs, yet their job forces them to deny or delay it. This is the opposite of why they went into healthcare.

Another indication of the emotional toll is what Dr. Peeno noted about job postings. She pointed out that many listings for insurance claims reviewer positions explicitly warn that candidates "must be able to endure extreme stress." That line acknowledges that these jobs involve ethical stress, the kind that can weigh heavily on one's conscience and mental well-being.

Over time, without intervention, moral injury and chronic stress can manifest as diagnosable mental health conditions. Some insurance workers develop full-blown PTSD symptoms: hypervigilance, emotional numbness, or intrusive memories related to traumatic cases. Others experience severe burnout, where they become emotionally exhausted and detached, merely going through the motions at work.

Ironically, the insurance industry that profits from limiting mental health benefits also creates significant mental health issues among its own workforce. And the culture in corporate insurance environments has not always been supportive of employees seeking help. Admitting you are struggling might be seen as weakness.

As Dr. Joseph Betancourt of the Commonwealth Fund put it in 2023, issues like burnout and moral injury in healthcare pose "a clear and present danger to the future of healthcare, and we ignore them at our own peril," a statement that applies not only to clinicians but to the often overlooked insurance workforce as well.

Understanding this emotional toll helps contextualize insurance employees' actions. The person denying your claim or reading a rejection script may well be suffering themselves, caught between their desire to help and a system designed to limit care. This doesn't excuse the system, but it suggests that many within it are potential allies rather than enemies.

For patients, this insight offers a strategic advantage: approaching insurance interactions with awareness that the employee might be sympathetic but constrained can open doors.

The moral injury affecting insurance workers also represents a vulnerability in the system itself. As more employees burn out, speak out, or opt out, insurers face increasing pressure to address these ethical concerns, pressure that patients and advocates can leverage for change.

INTERNAL RESISTANCE MOVEMENTS

Within the rigid hierarchies of insurance companies, acts of internal resistance do occur. While open rebellion is rare, many employees find ways to push back against policies they find egregious, by using formal complaint channels, covertly leaking information, or helping patients navigate the system.

Some larger insurers have formal ethics and compliance departments, with mechanisms for employees to report concerns. In theory, an adjuster or medical director who feels the company is engaging in unethical denials can file an internal report. Dr. Debby Day attempted this route when she was at Cigna. Faced with what she felt was an improper mandate to prioritize quantity of denials over quality, she raised concerns through appropriate internal channels, essentially blowing the whistle internally.

What happened? According to documentation, Human Resources and compliance personnel responded that management acknowledged Dr. Day's attention to detail but reminded her that "there are metrics in place that he must hold everyone to." In other words, her complaint was duly observed but dismissed; the company found "no wrongdoing" in enforcing productivity quotas. This outcome is unfortunately common. Internal investigations often side with the company's financial logic unless a law is being blatantly broken.

Some of the most impactful resistance comes in the form of employees becoming anonymous sources for external oversight. Dr. Linda Peeno recalled that she received vital information from "moles inside [insurance] companies who 'hate what they do.'" These insiders secretly send internal memos, denial criteria, or data that can be used in court cases and public testimony. This indicates an undercurrent of dissent within companies by staff who can't change the system from within but will expose it through leaks.

Even at the individual level, employees enact resistance in small ways. A customer service rep might compile a list of unfair denials and slip it to a state insurance department. An adjuster might deliberately bend a rule now and then, approving an iffy claim because they know the patient really needs it. A medical director might choose to take extra time on each case, technically violating their quota, as a form of protest by quality.

Dr. Michaels described his own subtle resistance tactics: "I would call treating physicians directly, coaching them on exactly what to document to satisfy our criteria. Officially, I was 'clarifying' the medical necessity. Unofficially, I was helping them navigate our arbitrary rules to get patients the care they needed."

Frontline staff sometimes coach patients on the appeals process more than required, out of sympathy. One current insurance nurse anonymously admitted: "When I know a denial is wrong but can't override it, I'll tell the patient exactly what to say in their appeal letter. I'll even suggest specific phrases that trigger mandatory review."

This kind of "resistance from within" is rarely dramatic or public, but it represents employees trying to reconcile their work with their ethics. For patients, it suggests that even within a seemingly hostile system, allies may exist—insurance employees who will quietly help if given the opportunity.

Understanding these internal resistance movements offers strategic insight for patients and advocates. When dealing with insurance, it's worth remembering that not everyone inside the company fully supports its practices. Looking for those potential allies, the adjusters, nurses, or doctors who might stretch rules to help, can sometimes make the difference between denial and approval.

As Dr. Michaels put it, "The system is designed to deny by default. But individual humans within that system still have some discretion. Approaching them with respect, clear documentation, and an understanding of their constraints can sometimes help them find a way to approve what's needed."

WHISTLEBLOWER CAREER CONSEQUENCES

Whistleblowers in healthcare and insurance are often hailed as heroes by the public for exposing wrongdoing. But inside their companies, they are usually regarded as traitors, so personal consequences can be severe. In the insurance industry, where confidentiality agreements and corporate loyalty are heavily emphasized, those who speak out face losing not only their jobs but also their careers and sometimes even their sense of security.

One common outcome is immediate termination or forced resignation. Once someone is identified as having leaked information or raised concerns publicly, the company typically moves swiftly to remove them. Officially, it might be framed as a policy violation or simply that the person "wasn't a good fit."

In Dr. Debby Day's case, she preemptively left Cigna after recording evidence of its practices, but Cigna's response to the media was to cast her as a disgruntled ex-employee. By labeling whistleblowers as "disgruntled," companies aim to undermine their credibility, suggesting they're speaking out of bitterness rather than integrity. This is a standard PR tactic that almost every insurance whistleblower has encountered.

For the whistleblower, being dismissed as just a malcontent can be frustrating, but it's often just the beginning of their career troubles. The insurance industry is relatively tight-knit, especially within individual sectors. Gaining a reputation as a whistleblower can blacklist a person from getting hired by other insurers. Even without a formal blacklist, word gets around.

Beyond career roadblocks, some whistleblowers face active retaliation and harassment. Dr. Linda Peeno's experience is a stark example. After testifying against Humana, becoming an outspoken critic of HMO practices, she received chilling anonymous threats. She recounted getting a call with a gravelly voice saying, "You better stop doing this stuff," following one of her TV interviews. Later, another caller warned that if she didn't cease her public testimonies, "harm would come" to her or her family.

Peeno believed she was put on an industry "hit list." She had to install a security system at home in addition to getting the police involved due to the persistence of threatening calls. While Peeno's case is extreme, it underscores that whistleblowing can become very personal and scary.

Legal protections for whistleblowers exist, but they are limited and hard to enforce. Under various laws (like the False Claims Act, or OSHA regulations for health insurance under the ACA), an employee is theoretically protected from retaliation for reporting certain types of violations. In practice, however, a company can find myriad reasons to fire someone that aren't an overt backlash or retaliation. And getting relief through a lawsuit can take years and huge personal cost.

The emotional and financial toll on whistleblowers is considerable. They frequently lose their steady income and may struggle to find a new job, leading to financial strain. They might also lose work friends or professional contacts who distance themselves. Psychologically, whistleblowers can feel isolated since they've broken the unspoken code of silence. They may even fail to get support from people who privately agree with them.

For patients and advocates, whistleblowers provide invaluable insights into how the system really works—exposing denial quotas, algorithmic claim rejections, and internal priorities that put profits over patients. Their revelations have prompted investigations, regulatory changes, and greater public awareness.

As one whistleblower put it: "I lost my career, but I helped change a policy that was hurting thousands of patients. That's the trade-off you make as a whistleblower. You sacrifice your personal security for the greater good. I still don't know if it was worth it for me personally, but I know it was the right thing to do."

Understanding the harsh consequences whistleblowers face helps contextualize why more insurance employees don't speak out, despite witnessing problematic practices. The system is designed to make silence the safer choice. For patients and advocates, supporting whistleblowers—through legal defense funds, public validation of their claims, and employment opportunities—is crucial to encouraging more truth-telling from within the industry.

LIFE AFTER LEAVING THE INSURANCE WORLD

What happens to insurance employees who decide they've had enough and leave the industry, especially those who left on principle? These industry defectors often find new ways to apply their knowledge, becoming voices for change or helping patients navigate the very systems they once operated.

A significant number of former insurance professionals choose to become advocates for patients or health system reformers. Freed from corporate obligations, they can finally speak openly about what they saw and work to improve it.

Wendell Potter is a prime example. After 15 years at Cigna, he resigned abruptly in 2008 with no other job lined up. In the years since, Potter reinvented himself as a prominent advocate for affordable healthcare. He has written books and articles exposing insurance industry tactics and co-founded organizations that campaign for major reforms.

Potter has noted that he sleeps better at night now that he's working to fix the problems he once was part of. For him, and many like him, leaving the industry was liberating. It allowed them to realign work with values.

Dr. Linda Peeno also charted a new path aligned with patient advocacy. After blowing the whistle on Humana, she did not return to any insurance company. Instead, she served as an expert witness in court cases, essentially testifying on behalf of patients who were wrongfully denied care. With her deep knowledge of how insurers make decisions, she became a powerful asset for patients fighting back.

Many ex-insurance employees gravitate towards the nonprofit sector or public service. They join think tanks, patient rights groups, or community health organizations. For instance, some former insurance executives have taken roles in healthcare policy making such as advising government agencies or legislative committees, where they can push for rules that address the abuses they witnessed.

Another route is consulting or advisory services. Former claims adjusters or medical directors sometimes offer their expertise to hospitals, physician groups, or large employers who purchase health plans. In those roles, they help the other side navigate insurance complexities or negotiate better terms.

For example, a former insurance case manager might become a patient advocate in a hospital, helping patients deal with insurance, using their knowledge of the insurer's playbook to get approvals that would otherwise be denied. Some have started or joined companies that assist consumers with medical billing advocacy, overturning wrongful denials for a fee or percentage of recovered funds.

There are also those who join the burgeoning health tech and insurance startup scene, often with the aim of making insurance more consumer-friendly. After leaving big insurers, some former employees have helped launch or run startups that promise to simplify insurance, create more transparency, or fill gaps in coverage.

Not everyone goes into advocacy or related fields, of course. Some insurance defectors do a complete career 180. The stress or disillusionment was such that they choose to work in a totally different domain—say, teaching, real estate, or running a small business—something where they won't face the same moral quandaries.

"After ten years denying claims, I couldn't do it anymore," one told me. "I retrained as a home health aide because I wanted to actually help people instead of hurting them. The pay is worse, but I can look at myself in the mirror again."

Interestingly, a few former insurance CEOs and executives have, later in their careers, come out in favor of sweeping changes like single-payer healthcare or stronger government oversight. This is a form of defection at the ideological level. For instance, one former Aetna CEO, Mark Bertolini, after leaving his post, expressed that we should debate single-payer and acknowledged the flaws in the current system.

For the defectors who take on public advocacy, a key part of their work is educating others about the internal workings of insurance. By writing books, doing interviews, or consulting for journalists and filmmakers, these former employees ensure that the opaque processes of insurance become more transparent to the world.

Their firsthand credibility makes it harder for industry spokespeople to dismiss every critique as "misinformation." Over time, the voices of defectors have contributed to gradual improvements: for example, the ACA included provisions (like requiring insurers to spend at least 80-85% of premiums on medical care) in part because people who knew the tricks of the trade advised lawmakers on what was needed.

These industry defectors collectively serve as the conscience of the system from the outside, reminding their former employers that healthcare, at its core, is about patients and not profits—a lesson they learned the hard way, and are determined to not let the world forget.

MOVING FORWARD

Through the stories of claims adjusters, medical directors, customer service representatives, and industry defectors, we've pulled back the curtain on how health insurance really operates in America. We've seen denial quotas that force employees to reject legitimate claims. We've witnessed doctors pressured to process 60,000 denials in a month with barely a second's review per case. We've heard from customer service representatives trained specifically to deflect and deny rather than resolve problems.

But we've also discovered something equally important: the system is operated by humans, many of whom are deeply uncomfortable with its workings. They experience moral injury, develop resistance strategies, and sometimes defect entirely to become powerful advocates for change.

This insight is more than just interesting—it's tactically valuable for anyone fighting insurance denials or advocating for system change.

The industry wants patients to feel powerless and alone when facing denial letters. But as we've seen through the experiences of insurance employees themselves, the system has vulnerabilities. These ethical tensions, procedural weaknesses, and human elements can be leveraged to get the care you need.

PART III:
Fighting Back

7

YOUR HEALTHCARE RIGHTS PLAYBOOK

"It always seems impossible until it's done."
— *Nelson Mandela*

The letter arrived in Melissa's mailbox on a Tuesday, buried between a cable bill and a coupon circular. The crisp, corporate letterhead belied its devastating contents: "Your claim for the immunotherapy treatment recommended by your oncologist has been denied as experimental and not medically necessary."

Melissa's stomach dropped. After helping Melissa battle stage-3 breast cancer for eighteen months, her oncologist had recommended a promising immunotherapy treatment that could significantly improve her chances of remission. With a 7-year-old daughter depending on her, Melissa couldn't accept this decision.

But like most Americans, she had no idea how to fight back.

"I remember sitting at the dining table, staring at that letter," Melissa told me. "I thought that was it. Game over. My doctor recommended this treatment to save my life, but some faceless insurance reviewer who'd never even met me had the final say? It felt like a death sentence."

It isn't. What Melissa didn't know, and what most Americans don't know either, is that insurance denials are just the beginning of a process, not the end. In fact, data consistently shows that about half of all insurance appeals ultimately get approved. This means that when your insurer denies a claim, there's roughly a 50-50 chance they're wrong, or at least that they'll reverse their decision when challenged.

Let that sink in. The system is so fundamentally flawed that when formally challenged, insurance companies admit they were wrong half the time.

I'm consistently amazed by how many Americans don't realize they have the right to appeal insurance decisions. Under the ACA, all non-grandfathered health plans must allow an internal appeal and then an independent external review for denied claims. Yet many consumers remain unaware of these protections. In a recent survey, over half of people who received an unexpected medical bill didn't challenge it, mainly because they weren't sure they could.

This chapter is your comprehensive playbook for fighting back. I've combined insights from healthcare attorneys, insurance industry veterans, patient advocacy organizations, and the frontline experiences of thousands of families to create a step-by-step guide for navigating insurance denials and appeals. Whether you're fighting for yourself or a loved one, these strategies can mean the difference between receiving life-changing care or being left at the mercy of a profit-driven system.

Three months after receiving that denial letter, Melissa's insurance approved the immunotherapy treatment. The difference wasn't in her medical condition or the treatment itself but in her brave decision to fight back—systematically, strategically, and relentlessly.

INSURANCE POLICY ARCHAEOLOGY: UNEARTHING YOUR TRUE COVERAGE

Before you can effectively challenge an insurance denial, you need to understand exactly what your policy does and doesn't cover. This isn't as simple as reading the glossy brochure you received during open enrollment or glancing at the summary of benefits.

"The single biggest mistake patients make is not having their full policy documents," explained a former insurance appeals coordinator who now works as a patient advocate. "The insurance companies count on you never reading the fine print."

Your excavation begins with obtaining these critical documents:

- **Certificate of Coverage (COC) or Evidence of Coverage (EOC):** This comprehensive document details what services are covered, under what conditions, and what's excluded.

- **Summary Plan Description (SPD)**: For employer-sponsored plans, this document provides additional details about how your plan works.
- **Medical Policies**: These internal guidelines define how the insurer interprets "medical necessity" and other key terms.

Finding these documents can be surprisingly difficult. They may be buried on your insurer's website, accessible only through your online account, or not even publicly available. Insurance companies aren't exactly motivated to make them easy to find.

"They sent me to a customer service portal that was broken," reported one Counterforce Health user fighting for his mother's physical therapy coverage. "Then they told me the documents would arrive by mail within 10 business days. After two weeks of nothing, I had to call three more times before they finally emailed them."

If you encounter similar resistance, remember: Under federal law, insurers must provide these documents upon request. Be persistent. Call your insurer's customer service line and specifically request your complete Certificate of Coverage and any relevant medical policies. If you have employer-sponsored insurance, your HR department may be able to provide these documents more quickly.

Once you have these documents, don't be intimidated by their length. Most run dozens or even hundreds of pages, but you don't need to read every word. Instead, focus on these critical sections:

1. Definitions Section

This section is the Rosetta Stone for understanding your policy. Insurers use very specific definitions for terms like "medically necessary," "experimental," and "investigational." These definitions determine what gets covered.

For example, one major insurer defines "medically necessary" as services that are:
- Appropriate and consistent with the diagnosis
- In accordance with accepted medical standards
- Not primarily for the convenience of the patient or provider
- The most appropriate supply or level of service which can be safely provided

These definitions are the foundation of your appeal. If your insurer has denied a treatment as "not medically necessary," their decision must align with their own definition. If it doesn't, you have powerful grounds for appeal.

2. Exclusions Section

This section lists what the policy explicitly won't cover. Common exclusions include:
- Cosmetic procedures
- Experimental or investigational treatments
- Weight loss procedures
- Certain infertility treatments

The exclusions section often contains surprises. One CareYaya family discovered their policy excluded "any service for which there is no legal obligation to pay." This vague language was used to deny coverage for treatment provided at a research hospital, even though the treatment itself was standard care.

3. Prior Authorization and Referral Requirements

Many policies require pre-approval for certain services or referrals for specialists. Missing these requirements can trigger automatic denials, even if the service would otherwise be covered.

4. Appeals Process Information

This section details how to challenge a denial, including important deadlines. Most policies allow 180 days to file an internal appeal, but the timeframe can vary.

As you review these documents, take detailed notes and highlight relevant sections So you can build the foundation for your appeal.

"When I referenced their own definition of 'medical necessity' in my appeal letter," Melissa told me, "I could tell from their response that they were shocked. Most people don't do their homework."

UNDERSTANDING WHY YOU WERE DENIED

Every denial letter contains clues about how to overturn it. The key is understanding what the insurer is really saying and not saying.

Let's decode the most common denial reasons:

"Not Medically Necessary"

This is the most frequent denial reason, appearing in approximately 60% of cases. When insurers claim a treatment isn't "medically necessary," they're

asserting that:
- The treatment isn't appropriate for your condition, OR
- There are more conservative options that should be tried first, OR
- There's insufficient evidence that the treatment will help

What they don't tell you is that these decisions are often made by administrators following rigid algorithms, not doctors familiar with your case. More importantly, these decisions are frequently overturned. California's Department of Managed Health Care reports that approximately 60% of "medical necessity" denials are reversed upon independent review.

"Experimental or Investigational"

This denial reason typically applies to newer treatments or off-label uses of approved medications. Insurers claim these treatments lack sufficient evidence of effectiveness or safety.

What they don't mention is that their definition of "experimental" may be outdated or overly restrictive. Many treatments insurers label as "experimental" are actually standard practice at major medical centers.

These denials have even higher overturn rates, around 80% according to some state data. This suggests insurers are using this category to deny treatments that have substantial evidence behind them.

"Out-of-Network" or "Non-Contracted Provider"

These denials occur when you receive care from providers outside your insurer's network. While seemingly straightforward, these denials often involve complex issues:
- The service may not have been available in-network
- You may have been referred to an out-of-network provider by an in-network doctor
- You may have received emergency care where network status shouldn't matter

What insurers don't reveal is that many states have "network adequacy" laws requiring coverage for out-of-network care when appropriate in-network providers aren't available. These laws are particularly relevant for specialized care or rural patients.

"Pre-Authorization Required"

These denials occur when your doctor provides a service without obtaining the insurer's prior approval. While these denials can be difficult to overturn,

exceptions exist for:
- Emergency situations
- Cases where the provider attempted to obtain authorization but couldn't
- Situations where the requirement wasn't clearly communicated

"Coding or Billing Error"

Sometimes denials stem from administrative issues: incorrect procedure codes, missing information, or documentation problems. These denials are often the easiest to overcome, requiring simple corrections rather than complex appeals.

Understanding the true nature of your denial is crucial because it determines your appeal strategy. Read your denial letter carefully, noting:
- The specific reason given for the denial
- Any policy provisions or criteria cited
- The deadline for filing an appeal
- The address where appeals should be sent

If the denial reason is unclear or vague, call your insurer and ask for clarification. Under federal law, they must provide a specific reason for the denial and explain the criteria used to make their decision.

"My insurer initially denied my mother's skilled nursing facility care as 'not medically necessary,'" explained Robert, a CareYaya family caregiver from Charlotte. "When I pressed them, they admitted the real issue was incomplete documentation from the hospital about her inability to perform daily activities. Once we submitted that information, they approved the claim without a formal appeal."

BUILDING YOUR APPEAL ARSENAL

A successful appeal requires evidence. Think of your appeal as building a case in court. You need compelling evidence that systematically dismantles the insurer's rationale for denial.

Your appeal arsenal should include:

1. A Powerful Appeal Letter

Your appeal letter sets the tone for your entire case. It should be clear, professional, and direct. Remember, this isn't a place for emotional pleas. It's a logical argument demonstrating why the denial was incorrect.

A strong appeal letter includes:
- Your name, policy number, and claim information
- A clear statement that you're appealing the denial
- A concise explanation of your medical condition
- Specific reasons why the denial was incorrect, citing policy language
- A summary of the supporting evidence you're including
- A clear request for what you want (approval of the claim)

Frame your letter as a logical argument rather than a complaint. For example, instead of writing "It's unfair to deny my MRI," write "The denial of the MRI does not align with your policy's definition of 'medical necessity' for the following reasons…"

2. Letter of Medical Necessity from Your Physician

This may be the single most important document in your appeal. Ask your doctor to write a detailed letter explaining:
- Your diagnosis and medical history
- Why the recommended treatment is medically necessary
- What other treatments have been tried and why they were insufficient
- What could happen if you don't receive the recommended treatment
- How the recommended treatment aligns with standard medical practice

The strongest letters explicitly address the insurer's stated reason for denial. If they deny a treatment as "experimental," your doctor should cite studies demonstrating its effectiveness.

"My oncologist initially wrote a brief, two-paragraph letter," Melissa shared. "When I explained what we were up against, she rewrote it as a two-page detailed analysis with citations from five recent studies. That made all the difference."

3. Medical Records and Test Results

Include relevant medical records that support your case. This might include:
- Lab results or imaging studies
- Consultation notes from specialists
- Hospital discharge summaries
- Records documenting failed alternative treatments

Highlight or tab the most important information. Don't make reviewers search for relevant details.

4. Scientific Evidence

For denials of treatments labeled "experimental" or "investigational," scientific evidence is crucial. Include:
- Peer-reviewed studies supporting the treatment
- Clinical guidelines from medical societies
- FDA approval documents (if applicable)
- Expert consensus statements

You don't need to be a medical researcher to find this evidence. Ask your doctor for relevant studies or search PubMed (pubmed.ncbi.nlm.nih.gov), a free database of medical research. Many medical journals provide free access to abstracts (summaries) even if the full articles require subscription.

5. Precedent Information

If you know other patients with your same insurer who have received the denied treatment, this information can be powerful. While you may not have access to their medical information, you might find:
- Support groups where patients share their experiences
- Patient advocacy organizations that track approval patterns
- Published cases regarding similar disputes

One individual we served through Counterforce Health discovered via an online support group that patients in a neighboring state with the same insurance plan routinely received coverage for a treatment she was denied. This information helped her successfully argue that the denial was inconsistent with the insurer's own practices.

6. Expert Opinions

In complex cases, independent expert opinions can strengthen your appeal. These might include:
- Evaluations from specialists not involved in your care
- Letters from researchers specializing in your condition
- Assessments from medical directors at other facilities

Organizing these materials professionally demonstrates you're serious about your appeal. Consider creating a binder with labeled tabs or a well-organized digital file if submitting electronically.

7. Leverage New Legal Protections

Recent laws offer additional shields against insurance abuses. The No

Surprises Act, implemented in 2022, protects patients from surprise out-of-network bills in emergencies or when inadvertently treated by an out-of-network provider at an in-network facility.

If you receive such a bill, you're legally responsible only for your normal in-network cost-sharing amount. The rest is between the insurer and provider to negotiate. Don't pay more than your in-network rate, and file a complaint if the bill violates this protection.

Another important update is the fix to the ACA's "family glitch." Previously, if your employer offered "affordable" self-only coverage, your family couldn't get ACA subsidies even if the family premium was unaffordable. Thanks to a 2023 rule change, families stuck in that predicament can now qualify for subsidized marketplace plans.

This was projected to help nearly 1 million Americans obtain more affordable insurance. If you have an expensive employer family plan, check whether your dependents might save money by switching to a marketplace plan.

THE ESCALATION LADDER

Insurance appeals follow a multi-level process, and understanding each rung of the ladder is essential for success.

Level 1: Internal Appeal

Your first appeal goes directly to your insurance company. Under the ACA, all health plans must have an internal appeals process.

For standard appeals, insurers typically have:
- 30 days to respond to pre-service claims (treatment you haven't received yet)
- 60 days to respond to post-service claims (treatment you've already received)

For urgent cases, you can request an expedited appeal, which requires a response within 72 hours.

Internal appeals are reviewed by insurance company employees who weren't involved in the initial denial. While this sounds promising, remember these reviewers still work for the insurer and may follow the same guidelines that led to the initial denial.

"My first internal appeal was denied with almost identical language to the original denial," shared one patient, whose specialized physical therapy was initially rejected. "It felt like they just rubber-stamped it."

This is why persistence is crucial. Many insurers count on patients giving up after the first rejection. Don't be that patient.

Level 2: Second Internal Appeal

Many plans offer a second level of internal appeal, often reviewed by a panel rather than an individual. This panel typically includes medical professionals with relevant expertise.

If your plan offers a second internal appeal, use it. This gives you another opportunity to make your case before moving to external review. It also creates a more comprehensive record if you need to escalate further.

Level 3: External Review

If your internal appeals are unsuccessful, you can request an external review by independent medical experts. This is your most powerful option.

External review became available nationwide under the ACA. The review is conducted by independent medical professionals with no financial ties to your insurer.

For standard external reviews, decisions typically come within 45 days. For urgent situations, expedited external reviews must be completed within 72 hours.

The statistics on external reviews are eye-opening:

- In Pennsylvania, 50.1% of appealed denials were overturned by external review
- In California, 60-80% of certain types of denials were reversed
- Nationwide, external reviews reverse insurance company decisions in approximately half of all cases

Why are these numbers so high? Because external reviewers have no financial incentive to deny care. They simply evaluate whether the treatment is medically appropriate according to accepted standards.

To request an external review:

- Wait until you've received a final denial from your insurer's internal process
- Submit a request to your state's external review program (usually through the Department of Insurance)
- Include all the evidence from your internal appeal, plus any new information

There are some limitations to external review. It's generally only available for denials based on medical judgment, not contractual issues. For example, if your policy explicitly excludes a specific treatment, external review may not help.

Level 4: Regulatory Complaints

Another powerful escalation option is filing a complaint with your state's insurance commissioner or department of insurance. These agencies enforce insurance regulations and can intervene when insurers violate the law.

Regulatory complaints are particularly effective for:
- Delays in processing claims or appeals
- Failure to provide required information
- Violations of state mandates or network adequacy requirements
- Pattern of denials for covered benefits

In some states, the insurance department will actively investigate your case and advocate on your behalf. In others, they may simply forward your complaint to the insurer and monitor the response.

"The turning point in my case came when I filed a complaint with the state insurance department," explained Fiona, whose son's autism therapy was repeatedly denied. "Suddenly, the insurer assigned a special case manager who actually returned my calls and fast-tracked my appeal."

Level 5: Legal Action

When all other options fail, legal action may be necessary. This is particularly true for high-dollar claims or life-threatening situations.

For employer-sponsored plans covered by ERISA (the Employee Retirement Income Security Act), the legal landscape is complex. ERISA preempts many state consumer protection laws, limiting the remedies available to patients.

For individual plans or those not governed by ERISA, state laws may provide stronger protections and the potential for additional damages.

Legal action should generally be a last resort due to the cost, time, and stress involved. However, simply involving an attorney can sometimes prompt insurers to reconsider their position.

"I never had to file a lawsuit," Melissa told me. "After my external review request was submitted, I had an attorney send a letter outlining the potential legal issues with their denial. They approved my treatment within days."

PHYSICIAN ALLIES

Your healthcare providers can be powerful advocates in your appeals process, but they need specific guidance to be effective.

Many doctors are frustrated by insurance denials but unsure when it comes to helping their patients fight back. They're experts in medicine, not insurance appeals. Your job is to make it as easy as possible for them to support your case.

Securing an Effective Letter of Medical Necessity

The quality of your doctor's letter can make or break your appeal. Here's how to ensure it's as strong as possible:

- Schedule a dedicated appointment to discuss your appeal. Don't try to address this during a routine visit.
- Bring a template or outline for the letter, including key points that need to be addressed.
- Share the insurer's denial reason so your doctor can directly counter it.
- Ask for specificity. Instead of "The patient needs this treatment," the letter should explain exactly why you need it and what could happen without it.
- Request citations to clinical guidelines, studies, or medical literature supporting the treatment.

Many doctors will appreciate this structured approach. It saves them time while ensuring their letter addresses the critical issues.

Arranging Peer-to-Peer Reviews

Many insurers offer peer-to-peer reviews, where your doctor can speak directly with the insurance company's medical director. These conversations can be highly effective, but they require preparation.

Before the peer-to-peer review:
- Ensure your doctor understands the specific denial reason
- Provide them with any relevant research or guidelines
- Suggest key points to emphasize during the call

Some doctors may be reluctant to participate in peer-to-peer reviews because they're not compensated for their time. If necessary, ask if you can pay for a consultation specifically for this purpose.

When Your Doctor Won't Help

Unfortunately, some physicians are unwilling or unable to assist with appeals. They may be overwhelmed with administrative burdens, concerned about legal implications, or simply uncomfortable advocating against insurance companies.

If you face this situation:
- Be direct about what you need and why it's important
- Offer to draft the letter yourself for them to review and sign
- Consider seeking a second opinion from another provider
- Contact a patient advocacy organization for your condition, which may be able to connect you with more supportive providers

Remember, you have the right to access your medical records even if your doctor won't actively support your appeal. These records can still form the foundation of your case.

STATE INSURANCE COMMISSIONERS

State insurance commissioners and departments are powerful but underutilized resources in the fight against unjust denials.

These regulators are charged with protecting consumers and enforcing insurance laws. They can be particularly helpful when:
- Your insurer violates state-specific regulations
- You experience unreasonable delays in processing claims or appeals

- Your insurer fails to provide required information
- You need guidance on navigating the appeals process

State-Specific Protections

Insurance regulation happens primarily at the state level, creating a patchwork of protections that vary depending on where you live. Some states have robust consumer protections, while others offer them only minimally.

Key state-specific protections may include:
- Network adequacy requirements: Laws requiring insurers to maintain sufficient in-network providers or cover out-of-network care when necessary.
- Coverage mandates: Requirements to cover specific conditions or treatments, such as autism therapy, fertility treatments, or gender-affirming care.
- Surprise billing protections: Laws limiting patient liability for unexpected out-of-network charges.
- External review standards: Processes for independent review of denied claims, sometimes with specialized standards for different medical conditions.

To find your state's protections, contact your insurance department directly or visit the National Association of Insurance Commissioners website (naic.org).

Filing an Effective Complaint

When filing a complaint with your state insurance department:
- Be concise but comprehensive. Include all relevant details, but avoid emotional language.
- Clearly state what laws or regulations you believe were violated. This isn't required, but it helps regulators identify issues quickly.
- Attach key documents, including denial letters, appeal correspondence, and relevant medical records.
- Specify what resolution you're seeking, whether it's approval of care, reimbursement for services, or investigation of a pattern of denials.

Most states allow you to file complaints online, by mail, or by phone. The process typically takes 30-60 days, though urgent situations may be addressed more quickly.

The Impact of Regulatory Pressure

Even when regulators can't directly overturn a denial, their involvement can create significant pressure on insurers.

Insurance companies are subject to regular audits and reviews by state regulators. Complaints become part of their record, sometimes triggering broader investigations if patterns emerge. No insurer wants to be the subject of a regulatory investigation, which can trigger fines, negative publicity, and increased oversight.

This dynamic creates leverage for patients. Simply copying the state insurance department on your appeal correspondence may even prompt a more favorable response from your insurer.

LEGAL INTERVENTION POINTS

While most denials can be successfully appealed without legal help, some situations warrant attorney involvement.

When to Consider Legal Representation

- High-dollar claims: When significant sums are at stake, the return on investment for legal help improves.
- Life-threatening denials: When a denial puts your life at risk and expedited appeals aren't working.
- Pattern of denials: When your insurer repeatedly denies legitimate claims despite successful appeals.
- Complex legal issues: When your case involves multiple parties, complicated regulations, or novel legal questions.
- Exhausted administrative remedies: When you've completed all available appeals without success.

Types of Legal Assistance

Not all legal aid requires full representation in a lawsuit. Consider these options:

- Consultation: A one-time meeting to evaluate your case and develop a strategy.
- Letter-writing: An attorney-authored letter can signal to insurers that you're serious about your rights.
- Appeal assistance: Some attorneys will help draft and review appeals without formally representing you.
- Limited representation: An attorney might handle specific aspects of

your case rather than taking it on entirely.

These options can be more affordable than full representation while still providing valuable expertise.

Finding the Right Attorney

Look for attorneys who specialize in:
- Health insurance disputes
- ERISA litigation (for employer-sponsored plans)
- Patient advocacy
- Consumer protection

Resources for finding appropriate legal help include:
- Patient advocacy organizations for your condition
- Your state bar association's referral service
- Legal aid organizations for lower-income individuals
- Law school clinics, which often provide free or low-cost assistance

Legal Precedents Worth Knowing

Several court cases have established important rights for patients:
- Rush Prudential HMO v. Moran (2002): This Supreme Court case upheld states' rights to require independent review of denied claims, establishing the foundation for today's external review processes.
- Harlick v. Blue Shield of California (2012): This case established that state mental health parity laws can override insurance policy exclusions, requiring coverage for residential treatment of severe mental illnesses.
- Wit v. United Behavioral Health (2019): This landmark case found that UnitedHealthcare's behavioral health subsidiary used overly restrictive guidelines to deny mental health and substance abuse treatment claims. The court ordered reprocessing of over 67,000 claims.

Understanding these precedents can help you frame your appeal in terms of established legal principles.

PATIENT ADVOCACY SERVICES

When navigating particularly complex denials or when you lack the time or energy to fight alone, professional patient advocates can be invaluable allies.

Types of Advocacy Services

- Independent Patient Advocates: Private professionals who provide personalized assistance for a fee. They typically charge hourly rates ($100-$300/hour) or flat fees for specific services.
- Nonprofit Advocacy Organizations: Condition-specific organizations that provide free or low-cost assistance.
- Hospital Patient Advocates: Many hospitals employ advocates who can help navigate insurance issues, particularly for in-patient care.
- State Consumer Assistance Programs: Created under the ACA, these programs provide free help with appeals and complaints.

What Patient Advocates Can Do

Patient advocates offer diverse services, including:
- Reviewing denial letters and coverage policies
- Drafting appeal letters and collecting supporting documentation
- Communicating with insurers and providers
- Preparing for external reviews
- Filing regulatory complaints
- Connecting you with appropriate legal resources

They bring expertise in insurance systems, medical coding, and appeal strategies that most patients lack.

Finding the Right Advocate

When selecting a patient advocate:
- Verify their credentials and experience with insurance appeals
- Ask about their success rate with cases similar to yours
- Understand their fee structure and what services are included
- Check references or testimonials from other clients

Two professional organizations maintain directories of credentialed advocates:
- The Alliance of Professional Health Advocates (aphadvocates.org)
- The National Association of Healthcare Advocacy (nahac.com)

STRATEGIC APPROACHES TO COMPLEX CASES

Beyond the specific tools and tactics we've covered, several strategic principles can increase your chances of success:

1. Document Everything

Keep detailed records of:

- Every conversation with your insurer (date, time, representative name, what was discussed)
- All correspondence, including emails, letters, and faxes
- Submission of appeals and supporting documents (use certified mail or delivery confirmation)
- Promises made by representatives about coverage or appeal status

This documentation serves two purposes: it holds insurers accountable and provides evidence if you need to escalate your case.

2. Be Persistent but Professional

Insurance systems are designed to wear you down, counting on patients to give up after the first or second denial. Remain persistent, but always professional. Anger and frustration are natural responses to unjust denials, but they rarely help your case. Insurance representatives and reviewers are more likely to go the extra mile for patients who treat them with respect.

3. Know When to Escalate

Some denials can be resolved with a simple phone call. Others require multiple levels of appeal and regulatory involvement. Developing a sense for when to escalate can save time and energy.

It's time to escalate when:

- You receive the same response multiple times
- Representatives can't explain the denial reason clearly
- Your appeal contains strong evidence that's being ignored
- Time-sensitive treatment is being delayed

4. Create a Sense of Urgency

Insurance companies process thousands of claims daily. Making your case stand out often requires creating a sense of urgency.

Effective tactics include:

- Copying senior executives on correspondence
- Mentioning regulatory and legal options
- Setting explicit deadlines for response
- Using certified mail or delivery confirmation

5. Use Multiple Channels Simultaneously

Don't put all your eggs in one basket. Pursue multiple strategies simultaneously:
- File an internal appeal while preparing for external review
- Submit a regulatory complaint while pursuing peer-to-peer review
- Engage your employer's HR department while working with your doctor

This creates multiple pressure points and increases your chances of finding a solution.

TAKING BACK CONTROL: MELISSA'S VICTORY AND YOURS

Remember Melissa, the breast cancer patient we met at the beginning of this chapter? Her story illustrates how these strategies work together to overturn even the most challenging denials.

After receiving her denial letter, Melissa:
- Obtained her complete policy documents and identified the insurer's definition of "experimental" treatments
- Worked with her oncologist to create a detailed letter of medical necessity with citations to recent studies
- Collected evidence showing the treatment was standard care at major cancer centers
- Filed an internal appeal, which was denied
- Requested external review while simultaneously filing a complaint with her state insurance commissioner
- Consulted an attorney who sent a letter outlining potential legal violations

Three months after the initial denial, Melissa received approval for her treatment. The insurer never acknowledged any error, simply stating that "additional information" had led to a reconsideration.

Melissa's case required persistence, strategic thinking, and help from multiple allies. But the reward was worth the effort.

Insurance denials are not final verdicts but opening moves in a negotiation. The system is designed to intimidate you into surrender, but armed with knowledge and determination, you can fight back effectively.

I've seen many families successfully challenge insurance denials using these exact strategies. Some appeals are resolved with a single phone call; others require months of persistent advocacy. But the pattern is clear: patients who fight systematically and strategically win far more often than those who accept the initial "no."

As you navigate your own appeals, remember that each successful challenge does more than secure your individual care. It sends a message to insurers that you are no longer willing to be a passive participant in a broken system. It demonstrates that you understand your rights and are prepared to assert them. Most importantly, it shifts the power dynamic in American healthcare, one appeal at a time.

The healthcare system may be designed to say "no," but with the right tools and tactics, you can turn that "no" into a "yes." Your health and financial security are worth fighting for. Don't let anyone, especially a faceless insurance bureaucracy, tell you otherwise.

QUICK REFERENCE GUIDE

When Your Claim Is Denied:

- Get the full denial explanation in writing
- Obtain your complete policy documents (Certificate of Coverage, Medical Policies)
- Understand the specific reason for denial
- Request a peer-to-peer review between your doctor and the insurer's medical director
- File an internal appeal within the deadline (typically 180 days)
- Request an expedited review for urgent situations (72-hour response required)
- Pursue external review if internal appeals fail
- File regulatory complaints with your state insurance commissioner
- Consider legal consultation for complex or high-value cases
- Engage patient advocacy services when additional support is needed

Building Your Appeal:

- Craft a clear, fact-based appeal letter
- Obtain a detailed letter of medical necessity from your doctor
- Include relevant medical records with key information highlighted

- Add scientific evidence supporting the treatment
- Reference similar cases where treatment was approved
- Address every point in the denial letter
- Submit via certified mail or with delivery confirmation
- Follow up regularly on the status of your appeal

Key Deadlines to Remember:

- Internal appeals: Generally 180 days from denial
- External review: Typically 4 months after final internal denial
- Expedited appeals: Request when treatment is urgently needed
- Regulatory complaints: File while appeals are in process, not after

Resources for Additional Help:

- Patient Advocate Foundation: 1-800-532-5274, patientadvocate.org
- Your state insurance department: Find contact information at naic.org
- Condition-specific advocacy organizations: Search "[your condition] patient advocacy"
- Professional patient advocates: aphadvocates.org, nahac.com

To receive a complimentary companion guide with comprehensive resource lists and templates, please visit insuredtodeath.org.
If you find this book helpful, sharing your thoughts on Amazon, Goodreads, or even Reddit makes a real difference. Your feedback not only helps others discover the book but also supports the community we're building.

Scan QR code for relevant links

8

THE TECH REVOLUTION

"The secret of change is to focus all of your energy not on fighting the old, but on building the new."

— *Socrates*

I once received a frantic call from Dorothy, a 72-year-old retiree caring for her husband with Parkinson's disease. She had just received a bill for $4,200 for an MRI that her insurance had inexplicably denied. While trying to help Dorothy navigate this crisis, I asked her "Did you know what this MRI would cost before you got it?"

She laughed bitterly. "Know the cost? My doctor said I needed it, so I got it. Nobody tells you what things cost until the bill arrives." She shrugged. "That's just how healthcare works."

Dorothy's experience reflects what millions of Americans face daily: a healthcare system deliberately designed to keep us in the dark. For decades, we've accepted this darkness as inevitable, that secret pricing, fragmented medical records, and impenetrable denial notices are simply "how healthcare works."

But something remarkable is happening. As politicians debate and corporations deflect, a quiet revolution is underway. Across America, innovators are creating technological tools that hand power back to patients. These tools shine light into healthcare's darkest corners, giving ordinary people the ability to compare prices, access their records, challenge denials, and connect with providers in ways that were impossible just a few years ago.

As someone who's spent years in both the business world and healthcare advocacy, I've witnessed firsthand how technology is changing the power balance. I've seen families use smartphone apps to find services at a quarter of the price they were initially quoted. I've watched older adults in remote areas access specialists through telehealth who would have been unreachable otherwise. I've helped parents of children with special needs use AI-powered systems to overturn insurance denials that would have previously gone unchallenged.

Technology alone won't fix American healthcare. The problems run too deep and profit motives too strong. But these innovations give us something essential in any fight against a powerful opponent: weapons to level the playing field. They provide ordinary people with the information, efficiency, and advocacy that were once exclusive to industry insiders.

In the pages ahead, I'll walk you through technologies that are helping patients take back control. For each, I'll explain how they work, share examples of their impact, and provide practical guidance on using them effectively. Some are as simple as downloading an app. Others involve more significant changes in how you approach healthcare.

Consider this your technological arsenal in the fight for healthcare justice.

PRICE TRANSPARENCY TOOLS

In January 2021, the federal Hospital Price Transparency Rule took effect, requiring hospitals to post their prices for services and negotiated insurance rates publicly. The goal was to empower consumers and stimulate competition. But compliance has been spotty at best. A 2024 audit found that about 46% of hospitals still weren't fully complying with the requirements. And even those who posted data often presented it in formats so messy and confusing that meaningful comparison was virtually impossible.

This is where technology steps in to make sense of the chaos.

"Once I started using Turquoise Health's website, I felt like I had x-ray vision into healthcare pricing for the first time," said Marcus, a member of the CareYaya community whose father needed knee surgery. "I discovered that the same procedure would cost $32,000 at our local hospital but only $19,000 at a surgical center 30 minutes away. Both were in-network. That's a $13,000 difference with identical coverage!"

Platforms like Turquoise Health and Healthcare Bluebook compile the machine-readable price files from hospitals and provide searchable interfaces that let patients look up procedures and compare prices across facilities. What they reveal is shocking: a test might cost $300 at one provider and $6,200 at another in the same region. Such differences, once hidden, are now exposed.

The impact on real people's lives can be substantial. Last year, I worked with a family whose daughter needed a specialized scan for chronic migraines. Their hospital quoted $2,800 for the procedure. After we used Healthcare Bluebook to check fair prices, they found an imaging center offering the same scan for $450. The hospital mysteriously lowered their price when confronted with this information.

These tools don't just save money but are changing the fundamental power dynamic between patients and providers. Knowledge that was once exclusive to industry insiders is now in the hands of regular people.

For prescription drugs, the savings can be even more dramatic. 60% of Americans report paying for medications is a burden, and about 29% have foregone filling prescriptions due to cost. Apps like GoodRx have emerged to address this problem by comparing pharmacy prices for any given drug and offering coupons.

The difference can be staggering. We recently helped an elderly couple in Michigan who was paying $187 monthly for a common blood pressure medication. Using GoodRx, we found the same medication at a different pharmacy for $24. That's over $1,900 in annual savings from a free app that took two minutes to use.

GoodRx claims to have helped consumers save around $30 billion on prescription costs since its launch. Perhaps more importantly, it educates consumers that cash prices can sometimes be lower than insurance copays, a revelation that encourages smart shopping.

Beyond medications, new services help patients find upfront pricing for procedures. Companies like MDSave and Sesame offer online marketplaces where patients can search for procedures and see set cash prices from local providers, often at significant discounts for paying upfront. For instance, MDSave might list a knee MRI at one imaging center for $400 (all-inclusive) versus $1,500 at a hospital.

For the uninsured or those with high deductibles, these platforms can be game-changers. One CareYaya family with a $7,500 deductible saved over $4,000 on their son's outpatient procedure by using MDSave instead of going through their insurance, a counterintuitive move that demonstrates how broken our system has become.

While these tools aren't perfect as data quality varies and not all services are shoppable in emergencies, they represent a fundamental shift toward transparency.

Practical Takeaway

Before scheduling any non-emergency procedure or filling an expensive prescription, take 10 minutes to check pricing on comparison tools. The savings can be substantial, and the knowledge you gain might help in negotiating even if you can't switch providers.

MEDICAL RECORDS MANAGEMENT

In 2022, I witnessed the near-tragic consequences of fragmented medical records firsthand. A friend was hospitalized after taking two medications that, when combined, caused a dangerous drop in blood pressure. One had been prescribed by his cardiologist, the other by his primary care physician. Neither doctor knew what the other had prescribed because they used different electronic record systems that didn't communicate.

This scenario plays out countless times daily across America. Medical records have traditionally been siloed in various clinic offices or hospital systems, often on incompatible platforms. This fragmentation that leads to duplicate tests, incomplete information during care, and mountains of paperwork.

Technology is now empowering patients with easier control over their health information through digital platforms and even blockchain-based solutions for record-keeping.

A prime example is Apple Health Records on the iPhone. Launched in 2018, this feature allows patients to download and aggregate their medical records from participating hospitals and clinics. By 2022, it was connected to over 800 healthcare institutions covering 12,000+ locations in the U.S., U.K., and Canada.

"Having my entire medical history in my pocket has saved me repeatedly," shared Emma, a mother of a child with a rare genetic condition who uses CareYaya services. "When we traveled and needed urgent care, I could show the ER doctor my son's complete record. The doctor told me this probably prevented unnecessary tests and inappropriate medications."

Traditional patient portals like Epic's MyChart have also expanded their capabilities. More than 190 million patients actively use Epic's MyChart portal, allowing them to schedule appointments, message doctors, review test results, and update information. Epic has enabled features that merge data from multiple MyChart accounts, moving toward greater interoperability.

The scale of transformation is enormous. Nearly half the U.S. population can now log into a patient portal to retrieve their medical information. This instant access represents a seismic shift from the old process of requesting records via phone or fax and waiting days or weeks.

The benefits extend beyond convenience. When patients have electronic access to health information and digital tools for self-management, many studies document positive outcomes like better disease control and higher satisfaction. Access gives patients agency.

There are countless stories of patients catching errors or important details because they reviewed their records: noticing a lab value that was borderline high and following up, or realizing a medication was missing from the list and contacting their provider to update it.

Beyond mainstream apps, more cutting-edge solutions are exploring the use of blockchain technology for medical records. Blockchain, the technology underpinning cryptocurrencies, offers a decentralized and secure way to log access to health data.

Estonia provides a leading example: since 2016, the country's national health system has used blockchain to ensure the integrity of electronic health records and log all access events, making the data essentially tamper-proof. Every time someone views or edits an Estonian patient's record, a blockchain entry is created, providing an immutable audit trail that enhances trust and privacy.

While still experimental in the U.S., startups like Patientory have launched blockchain-based personal health record services that let individuals store their medical data on a network and share it securely with others as needed. The vision is to give patients full ownership of their health information, breaking down silos between providers.

Practical Takeaway

Sign up for your healthcare providers' patient portals, and if you use an iPhone, set up Apple Health Records to consolidate your medical information. After appointments, review your notes for accuracy. In emergencies, having quick access to your medication list, allergies, and recent tests can be lifesaving.

TELEMEDICINE NAVIGATION

When the pandemic hit, Fran, an 87-year-old receiving care through CareYaya in rural North Carolina, suddenly couldn't see her cardiologist. The 90-minute drive had been difficult before. Now it seemed impossible. "I was sure I'd have to stop treatment," she told me. Instead, her doctor's office helped her set up telemedicine visits. What surprised Fran wasn't just that she could see her doctor remotely, it was that her care actually improved. "Now I have monthly check-ins instead of twice-yearly visits. My blood pressure is better controlled, and I'm not exhausted from the drive."

Fran's experience reflects the telemedicine revolution catalyzed by COVID-19. Before 2020, only about 8% of Americans had ever had a telemedicine visit. But during the pandemic's height, telehealth accounted for an estimated 13% of all outpatient visits nationwide. In Medicare, the expansion was even more dramatic: 53% of beneficiaries used telemedicine at least once during the first year of the pandemic.

This wasn't just an emergency stopgap. It represented a fundamental transformation in how care is delivered. By late 2023, over 12.6% of Medicare beneficiaries were still receiving services via telehealth each quarter, and 86.9% of hospitals were providing telehealth services.

But access alone isn't enough. Patients need guidance on how to use virtual care effectively. This is where telehealth navigation tools become crucial.

Leading telehealth platforms like Teladoc, Amwell, Doctor on Demand, and MDLive offer 24/7 access to virtual physicians. The scale is impressive. Teladoc Health alone reported facilitating over 50 million virtual visits as of late 2022, with about one in four Americans having access to their services through employers or health plans.

These platforms have navigation built in: they greet users with symptom checkers or intake questionnaires that triage them to the appropriate provider type. For example, Teladoc might direct someone reporting anxiety to a behavioral health specialist instead of a general practitioner, while Amwell's app might flag that a video visit isn't suitable for chest pain symptoms.

One key benefit has been for rural communities and specialist access. Programs like Project ECHO have popularized a tele-mentoring model where rural clinicians present cases via video to specialist teams who guide them, effectively bringing specialty expertise to the community level. During the pandemic, regulations that restricted telehealth were waived, allowing people to do telehealth from home with insurance coverage.

This catalyzed a culture shift. One study cited by the American Hospital

Association found high satisfaction rates among both patients and clinicians with telehealth. Many issues can be resolved without an in-person visit, and telehealth can prevent costly complications by making care more accessible.

Health systems and insurers have begun offering telehealth navigators—sometimes real people, sometimes AI chatbots—that help patients schedule appropriate tele-visits and prepare for them. For example, an insurer's app might ask about symptoms and then guide patients to either a nurse chat or a doctor video visit. After the tele-visit, the app can remind patients to follow up or help them find an in-person provider if recommended.

The COVID-19 era also saw traditional healthcare providers ramp up their own telehealth offerings via EHR portals or dedicated apps. Patients suddenly had multiple choices: use their hospital's telehealth for continuity with regular doctors, or use on-demand services for after-hours convenience.

Mental health in particular has seen a revolution. Companies like BetterHelp and Talkspace connect patients with licensed therapists via video or text, dramatically lowering barriers to counseling. Many patients who would never have driven to weekly therapy sessions are willing to speak with a therapist from home.

For rural hospitals, telemedicine has provided critical specialist availability through programs like telestroke and tele-ICU. In a telestroke program, if a patient arrives at a small rural hospital with stroke symptoms, local doctors can initiate a video consultation with a neurologist at a larger center who can examine the patient via camera, review scans remotely, and guide treatment.

To help patients navigate this new hybrid care landscape, some health systems have created dedicated telehealth navigation roles—staff who proactively reach out to set up virtual care like post-hospitalization check-ins or chronic disease management visits. This ensures that patients who aren't tech-savvy still benefit.

Part of telemedicine navigation is identifying digital divide gaps and addressing them. For instance, connecting patients to programs providing free devices or internet hotspots for telehealth purposes. Libraries and community centers in some rural towns have become telehealth access points, offering private rooms with good internet connections.

Practical Takeaway

Check if your insurance plan or employer offers telehealth benefits, and set up access before you need it. For routine follow-ups, minor illnesses, or mental health support, consider telehealth as your first option. It's often faster, cheaper, and equally effective. If you live in a rural area, ask your doctor about specialist telehealth consultations rather than traveling long distances.

DIRECT PRIMARY CARE PLATFORMS

"My doctor gave me his personal cell number and told me to text anytime," Glenn, who books care for his father, told me with disbelief. "Yesterday, I sent him a photo of a rash, and he called me within an hour with advice. No appointment, no bill, no hassle."

Glenn wasn't describing some VIP concierge service for the wealthy but rather his DPC membership, which costs him $75 monthly.

As mentioned in Chapter 5, while insurance-based healthcare grows increasingly convoluted, a parallel movement in the form of DPC has emerged that aims to simplify routine care by bypassing insurance altogether.

The growth has been remarkable. According to the American Academy of Family Physicians, 9% of family physicians in 2023 reported operating a direct primary care practice, up from only 3% in 2022 —a striking jump in adoption within one year. Nationwide, as of 2024, there were more than 2,400 DPC practices operating in nearly every state, with membership increasing 241% from 2017 to 2021.

DPC platforms are essentially technology-enabled clinics or networks that leverage the DPC model. They combine membership payment with modern health IT, such as user-friendly patient apps, data analytics for preventive care, and often novel clinic designs.

Examples include Forward Health, One Medical, Crossover Health, and many independent local DPC clinics. Each operates differently, but they share core principles: transparent pricing, enhanced access, and a focus on preventive, holistic care.

One Medical, recently acquired by Amazon for $3.9 billion, charges an annual membership fee (around $199 per year) for individuals. With that membership, patients get 24/7 virtual care through an app, same-day or next-day in-person appointments, and seamless specialist referrals. By the end of 2022, One Medical had about 836,000 members across 200+ offices in 29 metro areas.

Meanwhile, Forward Health takes a tech-forward approach: their clinics feature body scanners and genetic tests, with a flat fee (around $149 per month) covering all primary care services. Forward doesn't accept insurance; everything from visits to basic labs is included in the fee.

For patients with high-deductible plans or those uninsured, DPC can provide substantial savings on routine care. A typical DPC practice charges $50-$100 monthly for adults, which works out to $600-$1,200 yearly. For that price, patients receive unlimited office visits, many in-office procedures at no extra cost, and commonly used lab tests and medications at wholesale prices.

The AAFP reports that 99% of DPC practices offer same-day appointments, and the average panel size for a DPC physician is around 413 patients —far lower than the 2,000–3,000 patients per doctor in traditional primary care. This allows longer visits (often 30-60 minutes versus 10-15 minutes) and greater availability. Many DPC practices provide physicians' personal contact information for quick questions, something unheard of in standard practice.

Real-world outcomes from direct primary care are promising. Qliance, an early DPC provider in Washington state, reported that their patients had fewer ER visits and hospitalizations compared to similar populations, along with higher satisfaction. Another provider, Access Healthcare in North Carolina, documented better control of chronic conditions because patients could communicate freely without worrying about copays.

From a technology perspective, many DPC platforms leverage apps and data to enhance the model. Members might have an app for chatting with their doctor, seeing health data, and integrating fitness tracker information. Some DPC companies use connected health monitoring devices to continuously gather data that physicians use to personalize care.

It's important to note that DPC works best for primary care and routine services. Patients still need some form of coverage for hospitalizations, surgeries, or specialist care. Many DPC physicians advise carrying a high-deductible health plan or catastrophic insurance for major expenses.

For patients considering DPC, technology helps find and evaluate options. Websites like DPC Frontier maintain maps of DPC clinics nationwide, and many practices clearly list pricing and services online for easy comparison.

Practical Takeaway

If you have a high-deductible health plan or find yourself paying significant out-of-pocket costs for primary care, investigate direct primary care options in your area. For a predictable monthly fee, you might receive more comprehensive and accessible care than through traditional insurance-based practices.

CROWDSOURCED HOSPITAL PRICING

"I couldn't believe the difference," a CareYaya family caregiver told me about his experience with crowdsourced pricing information. "My wife needed a colonoscopy. The hospital quoted $3,800, but someone in our community Facebook group had posted about getting the same procedure for $980 at an outpatient center. Same doctor, different location, one-fourth the price."

In the quest for healthcare transparency, one innovative approach has been crowdsourcing, that is, the power of patients to share real pricing information. If hospitals and insurers have been reluctant to fully reveal costs, patients have taken matters into their own hands by pooling their bills and price quotes.

One of the pioneering projects in this space is ClearHealthCosts, a journalism-driven startup founded by Jeanne Pinder. ClearHealthCosts built an online tool where users could share the prices they were charged for common procedures.

ClearHealthCosts grew by partnering with media organizations in various cities, including CBS News, spreading the word and increasing data contributions from community members. The site's interactive software lets patients input their prices and see maps or lists of prices others have paid in their area.

The impact of crowdsourced pricing transparency is tangible. In Louisiana, a pricing transparency bill had been stuck in the state legislature. After ClearHealthCosts launched a Louisiana project with local media, the bill suddenly gained traction. Lawmakers, spurred by constituents' stories of outrageous prices, moved forward on reforms.

On an individual level, many patients have used the information to save money. One woman needed a foot MRI and was quoted $2,400 at a hospital but after consulting the ClearHealthCosts database, she found a place offering it for $450. Another patient whose hospital billed a high price for a routine blood test showed the billing office that others reported the same test for a fraction of the cost, and the hospital reduced her charge.

Beyond ClearHealthCosts, other grassroots initiatives have emerged. Online forums on Reddit (r/HealthInsurance or r/MedicalBilling) feature threads where people share experiences and prices, asking "Is this reasonable?" and seeking advice. Some patients have created public Google spreadsheets listing costs for surgeries or childbirth at various hospitals.

Social media campaigns like #ShowMeYourBills encourages patients to post images of hospital bills (with personal info redacted) to draw attention to high prices and billing abuses. The viral nature of social media meant some hospital

CEOs faced the embarrassment of seeing their facility's bill for a $50 IV Tylenol retweeted thousands of times. In response, a few hospitals engaged, sometimes issuing refunds or stating they would review charging practices.

One unique strength of crowdsourced data is that it captures the prices actually paid, not just list prices. Hospital transparency postings might show chargemaster rates, but crowdsourced entries often include notes like "Of course, crowdsourced data has limitations. It may not be comprehensive or statistically representative. However, as an adjunct to official data, it provides real-world clarity that speaks in a language patients understand: dollars and cents from people like them.

Practical Takeaway

Before scheduling a procedure, search online communities and price transparency websites to see what others have paid. Share your own experiences afterward to help others. Knowledge is cumulative: the more people share, the more powerful the database becomes.

HEALTHCARE CRYPTOCURRENCIES AND BLOCKCHAIN SOLUTIONS

While blockchain technology shows promise for medical records, its applications extend further into insurance, payments, and incentivizing healthy behaviors. The convergence of blockchain and cryptocurrency with healthcare has spawned experimental models of decentralized insurance, healthcare-specific tokens, and blockchain-based payment systems.

One major use case is secure health data management via blockchain. By storing either health data or pointers to encrypted health data on a blockchain, it ensures that no single entity could compromise records. The data becomes tamper-evident and resilient. For example, a patient's complete medical history could be indexed in a blockchain entry; any provider with the patient's permission could retrieve the records and trust it's the full, unaltered set.

In the U.S., where patients often see multiple providers across different networks, a blockchain-based health information exchange could potentially connect those silos without requiring each hospital to formally agree on data sharing. Companies like BurstIQ have worked with Colorado's Medicaid program on a pilot using blockchain for patient profiles to test if it improved data integrity and portability.

Another domain is healthcare payments and cryptocurrencies. Involving multiple intermediaries (insurers, clearinghouses, banks), traditional healthcare payments can be slow. Cryptocurrencies offer near-instant settlement and low fees by cutting out middlemen.

A report by Digital Health Insights notes that crypto payments can reduce transaction costs and delays in healthcare, particularly for global payments. A patient in the U.S. can use cryptocurrency to pay a hospital in another country for surgery, avoiding hefty foreign transaction fees. Even domestically, a hospital can accept cryptocurrency for a bill and receive payment immediately.

Some providers have begun experimenting with this approach. In 2018, a private hospital in Florida announced it would accept Bitcoin and Ethereum, targeting international patients. A Manhattan dentistry practice did the same for high-end cosmetic procedures.

Smart contracts are another promising blockchain application for insurance: self-executing agreements that trigger payments based on predefined rules. In health insurance, a smart contract might automatically pay a provider once it receives proof that a covered service was provided or reimburse a patient for an approved expense. This can reduce claim processing from weeks to minutes.

Companies like Etherisc have built decentralized insurance protocols that can adapt for health insurance applications. Originally focused on flight delay insurance via smart contract, the underlying concept of parametric triggers and immediate payout could apply to certain health claims.

One prominent blockchain insurance concept involved the use of tokens for peer-to-peer insurance. For example, in China, MediShares created a mutual aid health cost-sharing community on blockchain where members contribute cryptocurrency into a pool. If someone has a medical event, the smart contract verifies it and disburses an agreed amount from the pool.

We've also seen the emergence of healthcare-specific cryptocurrencies. Dentacoin (DCN) was launched for the dental industry, envisioned as a token that dentists and patients would use for transactions and rewards. Patients could pay for care with Dentacoin, earn tokens through preventive activities, and dentists would benefit from loyal patients. The Dentacoin foundation also proposed smart contracts for a "dental assurance" program, effectively a subscription between patient and dentist written to blockchain.

In the insurance industry, even large incumbents have explored blockchain. Anthem (a major U.S. insurer) piloted a blockchain-based app where patients could scan a QR code at a doctor's office to instantly authorize sharing insurance information. Major insurers Aetna and UnitedHealth Group joined with IBM in the Health Utility Network to explore how blockchain could streamline provider directories and claims.

One advantage is fighting fraud: with a shared ledger, it's easier to spot duplicate claims or suspicious billing patterns across payers. The immutable audit trail of blockchain appeals to regulators for tracking delivery of opioids from manufacturer to pharmacy to patient, for example.

Looking globally, Estonia has positioned its entire health system on blockchain for security. The Dubai Health Authority has also set a goal to put all health records on blockchain. Meanwhile, in China, there's interest in blockchain to connect huge public health databases in a more patient-centric way.

While challenges abound in applying blockchain to healthcare—regulatory uncertainty, integration with legacy systems, and cryptocurrency volatility—the persistence of projects suggests strong belief in blockchain's core attributes: security, transparency, and decentralization.

Practical Takeaway

While blockchain healthcare applications are still developing, watch for opportunities to participate in pilot programs offering enhanced data control or lower-cost payment options.

AI ADVOCATES

When Marina, a single mother caring for both her son with special needs and elderly father, received a $42,000 hospital bill for her father's emergency gallbladder surgery, she was devastated. "I thought we'd lose our house," she told me. The bill seemed legitimate until an AI-powered billing review flagged something peculiar: her father had supposedly received the same CT scan three times in four hours, at $7,000 each. When Marina questioned this, the hospital quickly admitted a "coding error" and removed $14,000 from the bill.

AI is increasingly acting as a champion for patients: identifying billing mistakes, guiding appeals, answering coverage questions, and aiding in medical decision-making. The healthcare system generates massive amounts of data that can overwhelm humans but are perfect for machine learning algorithms.

One striking success of AI is in fraud detection and billing anomaly identification. Highmark, a large Blue Cross Blue Shield insurer, deployed AI in its payment integrity department with remarkable results: in 2019 alone, their AI-driven fraud prevention saved approximately $260 million. Over five years, their AI implementations saved over $850 million.

The AI achieved this by catching things like doctors billing for unrealistic hours, upcoding, or potential fraud patterns. For patients, this means fewer fraudulent charges hitting their deductibles or causing premium increases.

On a more individual level, AI helps patients directly with billing errors and disputes. Several startups offer services where you upload medical bills and insurance EOBs, and their AI analyzes them for inconsistencies or overcharges. For instance, an AI might flag that a certain blood test was charged twice, or that a "global fee" already includes a charge that was also listed separately.

If anomalies are found, the platform can auto-generate a dispute letter or assist in correction. These interventions can save patients hundreds or thousands of dollars. And as the systems learn from each success, they improve at catching similar issues for others.

AI also advocates through digital assistants and chatbots that explain insurance benefits in plain language. Many people find insurance terminology confusing. Terms like "deductible vs. out-of-pocket max" or "coinsurance after copay" baffle even savvy consumers.

AI chatbots on insurer websites or apps allow patients to ask questions like, "Why did I get charged $200 for my ER visit?" or "Is Dr. Smith in-network?" The AI parses the question, looks up plan details or claims, and provides an answer. For instance: "It looks like you hadn't met your $1,000 deductible at the time of the ER visit, so you were responsible for the $200 charge. You now have $800 remaining on your deductible."

These answers, which once required lengthy phone calls with customer service, can now be delivered instantly by AI that doesn't tire of explaining multiple times. This form of AI assistance demystifies insurance for patients, effectively advocating through education.

AI is also supporting medical decision-making for patients. Symptom checker apps (like Buoy, Ada, or Babylon) use AI to triage symptoms and provide recommendations such as "consider a telehealth consult" or "see a doctor within 24 hours." They provide preliminary evaluation that guides patients to the right care setting, potentially saving them from unnecessary ER trips or urging them to get timely care when needed.

A CDC report indicated tele-triage and symptom bots saw heavy usage during COVID surges, helping direct patients appropriately when systems were overwhelmed. The benefit is twofold: reducing system strain and giving patients confidence about what to do next.

Furthermore, AI can personalize health information. An app for diabetics might analyze blood sugar readings and dietary logs before giving tailored feedback: "Your blood sugars have been high in the mornings. Research shows having a small high-protein snack before bed can help. Also, make sure to take your insulin 30 minutes before dinner as prescribed." This is advice a doctor or diabetes educator might give, but the AI delivers it in real-time when needed. One program using an AI coach for hypertension saw significant blood pressure drops for participants, similar to medication adjustments. By being an ever-present advocate for healthy behavior, AI augments the limited time clinicians have for each patient.

In appeals and disputes, AI is stepping up dramatically. With platforms like our own Counterforce Health, patients can leverage AI to generate powerful, data-driven appeal letters in minutes. By simply uploading their denial letters and supporting documents, the AI trained specifically for this purpose analyzes the case, identifies key arguments, and crafts a personalized appeal citing relevant medical evidence and policy language in minutes.

AI tools can also analyze insurance formularies and medication lists to suggest cheaper therapeutic equivalents. If a patient is prescribed an expensive brand-name drug, an AI system might notify them and their doctor that a generic or different brand is significantly cheaper under their plan.

AI is even detecting insurance scams that affect patients. Systems monitoring transactions can discover patterns of unauthorized charges and alert authorities. This protects patients from the headache of clearing up insurance fraud on their records.

From an expert analysis standpoint, consultants note that healthcare's administrative complexity (approaching $300 billion in annual costs) is ripe for AI disruption. By 2022, 62% of healthcare executives had adopted AI-centric strategies, up from 33% in 2018, reflecting how mainstream AI has become in operational thinking.

For patients, executive buy-in means experiences will increasingly feature AI support behind the scenes. Hospitals use AI for better scheduling (less waiting), insurers use it to approve straightforward claims faster (quicker reimbursements), and providers use it for automated prior authorization approvals (less treatment limbo).

Practical Takeaway

Take advantage of AI-powered tools for bill review, symptom checking, and insurance appeals. When dealing with customer service, try AI chatbots first. They're often faster than phone calls and can explain benefits clearly. For chronic conditions, explore AI coaching apps that provide personalized guidance between doctor visits.

TECHNOLOGY AS THE GREAT EQUALIZER

The American healthcare system remains complex, but technology is shifting power to patients. Price transparency tools expose hidden costs, enabling informed decisions and encouraging fair pricing. Digital health records can break down data silos, giving patients control over their medical history. Meanwhile, AI-driven platforms help patients appeal denials, saving hours of time.

The real-world impact is clear: a woman saves thousands on an MRI through price transparency, a family overturns an insurance denial with an AI-driven appeal, a rural patient receives specialty care via telehealth, and millions cut medication costs through price comparison apps.

Despite progress, challenges remain. Because adoption is uneven, many Americans are unaware of these tools with some lacking access to digital solutions. Hospitals resist transparency, and trust in AI varies. Integrating new technology into an outdated system is slow. But momentum is building as policies like the Hospital Price Transparency Rule and health data interoperability laws lay the groundwork for lasting change. The COVID-19 pandemic accelerated telehealth adoption, proving the need for digital-first healthcare solutions.

The next wave of innovation is already taking shape: real-time insurance pricing (knowing exact costs upfront), personal health AI assistants, and augmented reality self-care tools. Expanded blockchain pilots might allow access to global health records. The challenge will be ensuring these advancements prioritize real patient needs by reducing confusion, lowering costs, and improving access.

Technology is shifting healthcare from a system where patients are passive subjects to one where they are informed, proactive partners. They can compare providers, track their records, seek second opinions remotely, and hold insurers accountable, all with digital tools at their fingertips.

While obstacles persist, one thing is clear: patients are no longer navigating healthcare alone. They have maps, headlights, and sometimes even an AI co-pilot guiding the way.

9

THE POWER OF THE PEOPLE

"Never doubt that a small group of thoughtful, committed citizens can change the world; indeed, it's the only thing that ever has."

— *Margaret Mead*

The email arrived in my inbox at 2:17 AM on a Tuesday. The subject line read simply: "Thank you" I almost skipped it, assuming it was spam. Running CareYaya means endless emails, and sleep was a precious commodity that night. But something made me click.

"Mr. Shah," it began. "You don't know me, but I've been following your work. Yesterday, after fighting my insurance company for 8 months over my daughter's leukemia treatment, they finally approved it. I was about to give up. Then I saw that Facebook group you mentioned in your podcast. I posted my daughter's denial letter there. Within 24 hours, 3,700 people had shared it. A local news reporter called. Then a state representative. By evening, the insurance company was calling me suddenly eager to 'resolve this misunderstanding.' My daughter starts treatment next week."

The email was from Rachel, a single mother from Tucson whose 12-year-old daughter had been denied a life-saving treatment. For eight months, she'd followed the traditional appeals process, gathering medical records, filing paperwork, making endless phone calls. Eight months of her daughter's condition worsening while faceless reviewers decided her fate.

Yet it took just 24 hours of collective action, strangers sharing her story, amplifying her voice, shining light on injustice, to accomplish what she couldn't do alone.

I've witnessed this pattern repeatedly, one in which collective action succeeds where individual patients fail. This chapter is about harnessing that power and showing how ordinary Americans are joining forces to challenge an insurance industry that profits from their suffering.

The healthcare industry wants you to believe you're alone in your struggle. They design denial letters to sound final and authoritative, counting on your eventual surrender. But what they fear most is exactly what Rachel discovered: when patients unite, share strategies, and demand justice together, the balance of power shifts. What you're about to read isn't just about organizing techniques but reclaiming your power in a system designed to strip it away.

I've seen what happens when patients stop fighting alone and start fighting together. The insurance executive earning millions denying claims suddenly becomes less confident when thousands of patients expose their practices simultaneously. The politician taking healthcare industry donations thinks twice when constituents pack town halls demanding accountability. The hospital billing department pursuing aggressive collections changes course when community members stand together against medical debt.

As we explore the tools and strategies of collective action, remember this: the healthcare industry's power relies on our isolation. Our power comes from our unity.

THE SOCIAL MEDIA REVOLUTION: WHEN DENIAL LETTERS GO VIRAL

"I never thought I'd be a Twitter activist," Allen told me, laughing slightly. "I'm a 58-year-old accountant. My kids had to set up my Facebook account."

Yet Allen's story illustrates how social media has become an unofficial "appeals court" for insurance denials. After his wife's breast cancer diagnosis, their insurer denied coverage for a specialized radiation treatment their oncologist recommended. The denial letter cited "insufficient evidence of medical necessity" despite multiple peer-reviewed studies supporting the treatment.

Allen spent three months navigating the insurer's internal appeals process. Each appeal was denied. The external review process would take another 60 days, time his wife didn't have.

"I was desperate," Allen recalled. "My daughter suggested I post the denial letter on Twitter. I thought it was ridiculous. I had maybe 40 followers, mostly family. But I did it."

The post included a photo of the denial letter with the insurer's name clearly visible, alongside his wife's oncologist's recommendation letter.

Within hours, the post had been shared thousands of times. Healthcare professionals commented, pointing out how the treatment was standard care. Other patients shared similar experiences. A healthcare reporter from a national outlet direct-messaged him for an interview.

Forty-eight hours later, Allen received a call from a senior medical director at his insurance company. The denial had been "reconsidered." Treatment was approved to begin immediately.

"The same company that ignored my appeals for months suddenly couldn't wait to help," Allen said. "The only difference was that now everybody could see what they were doing."

Allen's experience reflects a growing trend. Patients who exhaust traditional appeals turn increasingly to social media, where public pressure can accomplish in days what formal processes fail to do in months. Insurance companies, highly sensitive to reputation damage, often respond quickly to public exposure.

We're seeing this pattern repeatedly:

- When pediatric gastroenterologist, Dr. Shehzad Saeed, tweeted about a denied Crohn's disease medication along with the child's painful rash, he received a response from insurance the next day and eventually got the medicine approved.
- When professor Miranda Yaver received a $30,000 bill for her hospital stay, calling her insurance led to long wait times. It was only when she tweeted and tagged Aetna that they quickly responded and reversed the insurance denial.
- When Sally Nix took to social media after being denied expensive infusions for a chronic illness, her story attracted media attention—suddenly $36,000 in claims were marked "paid."

These aren't isolated incidents but evidence of a powerful pattern: public shaming works when private appeals fail.

The strategy works because it flips the power dynamic. In a private appeal, the insurer controls the process, timeline, and outcome. On social media, the patient controls the narrative by exposing the company's behavior to customers, regulators, journalists, and lawmakers.

AMAZING HOW QUICKLY THEY FIND THE 'MEDICAL NECESSITY' WITH THE RIGHT APPEALS PROCESS!

"What they fear most is patterns becoming visible," one doctor told me. "One denial can be dismissed as an unfortunate mistake. Hundreds of denials with identical language suggest deliberate policy."

The strategy isn't foolproof. Not every viral post gets results. Companies sometimes wait out the storm, betting that public attention will shift elsewhere. And the process favors patients with large social networks, compelling stories, and social media savvy, potentially deepening inequities.

For those considering this approach, healthcare advocates recommend:

- Be factual and specific. Include denial language, doctor recommendations, and specific treatment information.
- Tag the insurance company and relevant regulators. Make it impossible to ignore.
- Protect privacy. Redact personal information while keeping company names and denial language visible.
- Connect with advocacy groups. Organizations can amplify your message.
- Document everything. If your insurance company contacts you after your post, get commitments in writing.

Perhaps most importantly, when you see others posting their denial stories, share them. The patient who helped you today may be you tomorrow.

COMMUNITY ORGANIZING FOR HEALTHCARE

Social media offers one pathway for collective action, but many of the most significant healthcare victories have come through old-fashioned community organizing—bringing patients together in physical spaces to build power and demand change.

One voice in person can sometimes make a greater impact than hundreds of online comments. When your congressional representatives hold town hall meetings, attend and ask specific questions about healthcare. Share your story briefly. For example, "My sister was denied life-saving treatment by her insurer; what will you do to hold insurance companies accountable?"

Politicians can ignore statistics, but they can't easily dismiss a constituent looking them in the eye and describing how their child was denied care. Those moments change minds.

Many states now allow virtual testimony, making it easier to participate in the legislative process even with time constraints or mobility challenges.

Effective healthcare organizing takes many forms:

Local Protests, Direct Action, and Public Testimony

When traditional advocacy fails, communities are turning to direct action and public testimony to confront insurers. In July 2024, over 100 patients, nurses, and advocates protested at UnitedHealth Group's headquarters, calling out an epidemic of claim denials amid record corporate profits. Some engaged in civil disobedience, risking arrest to spotlight the life-or-death impact of these decisions. This "Care Over Cost" campaign has rallied hundreds at insurance offices nationwide, combining demonstrations, personal testimonies, and petition deliveries to put human faces on denial statistics. Insurance companies prefer to keep denials invisible, happening in private homes where patients suffer silently. When hundreds gather at their headquarters holding photos of loved ones hurt by denials, that invisibility is shattered. These actions, along with town halls and public forums, allow patients to share their stories directly with policymakers and insurers, breaking the silence that often surrounds denied care and demanding accountability in person.

Grassroots Lobbying

Community groups often coordinate letter-writing campaigns, phone banks, and scheduled office visits to legislators. These efforts are most effective when they highlight local impact.

Medical students and patients formed coalitions like #ProtectOurPatients in 2017, holding rallies and phone banks and writing op-eds to local newspapers to build support for healthcare protections. These coordinated campaigns ensure that patient voices break through the noise of professional lobbyists.

Civil Disobedience

Sometimes dramatic action is needed to force attention on life-or-death issues. The disability rights group ADAPT has staged "die-ins" in congressional offices to dramatize how policy changes threaten lives. AIDS activists in the 1980s chained themselves to pharmaceutical headquarters to demand medication access.

Such tactics reflect the severity of healthcare injustice. When administrative processes fail and people are dying from denied care, civil disobedience becomes a moral response to immoral systems.

For those looking to get involved in healthcare organizing, start by:
- Finding local healthcare advocacy groups. Organizations like Healthcare-NOW and state-level Health Care for All chapters welcome new members.

- Sharing your story. Effective organizing begins with personal narratives that reveal systemic problems.
- Attending town halls and public meetings. Your elected officials should hear directly from you.
- Supporting those already organizing. If direct involvement isn't possible, donations and social media amplification help.

Remember: the healthcare system counts on your isolation. Community organizing breaks that isolation, connecting your individual struggle to a movement for change.

LEGISLATIVE ADVOCACY

Citizen advocacy, where ordinary people engage directly with the legislative process, can achieve healthcare reforms that might otherwise stall amid industry opposition. While professional lobbyists outnumber patient advocates in capitol hallways, research shows legislators are significantly influenced by constituent stories, especially when they highlight local impact.

The most effective legislative advocacy combines compelling personal narratives with broad grassroots pressure. The No Surprises Act, which protects patients from unexpected out-of-network bills, gained momentum after patients with enormous surprise bills were invited to the White House to share their stories. Their experiences—an $18,000 urine test, a $109,000 out-of-network heart attack bill—put human faces on a complex policy issue and helped push the bill through Congress.

Currently, prior authorization reform bills are gaining traction in states and Congress, propelled by patient horror stories of delayed or denied care. Federal regulators have proposed rules to rein in prior authorization delays, responding to persistent patient testimony about harmful impacts.

For those pursuing legislative change, the most effective strategies combine direct engagement, sustained public pressure, and electoral accountability. Advocacy organizations often coordinate "lobby days" where patients visit multiple legislators to amplify impact. Legislators are drowning in statistics. What cuts through are authentic stories from constituents, especially when there's a clear ask attached.

When CareYaya family caregiver Chelsea described her mother's multiple prior authorization delays to her congressman, she brought the actual denial letters and a timeline showing her mother waited 47 days for approval of urgent cardiac care. That specificity made the harm tangible in ways statistics couldn't.

Volume also matters. While individual stories open hearts, mass constituent contact overwhelms inboxes and phone lines, forcing lawmakers to prioritize the issue. Organized campaigns that generate thousands of messages via emails, calls, or petition signatures can shift the political calculus, especially when paired with direct lobbying. Legislative committees often hold hearings before voting on healthcare bills. Being selected to testify provides a powerful platform to shape the conversation as committee testimonies become part of the official record.

Ultimately, legislators respond to electoral pressure. Advocacy groups mobilize voters around healthcare issues, support candidates who prioritize patients' interests, and hold officials accountable for their healthcare votes. Organizations like Protect Our Care emerged after 2017 to campaign for candidates pledging to uphold healthcare protections. The 2018 midterms saw many candidates win on healthcare platforms, demonstrating the issue's electoral power. Citizen-driven advocacy has directly contributed to major policy victories like surprise billing protections. Mental health parity laws, requiring insurance to cover mental health on par with physical health, gained momentum through family advocacy. Cancer patient navigation programs, pediatric care mandates, and rare disease research funding have all advanced through persistent citizen lobbying.

STATES AS LABORATORIES: REFORM SUCCESS STORIES

States have pioneered patient protections that later became federal policy. Before the No Surprises Act, 33 states had enacted some form of surprise billing protection, with 18 states implementing comprehensive laws covering both emergency and in-network hospital services. These state policies became templates for the federal legislation that now protects all Americans.

Similarly, state insurance departments have created strong external review systems that overturn unjust denials. California's independent medical review (IMR) system is particularly robust. New data shows 60% of "not medically necessary" denials and 80% of "experimental" treatment denials get reversed through IMR or insurer reconsideration. These high reversal rates both help individual patients and expose systemic problems in initial coverage decisions.

Other innovative state reforms include Maryland operating a unique all-payer hospital rate system that controls costs while reducing disparities, and Colorado and Washington implementing state-designed public option plans to lower premiums on their insurance exchanges.

For patients and advocates seeking state-level change, effective approaches include:

- **Ballot Initiatives Where Available**: In the 24 states with ballot initiative processes, citizens can bypass reluctant legislators and take reforms directly to voters. This pathway has proven particularly effective for Medicaid expansion and drug pricing reforms. The Fairness Project, a nonprofit that supports healthcare ballot measures, has helped win Medicaid expansion in six states through this process. Their success demonstrates how direct democracy can overcome partisan resistance when policies have broad public support.
- **State Regulatory Advocacy**: Insurance is primarily regulated at the state level, giving state insurance commissioners significant authority over insurer practices. Patients can file complaints with these regulators and push for stronger oversight.
- **Coalition Building in State Capitals**: Successful state reforms typically emerge from broad coalitions uniting diverse stakeholders around common goals. These "strange bedfellows" alliances—patient groups alongside business interests, physicians alongside community organizations—can overcome traditional political divisions. In New York's ongoing campaign for a state single-payer plan (NY Health Act), a coalition unites nurses, labor unions, faith communities, and small business owners who all see benefits in comprehensive reform.

The state-level approach offers several advantages: reforms can be tailored to local needs, implementation happens closer to affected communities, and success in one state often creates momentum elsewhere. Most importantly, state victories provide concrete evidence that reforms work, building cases for national adoption.

CLASS ACTION POWER

Class-action lawsuits allow many people harmed by the same practice to unite their claims, creating accountability that would be impossible to achieve case-by-case. For patients facing wrongful insurance denials, class actions offer several advantages:

- Power in numbers. While insurers can easily dismiss individual complaints, a lawsuit representing thousands of patients demands attention.
- Pattern exposure. Class actions reveal systematic practices rather than

"isolated incidents."
- Judicial oversight. Courts can order industry-wide changes that benefit even non-plaintiffs.
- Financial consequences. Significant settlements provide both justice for victims and deterrence against future abuses.

Recent class actions have challenged some of the insurance industry's most problematic practices:

In 2023, a class-action lawsuit was filed against Cigna after investigative reports showed the insurer was using an algorithm (called PXDX) to automatically deny claims in batches without proper individual review. Plaintiffs allege this practice affected potentially hundreds of thousands of claims, essentially cheating patients out of coverage.

Even more significant was the landmark Wit v. United Behavioral Health case, which exposed how a major insurer used internally crafted medical necessity criteria to systematically deny coverage for mental health and addiction treatment. After a trial, a federal judge excoriated UBH's practices and ordered reprocessing of over 67,000 claims. The case drew support from the U.S. Department of Labor and state attorneys general, showing how class actions can rally broader institutional allies.

Building effective class actions requires several elements:

Identifying Patterns and Plaintiffs

Advocacy groups often hear from numerous patients about similar denials, revealing patterns suitable for class actions. Patient support groups, social media communities, and healthcare providers can help identify potential plaintiffs experiencing the same insurance practices.

"We look for commonality and typicality," explained a consumer rights attorney. "Are many patients being harmed in the same way by the same policy or practice? Is it something systematic rather than individual reviewer error?"

The Cigna algorithm case began when investigative journalists noticed similar language in many denial letters, suggesting automated rather than individualized review. This reporting helped attorneys identify potential plaintiffs for the class action.

Building Legal Theories

Class actions typically claim violations such as breach of contract, bad faith insurance practices, consumer protection law violations, or ERISA violations (for employer plans). The strongest cases identify specific laws or contractual provisions the insurer has violated.

In the Wit case, attorneys argued that UBH violated its fiduciary duty under ERISA by developing review criteria designed to save money rather than reflect accepted clinical standards. This clear legal theory, supported by internal company documents, convinced the court that systematic reform was necessary.

Finding Litigation Partners

Class actions require substantial resources and expertise. Patients typically partner with:
- Consumer rights law firms that specialize in insurance cases
- Public interest legal organizations focused on healthcare access
- State attorneys general who may pursue parallel enforcement actions
- Patient advocacy organizations that can help organize plaintiffs

These partnerships combine patients' experiences with legal and strategic expertise.

The impact of successful class actions extends far beyond monetary settlements. They generate publicity that pressures the entire industry, expose internal practices that might otherwise remain hidden, and create precedents that strengthen patient rights.

In the UBH trial, for example, internal emails revealed executives prioritizing cost savings over patient care, galvanizing calls for stricter mental health parity enforcement nationwide. Even when insurers appeal initial verdicts (as UBH did), the exposure of their practices changes the public conversation.

For patients considering participation in class actions:
- Document everything. Save all denial letters, communications with the insurer, and medical records supporting your claim.
- Connect with advocacy organizations. Groups like the Patient Advocate Foundation can help identify potential class actions related to your issue.
- Share your story. Attorneys building class cases actively seek patients affected by particular insurance practices.
- Be prepared for a long process. Class actions often take years to resolve.

Class actions complement other advocacy strategies. While community organizing and legislative advocacy change rules going forward, litigation can address past harms and force compliance with existing laws. Together, these approaches create a comprehensive accountability system for insurance practices.

MEDIA AS MEGAPHONE

"I never wanted to be on the news," Elaine told me, her voice still carrying traces of disbelief. "I'm a private person. But when my husband's stroke treatment was denied, and we were facing $218,000 in bills, I was desperate."

A friend suggested Elaine contact the local newspaper's healthcare reporter. Three days after her story ran—detailing how the insurer claimed her husband's emergency airlift to a stroke center was "not medically necessary" despite following established protocols—the insurance company called.

"They said it was all a 'processing error,'" Elaine recalled. "The claim was suddenly approved in full. They even apologized for the 'inconvenience,' as if they hadn't spent months telling us the denial was final."

Elaine's experience illustrates how media coverage can transform individual insurance disputes. When journalists highlight patient stories, they create accountability that internal processes often fail to provide. Insurance companies fear reputational damage far more than individual appeals.

Advocacy groups have developed sophisticated strategies for working with media to expose healthcare injustices and drive reforms:

Cultivating Media Relationships

Successful advocates build ongoing relationships with health journalists and investigative reporters. They provide these journalists with compelling cases, data, and expert commentary that illustrate systemic issues.

"Reporters need both personal stories and broader context," explained a communication strategist. "The most effective approach combines a powerful individual narrative with data showing it's not an isolated incident."

Organizations often maintain "press-ready" lists of patients willing to be interviewed, making journalists' jobs easier. They also respond quickly to news hooks. If an insurance executive makes headlines or a healthcare policy is being debated, advocates are ready with relevant patient stories.

High-Impact Reporting Examples

Several investigative journalism projects have directly led to policy change:

"Bill of the Month" Series: A joint KFF Health News-NPR monthly series examines outrageous medical bills. Since 2018, it has analyzed nearly $6.3

million in medical bills and spurred numerous improvements. Some featured patients found their bills reduced after publicity, and the series put surprise billing on the national agenda. Two patients from this series were even invited to the White House to share their stories, experiences which helped drive Congress to pass the No Surprises Act.

Insurance Practice Investigations: As mentioned in previous chapters, CNN revealed a former Aetna medical director admitted under oath that he never reviewed patient records when approving or denying coverage. This report led California's Insurance Commissioner to launch an investigation into Aetna's practices. Similarly, a 2023 *ProPublica* exposé uncovered Cigna's algorithmic claim denials, triggering both class-action lawsuits and regulatory scrutiny.

Local News Impact: Local journalism remains powerful in healthcare advocacy. Local TV stations running "Patient Advocate" segments have helped countless individuals get unjust denials reversed. These human-interest stories not only aid specific patients but pressure insurers to review similar cases to avoid additional negative coverage.

Media-Driven Policy Change

Sustained media attention often creates momentum for legislative or regulatory action. Investigative reporting on insulin prices and resulting patient deaths created public pressure that contributed to both state insulin copay caps and Medicare insulin price negotiation in the Inflation Reduction Act.

Another example: after the *Los Angeles Times* ran a series about patients forced into expensive procedures because insurance refused simpler drug options, lawmakers began discussing reforms to step-therapy requirements.

For patients and advocates seeking media attention:

- Focus on clear injustice. The most compelling stories feature stark contrasts between medical recommendations and insurance decisions.
- Be specific and factual. Include denial language, coverage terms, and relevant timelines.
- Connect individual stories to systematic problems. Help reporters see how your experience reflects broader patterns.
- Prepare concise talking points. Media opportunities often provide limited time to tell complex stories.
- Consider privacy boundaries. Decide in advance what medical details you're comfortable sharing publicly.

While media exposure is powerful, it comes with limitations. Not every worthy case attracts coverage. Media attention can be fleeting. And the strategy favors those with compelling narratives and communication skills, potentially reinforcing inequities.

Nevertheless, strategic media engagement remains one of advocacy's most powerful tools. By partnering with journalists, patients transform private suffering into public accountability and often catalyze broader reforms.

"The insurance company counted on our silence," Elaine told me. "Going public felt uncomfortable, but it was the only thing that worked. Now I tell everyone don't suffer quietly. Your story has power."

BUILDING COALITIONS FOR HEALTHCARE REFORM

The most successful healthcare reforms have something in common: they emerge not from single-issue campaigns but from broad coalitions uniting diverse stakeholders. By bringing together patient advocates, healthcare providers, labor unions, business interests, faith communities, and more, these alliances create unstoppable momentum for change.

Coalition power extends beyond national legislation to focused reforms like prescription drug pricing. The alliance Lower Drug Prices Now brings together patient advocates, seniors' organizations like AARP, nurses' and teachers' unions, and businesses struggling with employee drug costs. This coalition coordinated rallies nationwide featuring patients and community members demanding Medicare drug price negotiation. Their sustained pressure contributed significantly to the drug pricing provisions in the 2022 Inflation Reduction Act.

Effective coalitions leverage each partner's unique strengths:
- Patient groups provide powerful personal stories and moral urgency
- Healthcare providers contribute clinical expertise and credibility
- Labor unions offer organizing capacity and political influence
- Faith communities bring moral authority and community connections
- Business interests present economic arguments and practical impact
- Policy organizations supply data and legislative expertise

This diversity creates a "surround sound" effect, addressing healthcare issues from multiple angles simultaneously and making it harder for opponents to dismiss the coalition as representing narrow interests.

"Coalitions work because they prevent divide-and-conquer tactics," explained a veteran organizer, Mehreen. "When patients, doctors, nurses, employers, and community leaders all demand the same reform, politicians can't play one group against another."

Particularly effective are partnerships between patient advocates and healthcare professionals. When physicians join patients in highlighting insurance abuses, it becomes impossible to dismiss complaints as misunderstandings of medical necessity. The American Medical Association has worked alongside patient coalitions to streamline prior authorization, with both groups testifying to the harm caused by unnecessary delays.

Even unusual "strange bedfellows" coalitions form around specific issues where interests align. For surprise billing reform, consumer advocates joined forces with large employers and insurers against physician staffing firms and hospitals—an unconventional alignment that helped overcome legislative gridlock.

Building effective healthcare coalitions requires several key elements:

Clear, Specific Goals

Successful coalitions unite around concrete objectives rather than broad ideals. "Lower drug prices" is less effective than "Allow Medicare to negotiate prices for the 20 most expensive medications."

The surprise billing coalition succeeded partly because its goal was specific and understandable: protect patients from unexpected out-of-network charges when they receive care at in-network facilities.

Diverse but Cohesive Membership

Strong coalitions include organizations representing different constituencies while maintaining sufficient alignment on core principles. This diversity strengthens the coalition's reach while giving members flexibility on secondary issues.

In New York's ongoing campaign for a state single-payer system (NY Health Act), the coalition involves nurses' unions, immigrant rights groups, disability advocates, and faith organizations. While these groups may differ on other policies, they find common ground in universal healthcare.

Coordinated Messaging

Effective coalitions develop shared language and messaging discipline. All participants communicate key points consistently while tailoring delivery to their specific audiences.

Strategic Division of Labor

Coalitions distribute responsibilities based on member strengths. Some organizations excel at grassroots mobilization, others at policy analysis, media relations, or direct lobbying. By coordinating these activities, coalitions maximize impact across multiple fronts simultaneously.

For those seeking to join or build healthcare coalitions:

- Start local. Community-level coalitions often achieve concrete victories while building capacity for larger campaigns.
- Identify shared interests. Focus on goals that genuinely benefit all potential partners.
- Respect differences. Strong coalitions acknowledge where members disagree while emphasizing common ground.
- Celebrate incremental wins. Coalition sustainability depends on regular victories, however modest.

The coalition approach to healthcare advocacy recognizes a fundamental truth: the problems patients face are interconnected and systemic, requiring solutions that transcend individual organizations or single-issue campaigns. By bringing diverse voices together in strategic alignment, coalitions create the breadth and depth of support necessary for meaningful reform.

YOUR ROLE IN HEALTHCARE CHANGE

Throughout this chapter, we've explored powerful strategies for collective action: social media campaigns that reverse denials, community organizing that changes corporate policies, labor actions that secure better benefits, legislative advocacy that creates new patient protections, class actions that challenge systemic abuses, media partnerships that expose injustice, and coalitions that drive comprehensive reform.

These approaches share a common theme of transforming isolated patients into connected advocates with collective power. They replace resignation with action, helplessness with agency.

You might wonder, "What's my role in this larger movement?" The answer depends on your circumstances, capacity, and interests, but everyone can contribute to healthcare change. Here are pathways for engagement:

Share Your Story

Your healthcare experiences have power beyond your individual case. By sharing them strategically, you can expose patterns and inspire others.

Consider posting denial letters on social media (redacting personal information but naming the insurance company). Submit your story to patient advocacy organizations or healthcare journalists. Testify at legislative hearings or regulatory forums: each shared experience builds the case for systemic reform.

"I was reluctant to go public with my insurance nightmare," said Dan, a caregiver we supported. "But after my story appeared in the local paper, three people contacted me with identical denials from the same insurer. We filed a group complaint with the insurance commissioner, and all our claims were eventually approved. My story helped others, and their solidarity helped me."

Join Existing Organizations

Countless groups work for healthcare justice, from national organizations like Families USA to state-level "Health Care for All" chapters to condition-specific advocacy groups. These organizations provide structure, resources, and community for emerging advocates.

Research shows that sustained engagement is more likely within supportive groups than through isolated action. Organizations also provide training, strategic guidance, and connections to broader movements.

Focus on Winnable Victories

While comprehensive healthcare reform remains a long-term goal, near-term victories build momentum and improve real lives today. Focus initially on concrete, achievable changes that directly address harm.

Leverage Professional Skills

Everyone has valuable skills for healthcare advocacy. Lawyers can review policies and assist with appeals. Healthcare professionals can explain medical necessity and industry practices. Communications experts can craft compelling messages. Business leaders can highlight economic impacts. Educators can develop accessible materials explaining complex systems.

Consider how your professional expertise might address healthcare injustices, then connect with advocacy groups that could benefit from those skills.

Build Bridges

Healthcare reform requires unlikely alliances across traditional divides. Look for opportunities to connect different constituencies around common healthcare concerns.

Practice Resilience and Self-Care

Healthcare advocacy can be emotionally taxing, especially when it stems from personal trauma. Sustainable activism requires boundaries, support systems, and self-care.

"I couldn't fight effectively while drowning in my own healthcare trauma," shared a patient advocate. "Finding a support group of fellow advocates helped me transform pain into purpose without burning out."

Remember the Power of Small Actions

Not everyone can lead organizations or file lawsuits, but small, consistent actions create meaningful change:
- Sharing accurate healthcare information in your community
- Supporting others navigating insurance appeals
- Contacting representatives about healthcare legislation
- Amplifying advocacy campaigns through social media
- Voting for candidates who prioritize patient protections

These seemingly modest contributions, multiplied across thousands of engaged citizens, create the foundation for transformative change.

THE PATH FORWARD

The healthcare system profits from your isolation. Insurance companies design denial letters to make you feel powerless and alone. Billing departments count on your shame about medical debt. Politicians hope your healthcare frustrations remain private complaints rather than public demands.

But as we've seen throughout this chapter, that isolation is an illusion. Millions share your healthcare struggles. Thousands are organizing to change the system. Hundreds of advocacy organizations stand ready to support your participation.

The path from individual suffering to collective power begins with a single step of connecting your personal healthcare experience to the larger movement for change. That connection transforms both you and the movement. Adding your unique voice to a growing chorus demanding a healthcare system that serves patients rather than exploiting them.

In the next chapter, we'll explore specific policy reforms that could fundamentally reshape American healthcare. But those reforms will remain theoretical without the organizing strategies we've discussed here. Policy without power rarely produces change.

The insurance executive denying claims, the hospital administrator implementing aggressive billing practices, the politician accepting healthcare industry donations—all are counting on your surrender. They're betting that you'll accept denial letters as final, pay inflated bills without questions, and keep healthcare frustrations private.

Prove them wrong. Share your story. Join with others. Demand better. The most powerful force in healthcare isn't technology, money, or politics. It's people united in the belief that healthcare should be a right, not a privilege.

When it comes to transforming American healthcare, that change begins with you.

10

THE THREE-LAYER SOLUTION

"A dream you dream alone is only a dream. A dream you dream together is reality."

— John Lennon

Diana Sanchez was a 35-year-old therapist in Texas with what she believed was excellent health insurance, Diana never expected to find herself on the verge of losing their home.

"We had insurance. Good insurance," she told me. "But after David's accident, the bills just kept coming. The insurance company kept saying these things weren't covered or were out-of-network. How was I supposed to know that when he was unconscious in an ambulance?"

Her husband David, a construction foreman, had fallen from scaffolding, suffering a traumatic brain injury and multiple fractures. Despite their "comprehensive" insurance policy, the Sanchez family now faced over $160,000 in medical debt. Their retirement savings were gone. Their credit was ruined.

"I did everything they tell you to do," she said. "I got a stable job with benefits. We saved. We had insurance. And one accident still destroyed everything we built."

I've sat with hundreds of families like the Sanchezes. These aren't people who've made irresponsible choices. They're your neighbors, your child's teacher, your colleague, your family members. And they're one medical emergency away from financial ruin.

But it doesn't have to be this way.

I am convinced that we need a fundamentally different approach—one that blends universal protection against catastrophic costs with the best aspects of market-driven innovation and consumer choice: an approach that would have protected the Sanchez family while preserving what actually works in American healthcare.

What we need is a three-layer solution.

This approach isn't partisan fantasy or academic theory. It's a practical, implementable strategy drawn from successful elements around the world and right here in America. And most importantly, it addresses the fundamental problems that are bankrupting families like the Sanchezes while avoiding the political gridlock that has blocked meaningful reform.

In this chapter, I'll walk you through each component of this solution, show you how the pieces fit together, and outline a realistic path forward.

A NEW FRAMEWORK FOR AMERICAN HEALTHCARE

Imagine a healthcare system where:
- No American ever faces financial ruin from medical bills
- You can see a primary care doctor whenever you need to without worrying about costs
- You have real control over your healthcare dollars and can choose the providers you want
- Prices are transparent, allowing you to make informed decisions
- Doctors spend their time caring for patients rather than fighting with insurance companies
- Competition drives innovation and keeps costs reasonable
- Technology enhances rather than complicates your healthcare experience

This isn't a utopian fantasy. It's entirely achievable through a comprehensive approach I call the Three-Layer Solution.

At its core, the Three-Layer Solution combines three fundamental elements:
- Universal Catastrophic Coverage: A public insurance program that protects everyone from financially ruinous medical expenses
- Expanded Health Savings Accounts (HSA): Empowering individuals to control their healthcare dollars for routine expenses

- Direct Care Revolution: Subscription-based healthcare models that eliminate insurance bureaucracy for everyday care

These three layers are reinforced by crucial supporting reforms:

- Aggressive antitrust enforcement to restore competition
- Comprehensive price transparency requirements
- Administrative simplification to cut wasteful paperwork
- Technology integration that actually serves patients and providers

Together, these elements create a healthcare system that balances universal protection with individual choice and market-driven efficiency.

This might sound ambitious, and it is. But each component has already proven effective in various contexts. The innovation lies in combining them into a cohesive system that addresses the fundamental flaws in our current approach.

While policies like the ACA may have been well-intentioned in expanding coverage, the implementation created unintended consequences that we must acknowledge. The complex regulations inadvertently favored large incumbents with resources to navigate the regulatory landscape, while disadvantaging smaller, more innovative healthcare organizations. This regulatory environment accelerated consolidation, leading to the rise of mega-insurers and health systems that now dominate markets across America.

The concerning reality is that major insurers like UnitedHealth now effectively control approximately 10% of physician practices through various subsidiaries, while the Aetna-CVS merger created a behemoth controlling both insurance and pharmacy benefits. This vertical integration has proven detrimental to patients, physicians, and healthcare quality, while benefiting corporate shareholders.

Rather than further expanding the government's role, we need targeted reforms that break up consolidated power, enforce stronger antitrust policies to prevent harmful mergers, and create incentives for innovation and competition among smaller healthcare entities. The Three-Layer Solution addresses these issues by combining universal protection with market mechanisms that reward innovation rather than regulatory expertise.

Let's examine each element in detail, starting with the foundation: ensuring no American ever faces bankruptcy from medical bills.

UNIVERSAL CATASTROPHIC COVERAGE

Remember Diana and David Sanchez? Their nightmare began when David suffered a severe accident. Despite having insurance, they faced over $160,000 in medical debt that destroyed their financial security. Under Universal Catastrophic Coverage (UCC), their story would have ended very differently.

Universal Catastrophic Coverage is exactly what it sounds like: a public insurance program that covers very high medical expenses for every American. It's designed to prevent exactly the kind of financial catastrophe the Sanchez family experienced.

Here's how it works:

Every American would have protection against ruinous medical expenses through a public insurance program. For lower-income Americans, this coverage would start from the first dollar of care. For middle- and higher-income households, coverage would kick in after they've spent a certain percentage of their income on healthcare.

Under one UCC proposal, a family of four earning $50,000 might have a $2,500 deductible, while a family earning $100,000 would have a $7,500 deductible. Above those thresholds, all costs would be covered.

If the Sanchez family had UCC, their maximum financial exposure might have been around $5,000 based on their income, not the $160,000 that devastated them. That's a life-changing difference.

Design Principles

Several key principles distinguish UCC from other reform proposals:

- Income-based protection: Unlike one-size-fits-all approaches, UCC recognizes that what's "catastrophic" depends on your financial situation. A $5,000 medical bill might be manageable for a high-income household but devastating for a low-income family. That's why deductibles would increase proportionately with income, providing full coverage for the poorest Americans while requiring those with more resources to pay a reasonable share.
- Universal coverage: Everyone is included automatically. No enrollment periods, no losing coverage when you change jobs, no complex eligibility criteria. This universality dramatically reduces administrative costs while ensuring no one falls through the cracks.
- Targeted government role: Rather than replacing the entire healthcare system, UCC focuses government intervention where it's most needed: protecting people from financial disaster. This targeted approach avoids disrupting aspects of the system that work well while fixing its most catastrophic failure.

- Preventive care exemption: Most UCC proposals exempt preventive services from deductibles, recognizing that an ounce of prevention is worth a pound of cure, both medically and financially.

Practical Funding Approaches

The obvious question: how do we pay for this?

The surprising answer: largely by redirecting money we're already spending.

Americans currently pay for healthcare through a complex patchwork of premiums, taxes, deductibles, and out-of-pocket costs. UCC would consolidate much of this spending into a more efficient and equitable system.

Several funding models are viable:
- Dedicated tax funding: A per-capita tax or income-based premium could fund UCC, replacing much of what people currently pay for private insurance. For most Americans, this wouldn't represent new spending but rather a shift from private premiums to a public program that offers better protection.
- Reallocating current subsidies: The federal government already spends hundreds of billions annually on healthcare subsidies—from tax exclusions for employer-sponsored insurance to ACA marketplace subsidies. Redirecting these funds could cover much of UCC's cost.
- Cost controls: By consolidating catastrophic coverage under one program, UCC could negotiate better rates for expensive procedures and hospitalizations, similar to how Medicare currently operates but with improved efficiency.

Several analyses suggest UCC could be implemented without increasing total healthcare spending and might even reduce it through administrative savings and better price negotiations.

Implementation Paths

How do we get from here to there without massive disruption? Several implementation paths are possible:
- Federal program with private administration: The government could contract with private insurers to administer identical catastrophic plans for all Americans, similar to how MA works today.
- Integration with existing programs: UCC could build on the ACA framework, modifying exchange plans to become catastrophic policies with income-based subsidies. Medicare could expand to cover catastrophic costs for all ages.

- State-based pilots: States could test UCC using innovation waivers, combining federal funds with state resources to create state-level catastrophic programs.
- Phased rollout: Implementation could begin with specific populations (children, older adults) or income levels, gradually expanding to cover everyone.

The key is maintaining existing coverage during transition while steadily moving toward the new system. No abrupt changes, no coverage gaps, just a methodical transition to better protection for all.

EXPANDED HEALTH SAVINGS ACCOUNTS

While UCC protects against major medical expenses, most healthcare involves routine services that fall below catastrophic thresholds. For these everyday needs, we need a financing mechanism that empowers patients while encouraging cost-conscious choices.

Enter expanded HSAs, or financial accounts that allow individuals to save tax-free dollars for healthcare expenses.

Current HSAs are severely limited. You can only contribute if you have a qualified high-deductible health plan. Contribution limits are relatively low ($4,150 individual/$8,300 family in 2024), and you can't use HSA funds to pay for insurance premiums or many types of direct care.

These limitations have prevented HSAs from reaching their full potential as a tool for patient empowerment. But with key expansions, HSAs could become a cornerstone of a more patient-centered system.

The Patient-Controlled Healthcare Dollar

Consider Josh, who has type 2 diabetes. Josh pays $350 monthly for insulin and supplies, plus quarterly endocrinologist visits at $200 each. Under today's system, he juggles insurance claims, prior authorizations, and pharmacy benefits managers, often paying full price until he meets his deductible.

With an expanded HSA, Josh could:
- Contribute significantly more pre-tax dollars to his account
- Shop for the best prices on insulin and supplies, using price transparency tools
- Pay a direct care endocrinologist a monthly subscription fee for unlimited care
- Maintain funds for emergency needs while covering routine expenses

The difference isn't just financial but also psychological. Instead of being a passive recipient of whatever care his insurance decides to cover, Josh becomes an active consumer making informed choices about his healthcare dollars.

Policy Changes to Empower Patients

Several key policy changes would transform HSAs into powerful tools for healthcare consumers:

- **Decoupling from high-deductible plans**: Anyone should be able to open and contribute to an HSA, regardless of their insurance status. This simple change would make HSAs available to millions more Americans.
- **Dramatically higher contribution limits**: Annual limits should increase substantially—perhaps matching 401(k) retirement contribution limits (around $23,000 in 2024). This would allow people to build significant healthcare savings over time.
- **Expanded qualified expenses**: HSA funds should be usable for insurance premiums, direct care memberships, and a broader range of wellness services. This flexibility would give patients more options for how they spend their healthcare dollars.
- **Seeding accounts for lower-income Americans**: To ensure equity, the government could contribute to HSAs for low-income individuals, similar to how some 401(k) plans offer employer matches. This would give everyone access to the benefits of patient-controlled healthcare dollars.

These changes would transform HSAs from a niche tax benefit primarily used by the affluent into a universal tool for healthcare financing and patient empowerment.

Making Patient Control Viable

For expanded HSAs to truly empower patients, several conditions must be met:

- **Price transparency**: Patients need to know what services cost before making decisions. Recent federal rules requiring hospitals and insurers to publish prices are a start, but we need comprehensive, user-friendly tools that make comparison shopping easy.
- **Consumer education**: Americans need better financial literacy around healthcare spending. Education campaigns and simple tools could help people make informed choices with their HSA dollars.

- **Sufficient funding**: To ensure HSAs don't just benefit the wealthy, policies must help lower and middle-income families build adequate balances. This could include tax credits, government contributions, or employer matches targeted at those with fewer resources.

When these conditions are met, patients can become true consumers in the healthcare marketplace, creating pressure for better service, lower prices, and more innovation.

DIRECT PRIMARY CARE

The third layer of the solution addresses how care is delivered and paid for, particularly for routine, predictable services. DPC is the most established model in this revolution. Here's how it typically works:

- Patients pay a monthly fee directly to their primary care practice, usually $50-100 for adults
- This fee covers all or most primary care services: check-ups, sick visits, basic procedures, often some lab tests
- No insurance billing or claims. The monthly fee is the only payment
- Physicians maintain smaller patient panels (600-800 vs. 2,000+ in traditional practice)
- Patients get longer appointments, same-day access, and often direct communication with their doctor

The benefits extend beyond convenience. By eliminating the insurance middleman, DPC practices operate with about 40% less overhead, allowing more resources to go toward patient care. And because physicians spend more time with patients, they can address problems before they become serious, potentially reducing downstream costs for emergency care and hospitalizations.

Expanding the Direct Model

The direct care revolution is spreading beyond primary care:
- **Direct specialty care**: Specialists in fields like endocrinology, cardiology, and gynecology are adopting subscription models for patients with ongoing needs. Instead of billing per visit, these specialists offer comprehensive care for a monthly fee.
- **Surgery centers with transparent pricing**: Facilities like the Surgery Center of Oklahoma publish all-inclusive cash prices for procedures, often 50-80% lower than hospital charges. These centers work directly with patients or employers, avoiding insurance markup and

administrative costs.
- **Transparent imaging and testing**: Companies like Green Imaging offer MRIs, CT scans, and other diagnostic services at a fraction of hospital prices, with clear upfront costs instead of the surprise bills that often come from traditional providers.
- **Membership-based urgent care**: Some urgent care centers now offer unlimited visits for a monthly fee, providing an affordable alternative to expensive emergency room visits for non-life-threatening issues.

Each of these models strips away the complexity, opacity, and administrative waste of traditional healthcare financing, replacing it with simple, transparent pricing and direct relationships between providers and patients.

Real-World Impact

The direct care model creates significant benefits for both patients and providers:

For patients:
- Predictable costs without surprise bills
- Better access to care when needed
- Longer appointments and more personalized attention
- No fighting with insurance companies
- Often lower total costs for routine care

For providers:
- More time with patients
- Drastically reduced paperwork and administrative burden
- Professional autonomy and clinical independence
- Sustainable practice model without burnout
- Ability to practice medicine according to their values

Early research suggests direct care models can also reduce overall healthcare costs. A Milliman analysis found DPC patients had 25-35% fewer hospital admissions and emergency room visits compared to traditionally insured patients. When combined with catastrophic coverage for major expenses, direct care can provide comprehensive protection at a lower total cost.

Barriers to Growth and How to Overcome Them

Despite its benefits, the direct care model faces several barriers to widespread adoption:
- **Regulatory uncertainty**: Many states lack clear definitions of direct care, creating concern that these practices might be regulated as

insurance. Legislation explicitly defining direct care as a medical service model (not insurance) would remove this barrier.
- **Payment restrictions**: Current IRS rules make it difficult to use HSA funds for direct care memberships. Policy changes allowing HSA payment for direct care would accelerate adoption.
- **Integration challenges**: Direct care works well for routine services but must coordinate with insurance for major expenses. Better integration between direct care practices and insurers or hospitals would create a more seamless experience.
- **Awareness and education**: Many patients and providers simply don't know these models exist or understand how they work. Education campaigns targeting both groups could accelerate adoption.

These barriers are significant but surmountable. With appropriate policy changes and continued growth, direct care could transform from a niche alternative to a mainstream approach for routine healthcare.

REINFORCING REFORMS FOR MAKING THE SYSTEM WORK

The three core layers—Universal Catastrophic Coverage, Expanded HSAs, and Direct Care—provide the foundation for a transformed healthcare system. But like any foundation, they need supporting structures to function optimally. Four key reforms would reinforce the Three-Layer Solution:

Antitrust Enforcement: Restoring Competitive Markets

Hospital prices in Northern California are approximately 70% higher than in Southern California. Why? One dominant health system, Sutter Health, controls much of the Northern California market, while Southern California has more competition.

This isn't an isolated example. Over the past two decades, healthcare has undergone massive consolidation, with hospitals merging into large regional systems and buying up physician practices. This consolidation drives up prices without improving quality.

Studies consistently show that hospital mergers lead to price increases of 20-40% in concentrated markets, with no reliable improvement in care quality. When a dominant system controls most hospitals and physicians in a region, they can essentially name their price. And they do.

Effective antitrust enforcement is essential to restore competition:
- **Blocking anti-competitive mergers**: Federal agencies should

aggressively scrutinize and challenge hospital, insurer, and physician practice mergers that threaten competition. Recent successes, like blocking the Anthem-Cigna and Aetna-Humana mergers, show this approach can work.
- **Challenging anti-competitive practices**: Beyond mergers, regulators should target practices that stifle competition, such as anti-steering clauses that prevent insurers from directing patients to lower-cost providers. California's successful case against Sutter Health, which ended such practices, provides a template.
- **Addressing cumulative effects**: Many healthcare markets face "death by a thousand cuts" as dominant systems acquire individual physician practices that, taken alone, don't trigger antitrust review. Regulators should examine these cumulative effects and challenge patterns of acquisitions that create market power.
- **Promoting new entrants**: Removing barriers to new competition, like restrictive Certificate of Need laws that prevent new facilities from opening, can introduce competitive pressure even in concentrated markets.

Without these efforts, the benefits of the Three-Layer Solution would be limited. Patients with HSAs can't effectively shop for better value if every provider in their area charges inflated prices. UCC would pay more than necessary if it must reimburse monopoly providers. Competition is the oxygen that allows market-based reforms to breathe.

Price Transparency: Empowering Informed Choices

Imagine buying a car without knowing the price until weeks after you drive it off the lot. Or ordering at a restaurant where prices are revealed only when the bill arrives. Sounds absurd, right? Yet this is exactly how healthcare has operated for decades.

Recent federal rules aim to change this. As of 2021, hospitals must publish their prices, including negotiated rates with insurers. Starting in 2022-2023, insurers must disclose their negotiated rates and provide online tools showing patients their expected costs.

Early compliance was poor—an early 2022 review found only 14% of hospitals fully compliant with transparency requirements. But enforcement is improving, with higher penalties for non-compliance and more hospitals publishing usable data.

The impact could be significant. When prices become transparent, several positive changes occur:
- **Patient empowerment**: With clear prices, patients can make informed choices about where to receive care, especially for non-emergency services like imaging, elective surgeries, or routine tests.
- **Provider competition**: When patients can compare prices, providers face pressure to justify price differences or reduce inflated charges. Early evidence suggests some hospitals have lowered prices for shoppable services in response to transparency.
- **Employer leverage**: Self-insured employers can use price data to
- negotiate better rates or design benefits that steer employees toward high-value providers. This creates market pressure for reasonable pricing.
- **Elimination of price outliers**: Transparency exposes extreme price variations, which makes such variations harder to maintain.

For the Three-Layer Solution to work optimally, we need to go beyond current requirements:
- **Real-time, personalized price estimates**: Patients should be able to get binding quotes before receiving care, reflecting their specific insurance status and deductible situation.
- **Integrated price comparison tools**: Price information should be integrated into provider directories, scheduling systems, and electronic health records, making cost comparisons seamless.
- **Quality transparency alongside price**: Price information is most useful when paired with quality metrics, allowing patients to assess value, not just cost.

With comprehensive transparency, patients with HSAs become true consumers, direct care providers can demonstrate their value proposition, and UCC can negotiate fair rates for catastrophic care.

Administrative Simplification: Cutting the Paperwork Burden

The U.S. healthcare system drowns in paperwork. Administrative costs consume between 15-30% of healthcare spending where hundreds of billions of dollars that could otherwise go toward actual care.

A primary care physician I spoke with, put it bluntly: "I spend more time fighting with insurance companies than I do with patients. That's not why I went to medical school."

The causes of this administrative waste are numerous:

- **Multiplicity of payers**: Providers deal with dozens of insurance companies, each with different forms, rules, and payment rates.
- **Complex benefit designs**: The proliferation of plan types, each with its own network, formularies, and authorization requirements, creates enormous complexity.
- **Prior authorization requirements**: Insurers often require approval for tests, medications, or procedures, forcing providers to submit documentation and wait for decisions.
- **Fragmented medical records**: Lack of interoperability between systems means information is often manually transferred or duplicated.

Several reforms could dramatically reduce this burden:

- **Standardized billing and clearinghouse**: Creating a single portal for all healthcare claims would eliminate the need to manage different submission processes for each insurer. Providers could submit claims once, in a standard format, and the clearinghouse would route them to the appropriate payer.
- **Simplified or eliminated prior authorizations**: Many services routinely approved could be exempt from prior authorization entirely. For others, automated, real-time authorization systems could replace manual reviews.
- **Unified quality reporting**: Rather than reporting slightly different metrics to each payer, providers could submit a single set of standardized quality measures, reducing duplicate reporting.
- **Global budgets or capitation models**: Payment models that provide fixed funding per patient (like direct primary care) eliminate the need for per-service billing, drastically reducing administrative burden.

The Three-Layer Solution would inherently reduce administrative costs. UCC provides a single, uniform catastrophic coverage mechanism. Direct care eliminates insurance billing for routine services. HSAs simplify payment for everyday expenses. But additional administrative simplification efforts would further reduce waste and improve efficiency.

Technology Integration: Tools That Actually Help

Healthcare technology often seems designed to complicate rather than simplify. But properly implemented, technology can enhance every aspect of the Three-Layer Solution:

- **Artificial Intelligence for administration**: AI can automate routine tasks like medical coding, prior authorization reviews, and documentation. This isn't science fiction and is already happening. AI transcription services can draft clinical notes while doctors focus on patients. Machine learning algorithms can review and approve straightforward insurance claims, reserving human review for complex cases.

- **Blockchain for secure data sharing**: Blockchain technology can create secure, tamper-proof records of healthcare transactions and data access. Estonia has implemented blockchain to secure its national health records, ensuring privacy while enabling appropriate information sharing. Similar approaches could build trust in health data exchange in the U.S.
- **Interoperability for seamless coordination**: Recent federal rules require healthcare systems to share data using standardized formats (FHIR APIs), potentially ending the era of siloed medical records. When information flows seamlessly between providers, patients receive better-coordinated care with fewer duplicate tests and medical errors.
- **Telemedicine integration**: The pandemic accelerated telemedicine adoption, demonstrating its potential to increase access while reducing costs for certain services. Integrating virtual care options into direct care models and HSA-eligible expenses can extend healthcare access, particularly in underserved areas.

Properly implemented, these technologies can make healthcare more efficient, accessible, and patient-centered. Rather than adding complexity, they can simplify processes, reduce errors, and enhance the human elements of care.

MAKING IT HAPPEN

Transforming American healthcare won't happen overnight. A realistic implementation would occur in phases over about a decade, allowing for testing, adjustment, and gradual transition without disrupting existing coverage.

Phase 0: Planning and Groundwork (Year 0-1)

The initial phase focuses on building political consensus, engaging stakeholders, and developing implementation details:

- Establish a bipartisan Healthcare Reform Task Force to flesh out policy details
- Draft comprehensive legislation incorporating all elements of the

Three-Layer Solution
- Identify states willing to serve as early adopters or pilot sites
- Begin developing technical infrastructure (enrollment systems, payment mechanisms)
- Launch public education efforts explaining the changes and benefits
- Use existing authority to strengthen antitrust enforcement and price transparency

During this phase, patients would see little change in their day-to-day healthcare experience, but the foundation for transformation would be laid.

Phase 1: Legislative Action and Initial Reforms (Year 1-2)

With planning complete, legislative action would set larger changes in motion:

- Pass comprehensive reform legislation establishing UCC, expanding HSAs, and supporting direct care
- Implement HSA expansion, allowing anyone to open accounts with higher contribution limits
- Fund direct care pilots in underserved areas to demonstrate the model's potential
- Strengthen price transparency enforcement and create user-friendly comparison tools
- Launch administrative simplification initiatives, starting with standardized billing
- Approve state innovation waivers for UCC pilots in selected states

In this phase, patients would gain access to expanded HSAs and better price information. Direct care options would begin expanding, and some states might implement early versions of catastrophic coverage.

Phase 2: Initial UCC Implementation and Market Transition (Year 3-5)

The core of the Three-Layer Solution would begin taking the following actions during these years:

- Launch Universal Catastrophic Coverage nationally, with income-based deductibles
- Establish coordination between UCC and existing coverage (employer plans, Medicare)
- Monitor costs and adjust parameters as needed based on real-world experience
- Support rapid expansion of direct care models through regulatory

clarity and payment mechanisms
- Implement standardized billing clearinghouse to reduce administrative burden
- Continue aggressive antitrust enforcement to maintain competitive markets

During this phase, patients would notice such significant changes as protection against catastrophic medical costs, more direct care options, and simpler, more transparent healthcare financing.

Phase 3: Full Integration and Optimization (Year 6-10)

The final phase would focus on refining the system and addressing any issues that emerge:
- Adjust UCC parameters based on experience (deductible formulas, covered services)
- Support mature HSA ecosystem with robust balances for most Americans
- Integrate direct care across the care continuum, including specialty and hospital services
- Evaluate impact on overall healthcare costs, quality, and access
- Make any necessary corrections or enhancements based on data
- Ensure long-term political sustainability through demonstrated success

By the end of this phase, the Three-Layer Solution would be fully implemented, providing universal protection against medical bankruptcy while empowering patients and fostering innovation.

ADDRESSING POLITICAL AND ECONOMIC CHALLENGES

No reform this comprehensive would be without challenges. Several potential obstacles must be addressed:
- **Political resistance**: Both progressive and conservative purists might oppose aspects of the Three-Layer Solution. Progressives might prefer a more comprehensive single-payer approach, while conservatives might resist any expansion of government's role. Building a coalition requires emphasizing the hybrid nature of the proposal—universal protection with market-based delivery.
- **Industry opposition**: Entities profiting from the current system, particularly insurers and hospital systems, may resist changes that threaten their business models. Engaging these stakeholders early and

identifying transition paths that allow them to adapt rather than simply oppose reform is crucial.
- **Implementation complexity**: Transitioning from our current patchwork to a more coherent system inevitably involves complexity. Careful planning, clear communication, and phased implementation can mitigate disruption.
- **Cost concerns**: While analyses suggest the Three-Layer Solution could be implemented without increasing total healthcare spending, upfront investments will be needed. Transparent accounting of both costs and savings, along with clear funding mechanisms, can address these concerns.

Despite these challenges, the Three-Layer Solution offers a pragmatic path forward that avoids the political deadlock that has stymied more ideologically pure approaches. By combining elements that appeal to different perspectives, it creates potential for a broad coalition supporting meaningful reform.

THE PROMISE OF A NEW AMERICAN HEALTHCARE

Let's return to Diana and David Sanchez. How would their experience differ under the Three-Layer Solution?

When David fell from the scaffolding, his catastrophic injuries would have been covered by Universal Catastrophic Coverage after a deductible matched to their income—perhaps $5,000 instead of the $160,000 they actually faced. Their HSA, built up through tax-advantaged contributions, would have helped cover that deductible. As for David's ongoing recovery needs, they could have chosen direct care providers offering transparent pricing and subscription-based rehabilitation services.

Instead of financial devastation and endless battles with insurance, they would have experienced a healthcare system that actually delivered on its promise of protection and care.

This isn't just about the Sanchez family. It's about the millions of Americans who deserve better than a system that threatens their financial security while delivering mediocre results at astronomical costs.

The Three-Layer Solution offers a path to healthcare that is:
- **Universal but not uniform**: Everyone gets protection against financial ruin, but individuals retain choice in how they receive and pay for routine care.
- **Market-oriented but not market-fundamentalist**: Competition

drives innovation and efficiency, but government ensures universal catastrophic protection.
- **Simple but not simplistic**: The system has clear, understandable layers but recognizes healthcare's inherent complexity.
- **Evolutionary rather than revolutionary**: It builds on what works in our current system while fixing what doesn't, allowing for manageable transition rather than disruptive change.

Most importantly, it's a solution that could actually happen. By avoiding ideological absolutism and focusing on pragmatic, proven approaches, the Three-Layer Solution offers a realistic path toward a healthcare system that works for all Americans.

The choice is ours. We can continue with a system that bankrupts families like the Sanchezes while delivering subpar results at exorbitant costs. Or we can embrace a new approach that combines the best of public and private solutions to create healthcare that is universal, affordable, and patient-centered.

The blueprint exists. The evidence supports it. Now we need the political will to make it happen.

Conclusion

TAKING BACK CONTROL

As founder and CEO of CareYaya, I've witnessed thousands of families navigate America's healthcare labyrinth. I've seen despair, yes—but I've also seen something powerful: when provided with knowledge and collective action, Americans can successfully challenge this broken system. From individual appeals to nationwide movements, from workplace advocacy to community solutions, paths to better healthcare exist right now.

The journey through this book has taken us deep into the machinery of American healthcare. We've peeled back the curtain on the denial industry, where algorithms reject claims within seconds without human review. We've followed the money to understand how insurance companies generate astronomical profits while patients find it challenging to afford basic care. We've mapped the deliberate complexity that keeps patients confused and compliant.

But we've also traveled beyond the systemic problems to witness their human cost. We've heard from cancer patients forced to abandon treatment, families bankrupted by medical bills, and children denied necessary care. We've listened to physicians handcuffed by corporate policies that override their clinical judgment. We've even heard from insurance industry employees themselves, trapped in a system that rewards them for denying care rather than facilitating it.

Most importantly, we've discovered that resistance is possible and often successful. When patients understand their rights and appeal denials, they frequently win.

OUT-OF-NETWORK AGAIN. TRY YOUR LUCK NEXT VISIT

The strategies shared throughout this book operate at multiple levels:

At the individual level, knowledge is indeed power. Understanding your insurance policy, documenting medical necessity, and mastering the appeals process can mean the difference between care and denial.

At the family level, coordination and planning are essential. When the Johnsons needed care for their 83-year-old mother with dementia, they initially thought nursing home placement was inevitable. Instead, through careful planning and combining resources—adult day care, in-home aides, and family caregiving supported by respite services—they created a sustainable plan that kept her home for three additional years.

At the workplace level, collective voice matters enormously. When employees organize around specific health benefit issues, companies often respond. After 20,000 of Google's contract and temporary employees participated in a walkout, the company announced requirements for its contracting firms to provide health insurance among other benefits.

At the community level, resilience through local solutions provides essential safety nets. Community health centers served 30.5 million patients in 2022, offering sliding-scale fees based on income. Free clinics, mutual aid networks, and local government initiatives like NYC Care fill gaps when the formal system fails. These community efforts not only alleviate immediate suffering but demonstrate alternative approaches to healthcare delivery.

At the political level, citizens who vote and advocate with healthcare in mind can drive significant policy changes. When elected officials know voters are watching healthcare votes closely, their calculus can change. Recently, public pressure helped achieve a federal $35 monthly insulin cap for Medicare beneficiaries.

The vision that emerges from these multi-level efforts isn't utopian but is practical and achievable. We've seen glimpses of it already in successful healthcare models both within America and abroad:

Universal coverage ensures no American goes without healthcare from birth to death, regardless of employment, income, or pre-existing conditions. We've made progress, with the uninsured rate reaching a record low of 7.7% in 2023, but a reformed system would close the remaining gaps completely.

Affordability and simplicity that make insurance comprehensible and care accessible without financial ruin. This means reasonable out-of-pocket costs, transparent pricing, standardized forms, and an end to surprise billing and network confusion.

Emphasis on primary care, prevention, and mental health that keeps people well rather than merely treating them when sick. Countries with the best health outcomes have robust primary care systems where providers have manageable patient loads and can spend time coordinating care.

Equity that eliminates the unconscionable disparities in access and outcomes that currently plague our system. The racial and socioeconomic gaps in health access would be addressed through targeted investments in underserved areas, culturally competent care, and programs addressing social determinants of health.

Smarter cost control that addresses the true drivers of healthcare expense—administrative waste, price gouging, and unnecessary care—rather than simply shifting costs to patients or restricting necessary treatment. Medicare runs with administrative costs around 2%, while private insurers often exceed 15-20%.

What stands between this vision and reality isn't a lack of resources or knowledge but a lack of political will and the outsized influence of industry players who profit from the current dysfunction. The healthcare industry spends billions annually on lobbying, advertising, and political contributions to maintain a status quo that serves corporate interests rather than public health.

But their power ultimately depends on our acceptance of their terms—on our capitulation to complexity, fragmentation, and injustice. When we refuse to concede, we reclaim power. When we share knowledge and resources, as the families in our stories have done, we create alternatives. When we unite our voices, as workers and communities across America are doing, we build momentum for change.

These individual stories might seem small against the backdrop of a $4.9 trillion healthcare industry, but multiplied across communities and sustained over time, they become the foundation of systemic change. Every successful appeal weakens the denial machinery. Every community clinic demonstrates a different model of care delivery. Every workplace campaign for better benefits shifts employer priorities. Every ballot initiative for Medicaid expansion extends coverage to thousands.

The truth is, our healthcare system resembles a house with a crumbling foundation. We can't just patch the walls indefinitely; at some point, we need to address the structural problems. Yet while we work on rebuilding that foundation, people still need shelter from the rain today. This dual approach of navigating today's system while building tomorrow's embodies what it means to be a healthcare citizen in America.

Think of it this way: when you board an airplane, the flight attendant explains that in case of emergency, you should put on your own oxygen mask before helping others. Similarly, the strategies in this book help you secure your own healthcare "oxygen mask," but they also show how we can collectively ensure everyone has access to clean air. We need not choose between practical self-protection and visionary reform—both are essential and complementary.

As we close this book, remember that your healthcare story isn't over. In fact, it's just beginning, with you as a protagonist in the continuing struggle to take back control of American healthcare. The universal, affordable, equitable, and humane healthcare we deserve is a practical possibility demonstrated in parts of our own system and in many countries around the world. The question isn't whether such a system can exist, but whether we have the collective will to create it.

The answer is up to us. By refusing surrender, by supporting one another, by raising our voices, and by demanding change at every level, we can reclaim the promise of American healthcare. A system worthy of our nation's resources and ideals, one that provides care and dignity for all, is within our grasp if we have the courage to reach for it.

The final page of this book is just the first page of your healthcare citizenship. The next chapter in American healthcare will be written by those who refuse to accept the unacceptable, who imagine a better system, and who take concrete steps to build it. Together, we can and will take back control.

To view references and supporting documentation related to the content of this book, please visit www.insuredtodeath.org

A Note from the Author

Thank you for reading *Insured to Death*. To help you take the next step, please visit www.insuredtodeath.org and enter your email to confirm your purchase. You'll receive a free companion guide for appealing health insurance denials packed with templates, checklists, and practical tips. It's our way of saying thank you and keeping the conversation going.

If this book informed, empowered, or moved you in any way, I'd be grateful if you'd take a minute to leave a review on Amazon, Goodreads, or even share your thoughts on Reddit (r/HealthInsurance, r/Healthcare, or wherever you think people could benefit). Reviews help more readers discover the book, and more importantly, they build a community of people who refuse to stay silent about a broken system. Your voice makes a difference.

If you'd like to connect directly or stay updated on the latest from Counterforce Health, find me on LinkedIn (linkedin.com/in/neal-shah-careyaya/) and say hello! I read every message and would love to stay connected even if my response time sometimes takes as long as waiting on hold with your insurance company.

This book is just the beginning. Together, we can build a movement that pushes for fairness, accountability, and dignity in healthcare.

Thanks for being part of it.

With gratitude,
Neal

Scan QR code for relevant links

About the Author

Neal K. Shah is the Chief Executive Officer of CareYaya Health Technologies, a social enterprise and applied research lab advancing health equity for aging populations using artificial intelligence and neurotechnology and recognized by LinkedIn as one of America's Top 50 Startups in 2024. He also serves as Chairman of Counterforce Health, an AI-driven platform that helps patients and providers navigate insurance claim denials. Shah is a Principal Investigator on multiple federally funded innovation grants, including one supported by the National Institutes of Health and the University of Pennsylvania to develop AI tools that assist patients in appealing denied health insurance claims. He also leads a separate NIH-funded collaboration with Johns Hopkins focused on improving dementia caregiving through AI tools that upskill and train caregivers.

Shah holds dual bachelor's degrees in economics and philosophy, with a minor in mathematics, from the University of Pennsylvania. Before founding CareYaya, Shah managed a $250 million hedge fund. His pivot to healthcare came after deeply personal experiences as a caregiver, which inspired a mission-driven focus on transforming care delivery through technology.

Today, Shah is building strategic partnerships and technical capabilities to position CareYaya as America's leading launchpad for care innovation—expanding access to affordable care, driving humanitarian progress, and fundamentally improving quality of life for vulnerable populations. Shah's work has been supported by the National Institutes of Health, Johns Hopkins AITC, and Harvard Innovation Labs. He is also a prominent thought leader in health innovation, with features and contributions in *CNBC*, *The Wall Street Journal*, *Barron's*, *STAT*, *Neurology Live*, and *TechCrunch*.

www.ingramcontent.com/pod-product-compliance
Lightning Source LLC
Chambersburg PA
CBHW070618030426
42337CB00020B/3839